Sport, Sexualities and Queer/Theory

Edited by Jayne Caudwell

Routledge
Taylor & Francis Group

LONDON AND NEW YORK

First published 2006
By Routledge
2 Park Square, Milton Park, Abingdon, Oxon OX14 4RN

Simultaneously published in the USA and Canada
by Routledge
270 Madison Ave, New York, NY 10016

Routledge is an imprint of the Taylor & Francis Group, an informa business

© Jayne Caudwell, selection and editorial matter; individual chapters, the
contributors

Typeset in Goudy by
GreenGate Publishing Services, Tonbridge, Kent
Printed and bound in Great Britain by
TJ International Ltd, Padstow, Cornwall

Library of Congress Cataloging in Publication Data
Sport, sexualities and queer/theory / edited by Jayne Caudwell.
        p. cm. – (Routledge critical studies in sport)
    Includes bibliographical references and index.
    ISBN 0–415–36761–1 –ISBN 0–415–36762–X (pbk.)
        1. Lesbians and sports. 2. Gays and sports. 3. Gay Games.
I. Caudwell, Jayne. II. Series.

GV708.8.S66 2006
796.08'664–dc22

                                                                    2006011002

British Library Cataloguing in Publication Data
A catalogue record for this book is available from the British Library

ISBN10: 0–415–36761–1 (hbk)
ISBN10: 0–415–36762–x (pbk)
ISBN10: 0–203–02009–x (ebk)

ISBN13: 978–0–415–36761–5 (hbk)
ISBN13: 978–0–415–36762–2 (pbk)
ISBN13: 978–0–203–02009–8 (ebk)

Contents

Contributors

Jayne Caudwell is Senior Lecturer in the Sociology of Sport and Leisure Cultures at the University of Brighton's Chelsea School, England. Her teaching and research focus on gender, sexuality and women's experiences of football cultures. She is keen to explore the relationships between sport cultures and queer 'identity', methodology and theory.

Judy Davidson is an Assistant Professor in the Faculty of Physical Education and Recreation at the University of Alberta in Edmonton, Canada where she teaches about sport, leisure and cultural studies. She is interested in questions about the production of genders and sexualities in various sporting and leisure contexts. Her current research focuses on sexuality, HIV/AIDS health discourses, and nationalisms at the Gay Games and Cultural Events.

Heidi Eng is Senior Research Fellow in gender/sexuality research at the University of Oslo, Centre for Women's Studies and Gender Research. She is currently involved in an interdisciplinary research group, 'The Queer Turn', which explores destabilising trends and practises relating to gender and sexuality in culture and research. She also teaches on Gender Studies and Sport/Leisure Studies programmes.

Dennis Hemphill, a Senior Lecturer in the School of Human Movement, Recreation and Performance at Victoria University, Australia, undertakes teaching in the area of philosophy of exercise science, sport and physical education; and conducts research in the area of sport technology, inclusive curriculum, and professional ethics. He is editor of the anthology *All Part of the Game: Violence and Australian Sport* (1998) and co-editor (with C. Symons) of the anthology *Gender, Sexuality and Sport: A Dangerous Mix* (2002).

Nigel Jarvis is a Senior Lecturer in Tourism Management at the University of Brighton. His PhD research examines the meaning of sport among gay Canadian and British male athletes at the grass-root level of provision. He has also published on sponsorship and commodification issues related to gay sport events. In addition to his interest in gender, sexuality and sport, Nigel's research and teaching is linked to the impacts of tourism, and issues centred on sport tourism, and sexuality and tourism.

Rebecca Lock is a PhD candidate in the Department of Sociology at the University of Alberta, Canada. Her doctoral research explores how female athletes articulate and make sense of their experiences of pain in an athletic context.

Mary G. McDonald is Associate Professor in the Department of Physical Education, Health and Sport Studies and an affiliate with the Women's Studies programme at Miami University in Oxford, Ohio, USA. Her scholarship focuses on feminist and cultural studies of sport, the media and popular culture, and explores power relations as constituted along the axes of race, class, gender, nation and sexuality. She is co-editor with Susan Birrell of *Reading Sport: Critical Essays on Power and Representation* and is the guest editor of a special issue of the *Sociology of Sport Journal* titled *Whiteness and Sport*.

Gareth Owen is a PhD candidate in the Faculty of Arts and Human Sciences at London South Bank University, England. His thesis looks at identities and emotions in sport.

Heather Sykes is at the Ontario Institute for Studies in Education at the University of Toronto, Canada. Her research interests include issues of sexuality, gender and the body in sport and physical education. She uses post-structural, psychoanalytic and queer theoretical frameworks to examine social, cultural and psychic dynamics of exclusion and discrimination. She has also produced a performed ethnography called 'Wearing The Secret Out' about homophobia and homoeroticism in physical education. Her work has been published in the *Journal of Curriculum Studies*, *Sociology of Sport Journal* and the *Journal of Gay and Lesbian Issues in Education* and she is Editor of the journal *Curriculum Inquiry*.

Caroline Symons, a Lecturer in the School of Human Movement, Recreation and Performance at Victoria University, Australia, undertakes teaching in the areas of ethics, social policy, sociology and the politics of sport, as well as sport event management and career and professional development in sport. She recently completed an award winning PhD on the social history of the international Gay Games.

Ian Wellard is based in the Centre for Physical Education Research, Canterbury Christ Church University, where he is a Senior Research Fellow in the Sociology of Sport. He is currently involved in a number projects related to the body, gender and physical activity.

Series Editors' preface

The very personal and highly sensitive issue of sexuality in sport and its link to sexual preference and homophobic discrimination incorporates controversy and complexity in abundance.For that reason, it is a topic that is not easily understood and *Sport, Sexualities and Queer/Theory*, edited by Jayne Caudwell, is breaking new ground towards a better analytic approach. The attempt to investigate sexuality in sport using 'queer' and 'queer theory' is a radical development in sports studies.It is a strong critique of established ideas and stereotypes of gender and sexuality which undermines the hegemony of heteronormativity and encourages us to explore new ways of thinking.This approach reflects an important aim ofthe Routledge Critical Studies in Sport series: to question assumptions about sport, to critique established ideas, and to explore new ones.

The collection is the result of a co-operative effort between the contributors, who attended a specially convened seminar to discuss the appropriateness and potential of using queer and queer theory as a common theme running throughout the book. As series editors, we were invited to the seminar and were very pleased to have played an active part in the proceedings, the outcome of which was the political decision of the contributors to focus on queer and queer theory so as to move beyond existing analyses of sexualities in sport and make a critical intervention in the field.It is the first sports sociology text with this specific focus and we anticipate that it will encourage further debate among faculty and students who are seeking explanations and understanding about the particular ways in which sexualities are experienced, represented and negotiated in different sporting contexts. Debate should be further stimulated by the different ways in which the contributors approach the use of queer and queer theory,

At the start of the book, the explanatory power of these two terms is explored, setting the scene for the range of sporting examples which provide the specific contexts for the other chapters. There is a strong relationship throughout the text between empirical material and theoretical analysis – a characteristic of other books in the Series. The ethnographic approach is an important methodological device in the book, used by several of the contributors to communicate very personal accounts of sexual discrimination in sport, together with reactions and resistances to it. Jayne Caudwell explains that, 'via a focus on gay, lesbian, bisexual, transgendered, transsexual and intersex, as well as heterosexual experiences, queer theory documents complex subjectivities and expands our knowledge of sexuality'. The hope is that the greater the accumulation of knowledge about prejudice, the greater is the potential to change it. The book as a whole, therefore, represents a challenge to sexual prejudice in sport and the relations of power that aid in its reproduction.

Sport, Sexualities and Queer/Theory fits well with the philosophy of the Series. It is interrogative; interventionist; and innovative, exposing the everyday sporting experiences of the sexual minorities who are frequently misunderstood, misrepresented, and maligned, and whose sexual preferences are normally concealed.It is a challenge to complacency and signals the need for further work and greater understanding of the complexities of sexualities in sport.

Jennifer Hargreaves
Ian McDonald
University of Brighton
Series Editors

Acknowledgements

This book is an edited collection and would not have been possible without the work of all the authors. I'd like to thank Heather Sykes, Mary McDonald, Heidi Eng, Nigel Jarvis, Ian Wellard, Judy Davidson, Caroline Symons and Denis Hemphill, Gareth Owen, and Rebecca Lock for taking the time to discuss, write, re-write and share their work.

I'd also like to thank work colleagues (University of Brighton and Leeds Metropolitan University) for supporting the idea to produce such a collection. In particular Alan Tomlinson for his encouragement and assistance in getting some of the authors together and John Spink for his critical eye and kindness.

Importantly, I'd like to thank the series editors, Jennifer Hargreaves and Ian McDonald, for their interest and efforts to help make it happen. In particular, I'd like to make a special thank you to Jennifer for sharing her views and experience, and offering guidance.

Finally, I'd like to thank those close to me for all the ways they have quite simply let me get on with it!

Introduction

Jayne Caudwell

Sport, Sexualities and Queer/Theory is the first anthology in the field of sports studies to investigate sexuality and its relation to 'queer' and 'queer theory'. It is the
result of much deliberation. In November 2004 several of the contributors, and
the series editors, gathered to discuss the content of individual chapters and the
overall intent of the collection. During the meeting it soon became evident that
contributors understood queer and queer theory differently. This is hardly surprising given that queer eludes easy definition and the idea of queer theory
continues to be contested. Despite disagreements, it was felt that queer and queer
theory offer valuable ways to analyse and critically discuss sport. The lack of consensus over how queer and queer theory can[not] provide rigorous explanation
developed as an issue in naming the book. Initially, it was agreed that it should be
entitled *Sport, Sexuality and Queer Theory*. However, after some thought the tensions have been articulated by the denotation Queer/Theory. The aim is to
denote how queer *and* queer theory are separate and merge, and how contributors
deploy and apply the terms in different ways. As the first sociology of sport text
to bring together such work, the book captures tensions and processes within
scholarship and between scholars in relation to sexuality, queer, theory and sport.
In this collection, the debates over queer and queer theory, and their relevance
to sport, provoke dismissal, contestation and resolution. Such debates are commonplace in the humanities and social sciences (cf. Beemyn and Eliason, 1996;
Blasius, 2001; Corber and Valocchi 2003; Hall, 2003; Jagose, 1996; Morland and
Willox, 2005; Seidman, 1996; Sullivan, 2003; Turner, 2000) but have been slow
to appear in the study of sport. That said, important contributions appear in key
sociology of sport journals (cf. Broad, 2001; Caudwell, 2003; Davidson and
Shogan, 1998; Lock, 2003; McDonald, 2001; Sykes, 1998). This edited book,
then, might be viewed as overdue; it is a timely contribution to the critical study
of sport, sexuality and the body.

As the first anthology of its kind the book has three broad aims, these are:

(i) to provide an accessible source of literature for those interested in sport and
the complexities of sexuality.
(ii) to provide discussion that blends theoretical ideas with research methodologies and research findings.

(iii) to contribute to debates surrounding queer and queer theory and provoke further work from within sports studies.

Queer and queer theory

'Queer' is used in numerous ways to describe activism, theory, politics, identity and community. It is widely accepted that 'queer' emerged from activism surrounding HIV/aids and sexual practice. Queer Nation, established in 1990 in the US was closely followed by Outrage in the UK. According to Cherry Smyth:

> Queer activists saw Outrage as distinctly anti-assimilationist compared to the parliamentary reform group, Stonewall, which has been established as a response to Clause 28 in 1989 ... Outrage activists are not interested in seeking acceptance within an unchanged social system, but are setting out to 'fuck up the mainstream' as visibly as possible.
>
> (Cherry Smyth, 1992: 19–20)

We can imagine 'the mainstream' as heteronormativity. Berlant and Warner (2000) describe heteronormativity as 'the institutions, structures of understanding, and practical orientations that make heterosexuality seem not only coherent – that is organized as a sexuality – but also privileged' (2000: 312). In this vein queer developed as a response to heteronormativity and presents protest via an incorporation of both activism and theoretical conceptualisation.

Broadly speaking, queer reflects a departure from lesbian and gay politics of identity to politics of difference, resistance and challenge. Its intention is to make [very] visible previously denied and silenced 'identities' and sexualities: 'bodies and sexual desires that do not fit dominant standards of gender and/or sexuality' (Beemyn and Eliason, 1996: 5). Despite departure from identity politics, queer does engage with the idea of identity to achieve its many aims. These aims often include: exposing the constructedness of sexuality; exposing the illusion/fiction of sexual identity; avoiding normative and essentialising identities; resisting regimes of the 'normal'; violating compulsory sex/gender relations; dismantling binary gender relations; and undermining heteronormative hegemonic discourses. Queer has worked as an effective challenge to heteronormativity because of branding and celebrating the marginalised and/or the excluded.

In a very rudimentary way, queer theory is the study of sexuality. It contests earlier explanations of sexuality, namely sexology and some aspects of psychoanalysis, and debates categorisation of sexual identity. From this starting point Jagose (1996) and Turner (2000) show how queer theory emerged as important criticism of how sexuality functions to maintain social relations of power. The imbrications of queer theory and feminism are difficult to ignore given the impossibility of separating out sexuality from gender, and of course from 'race', ethnicity and class. In this way queer theory is more complicated than a straightforward 'theory of sexuality' implies. Some authors continue to reference queer theory (Jagose, 1996; Morland and Willox, 2005; Seidman, 1996, Sullivan,

2003), others refer to queer studies (Beemyn and Eliason, 1996; Corber and Valocchi, 2003), queer politics (Blasius, 2001) and, unsurprisingly, queer theor*ies* (Hall, 2003). Queer theory, then, has many dimensions, reaching beyond sexuality but ultimately connected to sexuality and it is this range that attests the potential of queer and queer theory.

For me, queer theory is legitimised through its relation to knowledge production. Queer theory's intention to deconstruct sexuality resonates with post-structuralist critiques of the Enlightenment's reliance on binary opposites (e.g. heterosexual–homosexual) and advocacy of 'scientific' (truth) knowledge (e.g. sexology). In this vein, Seidman's description of queer theory as political theory of *knowledge* of difference can aptly explain queer theory's core. As Seidman suggests, queer theory is concerned with 'institutional practices and discourses producing sexual knowledges and ... ways these knowledges and social practices repress differences' (1996: 13). Clearly, there are links with post-structuralism's quest to expose the regulatory power of institutions, knowledge and discursive practices. Through a mapping or genealogy of existing knowledge claims, queer theory provides a critique of dominant discourses of heteronormativity. In addition, via a focus on gay, lesbian, bisexual, transgendered, transsexual and intersex, as well as heterosexual experiences, queer theory documents complex subjectivities and expands our knowledge of sexuality. Within such a project, which is in effect a move to disturb and destabilise the familiar, 'queer' can appear as adjective, noun and/or verb (Hall, 2003) and we witness its varied usages in some chapters in this book.

Sport, sexualities and queer/theory

Part I consists of two chapters that engage with dilemmas surrounding the study of sport and sexuality. Both are explicit in illuminating possibilities that queer theory offers and advocates its value to an analysis of sport. In many ways, these first two chapters provide insight that enables a clearer understanding of debates that arise in the remaining eight chapters. In Chapter 1, Heather Sykes offers a comprehensive mapping of developments in queer theory over the past two decades, and charts the contributions of different queer theorists. She starts by acknowledging the difficulties in establishing a simple version of queer theory and goes on to give a thorough and detailed account of arguments that have shaped the emergence of queer theory, and continue to forge its development. She is keen to rectify some earlier omissions through reference to 'race' and consistently highlights key authors that have, previously, appeared on the margins. The citations of studies of sport are regular and underpin the value of her call for *queering theories of sexuality in sport studies*. We are treated to an accessible discussion of key concepts and a wealth of cited materials. In all, the chapter is an important and convincing precursor to this collection, which grapples with applying queer/theory to sport.

In Chapter 2, Mary McDonald continues the emphasis to move beyond accounts of gender and sexuality that privilege white experience and authorship.

Her critical reflections on existing literature, from North American sport schol-ars, intend to open our eyes to the operation of whiteness. She challenges theoretical and political practices that help forge 'identity' as fixed, highlighting how whiteness remains unmarked in these processes. In addition, she demon-strates how the notion of a universal 'sexual identity' is in fact a fiction. The criticisms she makes provide an important reminder to not underestimate the powerful functioning of whiteness and to constantly question assumptions of 'queer citizenship'. For her, bodies are given meaning through compounded nor-malising discourses of whiteness and heteronormativity. She demonstrates how disidentification and José Muñoz's (1999) work, including readings of images of a 'famous negro athlete' and Sugar Ray Robinson, can disrupt these normalising discourses: 'Thus disidentification is a step further than cracking the code of the majority; It proceeds to use this code as raw material for representing a disem-powered politics or positionality that has been rendered unthinkable by the dominant culture' (Muñoz 1999: 31).

Sykes and McDonald provide crucial theoretical interjections that assist in establishing meaningful links between queer literatures generally and specific practices in sport. Both chapters make apparent how queer and queer theory can help develop new ways to study sport.

Part II is concerned with how queer/theory has helped researchers understand their research findings. The four chapters reflect research into specific sport com-munities, namely, intermediate and elite sport in Norway, men's softball in Canada, men's tennis in England and the Gay Games and Cultural Events. All are the result of PhD work and signal important contributions to the sociology of sport. Individual authors draw on queer/theory, to varying degrees, to explain their findings. Here we are introduced to practices, and communities, that regu-late and disrupt the [hetero]normative.

In Chapter 3, Heidi Eng focuses on Norwegian athletes who identify as lesbian and gay. She compares the different conditions men and women experience to do 'sex/uality' in their specific sport setting. Moreover, she looks at a particular sport activity, the social spaces of sport and locker room culture. In her discussions she refuses to name the sport. This is a result of her fidelity to Norwegian athletes who fear the tag will help identify them because athletes' populations, in the country, are small and recognisable. For Eng, sex/uality signifies sexual acts, desire and the erotic as well as sexual identity. She links interview research findings with theo-retical concepts; 'queer' and 'queering', referencing Foucault's (1990) work, on "silence itself", as significant to her analysis. She highlights the connections between queer theory and methodology through an emphasis on 'the unseen, the taboo, acts/practices/language that is 'not spoken' – outside known language, or seen as problematic speech acts' (p. 51, this volume). The chapter continues the debate outlined by Sykes and McDonald through the application of queer and queering, and placing experiences of sexual dissidents at the centre.

In Chapter 4, Nigel Jarvis presents findings from his ethnographic research on gay men's sporting masculinities in softball. He is keen to ascertain whether the practices within the team's subculture are queer acts of resistance or if they can be better understood through the familiar concept of masculine hegemony. To this end his introduction discusses how gay men and/in sport have been theorised to date. The research findings are organised to emphasise the importance of language, demeanour and image in the production of subcultural style. In contrast to experiences in the context of intermediate and elite Norwegian sport, language and demeanour are explicitly gendered and sexualised. The men articulate gay sexuality coherently. Their comments often challenge discursive heteronormative sexing and gendering of competitive sport; through baseball-inflected language players reference gay sexual acts and desires, gay sexual identities, and gender identities. Despite these valuable transgressions, the demeanour of some players reproduces dominant competitive sporting behaviours, namely behaviours that support the means of winning. Jarvis concludes with a discussion about how difficult it is for subordinate groups to challenge obdurate sporting practices that privilege the heterosexual. In the next chapter, Ian Wellard continues with this point in his exploration of the *limits of queer and sport*.

Wellard considers the emergence of a gay tennis club in the south of England. The formation of the club, as with similar sports groups that are created by sexual minorities, intends to provide a safe enclave for respite from the traditions and rituals of heterosexism. Taking up Butler's challenge to reveal 'queer acts', Wellard highlights some of the ways the tennis players have challenged dominant practices in sport. However, as with the previous chapter, the overwhelming realisation is that gay participants might prefer 'straight acts' as is highlighted by the pleasure of one research participant who commented, 'you'd never know it was a gay tennis club'. Again we witness the processes some gay athletes/players go through in order to assimilate: or put another way, the power of heteronormativity, in sport, to influence gay sensibilities.

The chapters by Jarvis and Wellard provide insights into gay men's experiences of sport. Such contributions are sometimes missing from the sports studies literature on sexuality. Both authors engage with seminal work by Brian Pronger, and their discussion demonstrates the importance of Pronger's earlier contributions to understanding gay men's involvement in sport and theoretical tensions surrounding how gay presence in sport might best be theorised.

In Chapter 6, Judy Davidson takes the focus to the Gay Games and the cultural events associated with the Games. Her interest in 'queer shame for gay pride' arose from archival research of the history of the Gay Games and the role of Dr Thomas Waddell (Gay Games founder). After offering a brief account of how the Gay Games emerged, Davidson concentrates on archival discourses of gay pride. She notes: 'The individual and organizational investments in expressing lesbian and gay pride were almost overwhelming, and too insistent to ignore' and sets out to establish the ways pride is 'linked to the original shaming', in other words 'the original refusal of an Olympic designation' (p. 94, this volume). Through in-depth consideration of shame and pride her chapter engages the psychic domain and its relation to the social domain. In this way she demonstrates the value of aspects of psychoanalysis to a detailed understanding of how heteronormativity helps produce gay pride.

Part III looks at how the body is given meaning in particular sport settings. We continue analysis of the Gay Games, in Chapter 7, with Caroline Symons' and Denis Hemphill's critical examination of the treatment of transgendered athletes. This is followed by, in Chapter 8, Gareth Owen's discussion on how gay men experience their bodies in competitive rowing; in Chapter 9, by Jayne Caudwell's concern with how femme-inine women, in football, are understood; and in Chapter 10 by Rebecca Lock's critical analysis of how pain is evoked in the [re]production of heterosexual femininity.

Caroline Symons and Denis Hemphill reflect on the following Gay Games: New York 1994; Amsterdam 1998; and Sydney, 2002. The inclusion of transgender athletes in these games is discussed. The chapter starts by illustrating how the sexed body is 'naturalised' in sport, leaving a legacy of an enduring two-sexed system. Such a foundational approach has huge implications for bodies that do not fall neatly into this absolute binary and the chapter explores how transgender participants have been treated by Gay Games policy. The New York Gay Games appear to be the 'first international sports event to include transgender participants within policy and procedures'. The Amsterdam games, despite having a coherent transgender policy, are criticised for reliance on medical and psychological criteria leaving many dissatisfied with the outcome. Throughout the chapter, the authors argue for an understanding of sex and gender that resists dominant sporting discourse and they highlight ways in which transgender activism has informed non-discriminatory practice. Sydney Gay Games are discussed in relation to improved practice, and the netball competition is cited as a case in hand.

To continue the focus on athletes' bodies, Gareth Owen, reiterating Davidson's emphasis on gay shame and pride, uses reflexive ethnography to show how his body and emotions are inseparable from understanding gender and sexual identities in competitive rowing. As a member of a gay rowing club and men's crew (coxed eight), he uses his 'body as an instrument of data collection' and explores the possibilities of sporting narrative. In her earlier chapter, Eng introduced the methodology of melding together research findings in order to re-tell a 'story' about research participants' experience and she referenced Toni Bruce's (1998) work as influential. Owen continues to galvanise this research methodology with his nerve-racking (for those of us who have raced in such events) narrative of pre-race rituals. It becomes apparent that there are possibilities for how gay masculinity can be materialised. However, Owen concludes that 'hegemonic masculinity is still reproduced by the mandatory performance of *competitive* masculinities in conventional sport'.

The final two chapters, in very different ways, consider femininity. In Chapter 9, Jayne Caudwell aims to explore the nuances of femininity and deploys 'femme' as a way to register potential to queer femininity. Her research with an 'out' lesbian football team from London demonstrates the value of collective 'identity' *and* the futility of promoting homogeneity. Clearly, the team struggles to establish a safe space to play within football's regime of heteronormativity. However, it is interactions between players, surrounding femme-inity and response to the materialisation of femme-inine bodies, which reveal the ubiquity and multiplicity of heteronormativity. Caudwell considers the possibility that lesbian players might reinforce the values, beliefs, and status of normative culture. Discussion highlights how femme-inine bodies are [mis]understood as fragile versions of football players and demands a re-reading of femme-ininity as subversive and having political power to offer potent disruption of the heteronormative.

Finally, in Chapter 10, Rebecca Lock 'considers the relationship between pain and heterosexual femininity in the context of women's ice hockey'. She argues that pain and heterosexuality are socially constructed as 'natural' and warns against viewing experiences of both as universal phenomena. In particular she offers detailed critical analysis of how discourses surrounding rape, birthing and medical treatment of pain for women, produce gendered grammar. From here, she demonstrates how this gendered grammar regulates heterosexual femininity in ice hockey, a sport in which 'some pain is inevitable'. Given the potentiality for pain in ice hockey, Lock illustrates the ways certain kinds of pain are refused via the rules of the game. She explores how pain that undermines the production of heterosexual femininity is countered to: 'allow women to experience pain that least contravenes their heterosexual femininity; prevent females from experiencing pain most associated with heterosexual masculinity; use strategies that heterosexually feminize female athletes'. In addition, she introduces psychic pain and challenges its erasure from analyses of pain. The inclusion of the psychic dimension of pain makes links with Davidson's (Chapter 6) and Owen's (Chapter 8) work on shame and further illustrates the intricacies of heteronormativity.

Concluding thoughts

In all, the book covers a range of issues related to sexuality and sport. It is impossible to ignore the 'Western' contexts being discussed. All the authors are white and the issues being addressed tend to, but do not always, reflect white-Western interests. The experiences documented in this collection are predominantly those of white athletes. In the first part of the book Sykes (Chapter 1) and McDonald (Chapter 2) call for change in relation to this point, this request is reiterated here; there is a need for further work on the intersectionality of sexuality, gender, 'race' and ethnicity, and an acknowledgement that whiteness and heteronormativity are inseparable in Western capitalist sports cultures (McDonald, 2001). Future research and writing determining the connections are essential. Such work appears elsewhere, as many of the authors highlight, and those interested in sport and sexuality must help prevent further lag.

The dominance of competitive sport and its concomitant rituals raises a concern that runs through many chapters. In parts two and three of the book, authors tend to use research findings to illustrate the blatant, and stubborn, [hetero]normative practices of competitive sport. Some suspect that transforming these cultural practices is near impossible while others are keen to identify moments of queer resistance. An ongoing critical analysis of competitive sport is obviously valuable to efforts for change, as is illustrated by Symons' and

Hemphill's (Chapter 7) account of the Gay Games and transgender participation. In addition, it is important to recognise that competition infiltrates many sporting endeavours and that competitiveness often remains embedded in playing for fun or recreation. Jarvis (Chapter 4), Wellard (Chapter 5) and Caudwell (Chapter 9) make this point, demonstrating how easy it is for participants to adopt dominant heteronormative discourses of competition and simultaneously dislocate these discourses.

In addition to a critical analysis of sporting practice the book offers work on methodology/ies. In this collection we witness a range of approaches. In many ways the focus on sexuality, something which is often stigmatised and silenced, stretches traditional methodologies. Eng (Chapter 3) and Owen (Chapter 8) take up sporting narrative as one way to access sexual silences, and Davidson (Chapter 6) interrogates archival material to expose the fiction of discourse surrounding pride and shame. Unsurprisingly given the focus of investigation, ethnography remains popular and several chapters contribute further to qualitative research now evident in sports studies (cf. Andrews et al., 2005).

Finally, the body emerges as a key site for exploring the tensions between sexuality, queer and queer theory. The body, in sport, becomes the anchorage for gender, sexuality and race, class, and ability. Heteronormativity appears as a useful concept to explain regulation of this materialisation. Authors tend to expose the social dimensions of the process and arrangement. However, some of the contributors have extended analyses to the physic domain, therefore highlighting the complex impact of heteronormativity on the body. In all, the book offers original contributions that intend to stretch our understanding of sexuality and sport beyond lesbian and gay studies and identity politics.

References

Andrews, D. L., Mason, D. S, and Silk, M. L. (2005) *Qualitative Methods in Sports Studies*. London: Berg.

Beemyn, B. and Eliason, M. (eds) (1996) *Queer Studies: A Lesbian, Gay, Bisexual and Transgender Anthology*. New York: NYU Press.

Berlant, L. and Warner, M. (2000) 'Sex in public', in L. Berlant (ed.) *Intimacy*. Chicago: Chicago University Press.

Blasius, M. (ed.) (2001) *Sexual Identities. Queer Politics*. Oxford: Princeton.

Broad, K. L. (2001) 'The gendered unapologetic: Queer resistance in women's sport'. *Sociology of Sport Journal*, 18 (2): 181–204.

Bruce, T. (1998) 'Postmodernism and the Possibilities for writing "vital" sports texts', in G. Rail (ed.) *Sport and Postmodern Times*. New York: SUNY.

Caudwell, J. (2003) 'Sporting gender: women's footballing bodies as sites/sights for the [re]articulation of sex, gender and desire'. *Sociology of Sport Journal*, 20 (3): 371–86.

Corber, J. and Valocchi, S. (eds) (2003) *Queer Studies: An Interdisciplinary Reader*. London: Blackwell.

Davidson, J. and Shogan, D. (1998) 'What's queer about studying up? A response to Messner', *Sociology of Sport Journal*, 15 (4): 359–66.

Foucault, M. [1976] (1990) *The History of Sexuality: Volume 1*. New York: Vintage.

Hall, D. (2003) *Queer Theories*. London: Palgrave.

Jagose, A. (1996) *Queer Theory: An Introduction*. New York: New York University Press.

Lock, R. (2003) 'The doping ban: Compulsory heterosexuality and lesbophobia'. *International Review for the Sociology of Sport*, 38 (4): 397–471.

McDonald, M. G. (2001) 'Queering whiteness: The peculiar case of the Women's National Basketball Association', *Sociological Perspectives*, 45 (4): 379–96.

Morland, I. and Willox, A. (eds) (2005) *Queer Theory*. London: Palgrave.

Muñoz, J. (1999) *Disidentifications: Queers of Color and the Performance of Politics*. Minneapolis: University of Minnesota.

Seidman, S. (ed.) (1996) *Queer Theory/Sociology*. London: Blackwells.

Smyth, C. (1992) *Lesbians Talk Queer Notions*. London: Scarlet Press.

Sullivan, N. (2003) *A Critical Introduction to Queer Theory*. Edinburgh: Edinburgh Press.

Sykes, H. (1998) 'Turning the closets inside/out: towards a queer-feminist theory in women's physical education', *Sociology of Sport Journal*, 15 (2): 154–73.

Turner, W. B. (2000) *A Genealogy of Queer Theory*. Philadelphia: Temple University Press.

Part I

Queer/theory and the study of sport

1 Queering theories of sexuality in sport studies

Heather Sykes

Introduction

Queer theory necessarily resists any straightforward definition, yet it is possible to trace the emergence of central queer theories and theorists during the past two decades. Queer theory refuses the notion of sexual identity *per se* and therefore expands well beyond issues facing lesbians and gay men in sport. Research influenced by queer theory alters how researchers and students in Sport Studies approach issues of embodiment, health and the body in sporting contexts. In this chapter I suggest how queer theory's critique of sexual identity and postmodernism's suspicion towards fundamental truths and categories might alter how we think about sexuality, desire and the body in Sport Studies.

Queer theory arose in the context of critiques of feminism by queers of color, sex debates between anti-pornography and sex-radical feminists, the rise of postmodern and post-structural theories, and the right wing backlash against homosexuality in the AIDS crisis (Seidman, 1994, 1996; Walters, 1996). Teresa de Lauretis has been attributed with coining the term 'Queer Theory' in 1991 in her introductory comments about a conference on theorizing lesbian and gay sexualities to remedy the masking of gay male privilege in the purportedly equitable phrase 'lesbian and gay' (Walters, 1996). Her theoretical premise was that queer theory would no longer regard homosexuality 'simply as marginal with regard to a dominant, stable' heterosexuality – or transgressive versus proper; deviant versus natural. A political movement called 'Queer Nation' was born in 1990 at a small meeting of mostly white gay men interested in direct action around lesbian and gay issues (Penn, 1995). A radically different Queer Atzlán was envisioned by Cherríe Moraga (1996) in which:

> we can work to teach one another that our freedom as a people is mutually dependent and cannot be parceled out – class before race before sex before sexuality...a new Chicano nationalism calls for the integration of both the traditional and the revolutionary, the ancient and the contemporary.
>
> (cited in Norton, 1996: 303)

Well before the term queer theory appeared, queer feminists of color such as Gloria Anzaldúa (1983; 1998) and Audre Lourde (1982) had been rewriting the meanings of and politics associated with queer, lesbian and dyke in communities of color. de Lauretis asked whether queerness can construct 'another discursive horizon, another way of living the racial and the sexual' or whether 'we are condemned to repeat our respective histories, even as we study them' (de Lauretis, 1991: 9). Thus, in this first anthology relating queer theory to sport, a pressing issue is whether queer sport studies are 'condemned to repeat' the same histories of exclusion, in particular the cycle of deracination that erases 'the specificity of "raced" gay existence under a queer rubric in which whiteness is not problematized' (Walters, 1996: 842) that gave rise to queer theory in the early nineteen-nineties. The task, as I see it, facing Sport Studies is to queer normative theorizing about desire and embodiment and sport without parceling out *class before race before sex before sexuality* (Moraga, 1996); to envision research that sets in motion another way of *living the racial and the sexual* (de Lauretis, 1991), and possibly to conceptualize the dynamics of love and hate in sport *without the alibis of race, sex and gender* (Britzman, 1995).

Essentialism versus social constructionism

Queer theory emerged from Gay and Lesbian Studies which tended to examine the social construction of gay and lesbian sexualities in localized, historical contexts. Lesbian and Gay Studies, in turn, emerged in response to debates between essentialist versus constructionist explanations about the origins and causes of homosexual identity. Briefly, essentialist theories attributed homosexuality to biological or timeless metaphysical causes. Biological essentialism assumes that biological influences, such as the 'Gay Gene' (LeVay and Harmer, 1994) precede cultural influences and set predetermined limits on the impact of social/cultural forces. In contrast, social constructionism (Wikipedia, 2005) examines ways that social reality is created, institutionalized and made into traditions by humans. It assumes that reality is reproduced by people acting on their interpretations and knowledge about reality. Perhaps most importantly for postfoundational sport research, social constructionism considers how human subjectivity imposes itself on seemingly objective, rational, biological 'facts'. For example, in the sociology of science Bruno Latour (Latour and Woolgar, 1986) showed how the very objects of scientific study are, in fact, social constructions produced within the social context of the laboratory and academic community. Within the context of physical fitness, Brian Pronger (2002) exposed how scientific and technological 'facts' about the physically trained body have been socially constructed through exercise texts. Similarly, John Hood-Williams revealed how the International Olympic Committee, in its attempts to create a definitive 'sex test' for athletes, was heavily involved in the ongoing, pervasive social construction of biological sex as either 'male' or 'female' when, he rightly asserts, 'there never will be a true sign of a true sex' (1995: 290).

In Lesbian and Gay Studies, early social constructionist work by scholars such as Ken Plummer, Lillian Faderman and Jeffery Weeks sought to explain the social meanings and changing forms of the modern homosexual. Weeks (1991) explicated how sexual identities 'are not necessary attributes of particular sexual drives or desires, and [they] are not, in fact, essential – that is naturally pre-given – aspects of our personality' (1991: 68). Marx's view that an individual is an ensemble of social relations, Freud's notion that unconscious forces beyond rational control subvert the conscious individual, and subsequent feminist rethinking of the relations between the psyche and male power are used by Weeks to support the following conclusions: 'First, that subjectivity is always fractured, contradictory, ambiguous, and disrupted; second, that identity is not inborn, pregiven, or 'natural'. It is striven for, contested, negotiated, and achieved, often in struggles of the subordinated against the dominant' (1991: 94).

Such social constructionist work in Lesbian and Gay Studies has fundamentally challenged trans-historical and essentialist approaches to researching 'homosexuality', although many studies have uncritically foregrounded white, colonial sexual formations.

Postmodernism and post-structuralism

Social constructionism is linked to postmodernism because both concede that knowledges are constructed; yet postmodernism scrutinizes how rationality is not as rational as it claims to be. Postmodern and queer theories shift away from nuanced accounts of how sexualities have been socially constructed towards even more radical versions of constructionism that critique enlightenment, humanist notions of the self and sexual identity. There has been an important conceptual shift from identity to subjectivity. In post-structuralism, as Andermahr *et al.* (2000) describe, the subject is split into conscious and unconscious aspects and is always in the process of being constituted through psychic and discursive systems, and 'the fluidity of subjectivity is such that it never fully coincides with identity' (2000: 268). This post-structural critique of a stable, unified humanist identity has been influential in the cultivation of queer theory. Thus, according to Lisa Duggan (1998), queer theories critique:

• humanist narrative of self and progress, such as the heroic progress of successive gay liberation movements;
• identity categories presented as stable and authentic;
• empiricist methods that claim to represent the transparent truth of experience.

The shift towards postmodernism emerged from the continual assertion of 'difference' within the 'sameness' of lesbian and gay communities. Many activists and intellectuals, acknowledging sexual and to a lesser extent racial, differences, sought out ways to enable and think about proliferating identities and identifications. The notion of a natural and stable heterosexuality had been heavily criticized in many areas of the humanities and social sciences. Increasingly, Queer Studies started to examine the historical process by which categories such as heterosexual, lesbian and gay came into being. For example, some early

approaches to queering theory responded by exploring the formation and reproduction of heterosexualities (Adams, 1997; Katz, 1995) whereas Michael Warner
(1993) noted that queer 'gets a critical edge by defining itself against the normal
rather than heterosexual' (1993: xxvi). Thus, queer theorists started to de/con-
struct heteronormativity rather than heterosexuality *per se* (Hennessy, 1995).
Queer theorists began to examine where the line between unacceptable and
acceptable sexual practices had been socially constructed. Seidman (1993) rea-
soned that if homosexuality and heterosexuality are a coupling in which each
presupposes the other, and which assumes hierarchical forms, then the epistemic
and political project of identifying a gay subject reinforces and reproduces this
hierarchical figure. Put another way, in order to maintain any binary between gay
and straight, homo and hetero, inside and outside, a boundary is required and it
is the 'production and management' (Namaste, 1994: 224) of such boundaries
that deconstructive queer theory interrogates (Sykes, 1998). Decolonial queer
theory examines boundaries or the *borderlands* from non-white, non-colonial and
non-heteronormative positions (Pérez, 2003). In summary, queer theorists
etched a space to think about the:

- construction of heterosexuality;
- heteronormativity which aligns the dominance of whiteness and late capitalism with heterosexuality;
- relations between hetero and the Other; and
- theories and practices that place queerness at the center in order to transform homosexual, gay, lesbian theory into a general social theory.

As a result, studies of gender and/or sexuality in sport increasingly take into
account the hierarchical relations and intersections between masculinity and femininity, sexual minorities and heterosexuality. One recent example is Jason
Laurendeau's (2004) analysis of the intersection of heterosexual masculinity and
femininity constructed through women's and men's songs in the sport of skydiving
in which he argues that men's songs tend to reinforce a hyperheterosexual masculinity whereas women's songs construct a strong heterosexual femininity which
simultaneously marginalizes non-normative femininities. Some studies utilize relatively stable, social constructionist frameworks for sexual identities to investigate
the operation of heteronorms. For instance Jan Wright and Gill Clarke's (1999)
study of women's rugby media in the UK and Australia identified the pervasiveness
of compulsory heterosexuality in print media while assuming the players themselves possessed relatively stable, politically valuable, lesbian or heterosexual
identities. Rather than examining the hierarchical relation between lesbian and
heterosexual identities, other researchers such as P. J. McGann (2004) conceptualize queer, sexual dissent, minority identities in relation to normative or compulsory
heterosexuality. McGann examined how sport privileges heterosexual over queer
desires by observing how institutions and individual men respond to the presence
of female bodies in the hypermasculine context of ice hockey. Queer theories were
used by K. L. Broad (2001) to frame how she observed queer politics within US

women's rugby in the early 1900s. Broad observed how players transgressed normative female gender, how sexual fluidity within women's rugby culture challenged a homo/heterosexual binary and how players deployed confrontational perversions or 'badass queer acts' (2001: 198). Gender–queer identifications have also been examined, primarily in the context of women's team sports. Debra Silverman (1993) analyzed how femme-identified athletes in the NCCA women's basketball league re-use the normative markers of femininity as expressions of self-representation. The work of Jayne Caudwell (1999; 2004; 2005) has been central to the analysis of queer identifications and practices, in particular butch and femme, lesbian and queer subjectivities in UK women's soccer.

Nikki Sullivan (2003) suggests that queer should be thought of as a set of actions, a verb, as something we do to theory; rather than something that is, a noun, an identity we have or the content that particular theories have. In the anthology *Thinking Queer*, editor Susan Talburt argues that,

> Queer has been said not to be a noun, for nouns stabilize in space and time but an adjective that cuts across identities, subjectivities and communities... but it draws from a history that has constructed queer as an identity [so] efforts to shift queer's meanings from noun to verb, from identity to practice, from modality of being to modality of doing will be neither linear nor complete but contextual and partial.
>
> (cited in Talburt and Steinberg, 2000: 4–5)

Judith Butler (1991, cited in Jagose, 1996) argued that if queer is to avoid the limitations of earlier lesbian and gay formations, it must be thought of as a category in constant formation: '[It] will have to remain that which is, in the present, never fully owned, but always and only redeployed, twisted, queered from a prior usage and in the direction of urgent and expanding political purposes' (cited in Jagose, 1996: 3).

Notwithstanding these attempts to summarize queer theory, Diana Fuss (1991) suggested that the dream of a common definition or no definition at all is just that – a dream. What we can do is look at the explanations and uses of queer theories – use them up, exhaust them, turn them inside out giving them new inflections and purposes in our own work.

Critical scholarship about HIV/AIDS representations and activism was a pivotal discourse in the emergence of queer theorizing (Cole, 1996; Crimp, 1988; King, 1993; Patton, 1990, 1994; Treichler, 1999). Since then, other queer theorizing has examined how transnational sexualities operate and travel across regional and national boundaries via globalization of health, education and sport discourses (Gibson-Graham, 2001; Morris, 1997; Patton and Sanchez-Eppler, 2000; Spivak, 1994). Informed by critical geography, Cathy van Ingen (2004) analyzed the intersections of health, AIDS, whiteness and class-based transphobia produced within/as the social space of queer sportscape of the Toronto Frontrunners (a lesbian, gay, bisexual and transgender running club). Expanding notions about transsexual, transgender and intersex embodiment is a central concern in the emerging field of Trans Theory (Elliot, 2001; Wilchins, 2004; Namaste, 2000; Prosser, 1998). Studies into transgender and transsexual issues in sport have been informed to different degrees by social constructionism, post-structuralist, gender and trans theory. Trans/gender theory, argued Tamar Meyer (2004), challenges the bi-polar gender system in sport which can allow researchers to imagine new athletic embodiments of 'person'hood that take into account gender variant and intersexed athletes. Semerjian and Cohen (2005) have interviewed transgender athletes in the United States to explore how they negotiate their identities within sport. From the start, Disability Studies have interrogated what gets counted as a 'normal' body, challenging taken-for-granted ideas about mobility, and productivity (Connolly, 2003) and even that any body is 'able' across different circumstances and times of life. Recent work in the sociology of the body and embodiment increasingly brings together Disability Studies, Crip Theory and Queer Theory (Clare, 2001; McRuer and Wilerson, 2003; Shildrick, 2002), which creates immense possibilities for future interdisciplinary approaches to studying sport.

Teresa de Lauretis' (1991) theoretical premise for queering theory was to reframe 'gay sexuality in its specific male and female cultural forms' as a form of social agency that is both interactive and resistant; participatory and distinct; equal and different; politically represented yet historically and materially specific. Queered theories are littered with different reworkings of this logic of the 'and'. This is the move from the logic of identity to the logic of the 'and', the limit (Pronger; 1998) and the boundary. de Lauretis (1991) sought to problematize both what had been said and understood – discursive constructions – and what had been left out – constructed silences – within Lesbian and Gay Studies. Along similar lines, in my methodological approach I differentiate between feminist understanding – which asks questions texts insist upon – and queer overstanding – which asks questions texts do not pose (Sykes, 2001). Examples of constructed silences include what Pérez (2003) calls the decolonial imaginary, Kristeva (1982) calls the abject, and what Britzman (1995) calls the unthought. These diverse queer approaches have the potential to initiate interdisciplinary conversations about desire, sex/uality and gender within Sport Studies in relation to racialization, global capitalism, feminism, post-structuralism and the unconscious.

Queering the history of sexology

Examining how an essentialist or constructionist explanation, theory or identity was produced or exceeded by something else has been the focus of some approaches to queer theory. Fine examples of this approach can be found in rereadings of the history of sexology. Indeed the idea that homosexuality is a biological condition has been shown to be a construction of nineteenth century medicine and sexology. The category of homosexuality was constituted from the moment it was characterized by sexologist Karl Westphal in 1870. As Foucault (1978) famously stated: 'the homosexual was now a species' (1978:.43), he went on to document how, before 1870, anyone might succumb to same-sex acts that were condemned in religious and civil law, whereas after 1870 same-sex acts became associated with a type of person. Homosexual acts were converted into a psychobiological condition.

The knowledge constructed by the science of sexology was extremely influential at the end of the nineteenth century. Sexologists such as Karl Heinrich Ulrichs, Richard von Krafft-Ebing and Havelock Ellis, who worked during the 1870s to the 1940s, coined many of the terms we still use today such as 'homosexuality', 'heterosexuality', 'sadism' and 'masochism'. Recent work on the history of sexology reveals how many more categories and labels were used, many of them now outdated such as 'invert' and 'uranian/uraniad'. The science of sexology changed Eurocentric discourses about 'deviant' sexual and gender identities in three important ways – decriminalization, medicalization and categorization. Rita Felski (1998) points out how it was not that new sexual discourses about the hysterical woman, the homosexual or the masturbating child simply produced new sexual identities; rather, that the history of sexology contains messy and surprising histories about the formation of modern sexual categories. Felski argues that it is as dangerous to reduce sexology to a repressive scientific discourse as it is to suggest that sexologists were heroic pioneers pushing the boundaries of sexual tolerance and understanding.

Sexual inversion has been interpreted as being synonymous with homosexuality. The trope of 'female souls trapped in male bodies' was often emphasized in social constructionist histories of the sexological discourse about Western homosexuality. Transsexual theorists such as Jay Prosser (1998) are showing how this commonplace idea within Lesbian and Gay Studies is an inaccurate and reductive interpretation. Prosser suggests inversion measured transgenderism rather than homosexuality. The sexological concept of the 'invert' included some types of homosexuality, it also encompassed a broader range of transgender identifications, including clear instances of a somatic desire to 'change sex'. Moreover early sexological discourse played an important part in recognizing transsexual subjects, and the development of medical and surgical aids to gender reassignment.

Theories of race and homosexuality have been closely intertwined, shaped by scientific racism (Somerville, 1994). Biological degeneracy theories about primitives underpinned sexologists' theories of homosexuality. In *Racial Castration* David Eng (2001) reveals a similar racial logic in Freud's developmental notion of homosexuality as a less mature, more 'primitive' version of heterosexuality. These theories were 'steeped in pervasive cultural anxieties toward 'mixed' bodies' (Somerville, 1994) that threatened the imagined purity of the white heterosexual male body. Thus the homosexual invert was constructed in terms of a 'mix of genders'. Dana Seitler (2004) recently used queer theory to point out how turn-of-the-century scientific construction and classification of perverse bodies is not only a history of homosexuality but, in fact, a story in which race, gender, physical deformation and bodily forms interact and coalesce. Seitler studied the medical photographs used by sexologists, including Havelock Ellis, to create and archive their categorizations. Rather than producing a stable homosexual subject, she argues that sexological and medical classifications produced 'queer physiognomy' across a number of unstable registers such as intelligence, age, race, gender variance and anatomical variance. Taking up a more contemporary issue within sport, Rebecca Lock (2003) argues that the construction of non-heterosexual femininity as 'ugly' underpins the construction of doping in sport as 'bad'. Such critical studies into visual anatomy and doping ethics illustrate the divergent topics being re-examined as a result of queer theorizing.

Michel Foucault and subjectification

Despite immense changes in theories of sexuality from the nineteenth to the twenty-first century, from sexologists through Freud to postmodern queer, Foucault points out an important continuum between the Victorians, the modernists and queers – that share the conviction that sexuality holds the key to our identity (or subjectivity). For many queer theorists, this reliance on identity is deemed to be more regulatory and exclusionary than progressive and liberating. This does not mean that identity no longer exists, or that all queer theories are anti-identity and do not draw from the socio-political effects of identity claims and movements. However, post-structuralist queer theorists started looking towards *identity as difference* rather than towards ever-increasing specific communities based on the possibility of *identity as self-presence*. This is a crucial move away from identity as essence or presence towards the idea that identity is relational, is constructed and implicated in an 'Other'. Basically this means acknowledging that identity is purchased at the expense or necessary exclusion of an 'Other'. Thus the logic of identity becomes the logic of a boundary.

In *Fear of a Queer Planet*, Michael Warner (1993) explained how identity poses such a problem because issues of sexuality cannot be captured by the languages designed to name them, hence attempts to fix sexual identities are over-determined by other conflicts. Foucault examined these conflicts by examining how people became subjects of scientific investigation, especially the 'new' sciences of sexology, psychiatry and eugenics. Foucault analyzed how power is produced and resisted at the everyday, local level of the body and how it feeds up to institutions such as schools, prisons and hospitals (Mills, 2003). In the sociology of sport Foucault's work has influenced work on surveillance, discipline, the gaze and technologies of the self, governmentality and neo-liberalism (Cole, *et al.*, 2004; Rail and Harvey, 1995). Foucault was concerned with how individuals are pressurized into creating themselves and their identities in a certain fashion. Individuals define themselves in relation to – or more accurately are constituted by – numerous discourses such as race, health, sex and nationality. At the level of the individual, it is a matter of subjectification:

- How the person is trained in certain ways of behaving, the extent to which a person is subject to power;
- How the person understands their own capacities – how they are subject to a body of ethics;
- How the person relates to others – accepts the situation as true.

Thus, individuals do not have 'free will' to construct a sexual identity, nor is it merely a matter of finding a way to gain agency to 'come out' or to 'be a queer on the team' in the face of oppressive power structures. Rather, Foucault focused on how sexuality came to be by looking at processes such as confessing; 'discovering' one's identity; coming out; how the search for the cause of homosexuality was integral to how we came to think about and DO homosexuality. For example Toby Miller (1998) described how rugby league player Ian Roberts' 'coming out' operated through his repeated Foucaultian confessionals. Annamarie Jagose (1996) explained that, although queer can never be outside the magnetic field of identity, 'queer is less an identity than a critique of identity' (1996: 3). Thus, 'homosexuals' can be thought about in terms uncoupled from, yet historically implicated, in individual or collective identities. In his anthropological study of Jewish sports and soccer clubs in Vienna, Austria, Matti Bunzl (2000) acknowledges that although coming out as Jewish or queer is the object of his study, 'coming out cannot be just a declaration of individual and collective authentification' (2000: 322). Rather he asserts how: 'As symptoms of modernity, Jews and homosexuals were demarcated to be silenced; as symptoms of postmodernity, they are invited to speak, but from the very position of difference that constituted them in the first place' (2000: 322).

Feminist sport scholars have foregrounded the regulation of gendered embodiment, contesting, yet at the same time drawing from Foucault's notion of the docile body. Examples of this approach can be found in Jennifer Wesely's (2001) exploration of how male and female bodybuilders negotiated their gender identities and Pirkko Markula's (2004) study of commercial fitness classes in which she assessed the possibilities for subjects to enact what Foucault called 'technologies of the self' within the fitness industry as a regime of power/knowledge that narrowly regulates the feminine body. Another strand of studies under the purview of sport has used a Foucaultian framework to analyze marginalized and normative sexualities *per se*, such as Brian Pronger's (1992) early analysis of gay male sensibilities (de-emphasis, irony, change) in *The Arena of Masculinity*. However Pronger's (2002) most recent analysis in *Body Fascism* uses Foucault's concept of the subjection of the body in tandem with Deleuze and Guattari's idea that flows of desire work to limit and free (territorialize and deterritorialize) the body. Pronger's work radically shifts the notion of desire from being an expression of, or being repressed in order to create, genital sexuality, gay sensibility or homosexual identity towards the concepts of puissance and pouvoir in which desire is: 'the force by which we move at all. The movement of desire is the essence of the body. As such, it is the process of all physical activities: walking, reading, writing, conversing, sitting, swimming, eating, defecating, thinking...' (2002: 76).

This type of work is representative of an expansive – what Eve Sedgwick (1990) called a universalizing – queer approach to theorizing desire. Such use of queer theory extends beyond what Britzman (1995) referred to as the alibis of race, class and gender into quite different and more diffuse registers of the body and embodiment. Also diverging from queer theory are critical postmodern spatial studies of sport which, Cathy van Ingen (2003) suggests, developed in part as a critique of Foucault, and seek to examine the heterogeneity of gender, sexuality, race and other subaltern relations. Yet another influential strand in this universalizing approach to queer theorizing has been influenced by Judith Butler's radical philosophy that draws upon Foucault in tandem with revisionist readings of Freudian psychoanalytic desire.

Judith Butler and performativity

As you begin reading post-structural work, you read that identity is 'fluid', it is not 'fixed'. Also, that identity is 'partial', 'incomplete' and 'fragmented'. You may have come across these descriptions elsewhere, and they may not seem real – it may not be how we 'really feel'. Yet again, such notions of the self can provide rich insights into the tensions and contractions of a vast range of sport experiences. Writing about men's rugby union in New Zealand, Richard Pringle (2001) used narratives of self that revealed how competing discourses, such as playing nice versus tackling hard, or homophobic bullying versus boy–boy friendship, made it difficult for him to maintain a coherent sense of self. What is at stake here, in post-structural, some queer work and certainly in Butler's work, is a significant challenge to humanism, to the idea that the self can fully know itself, that it achieves the status of 'being' from which the self, or a subject, can act. For Butler, sex, gender and sexuality are not stable, fundamental 'facts' underpinning our existence; rather identities are taken on through the violent foreclosure of identities that do *not* matter.

Butler uses psychoanalytic theories of the subject and subjection, of performativity and identification, that underpin more superficial claims that identity is always incomplete and partial. In *The Psychic Life of Power*, Judith Butler (1997) argued that contemporary heteronormative culture is based on widespread refusing – or disavowing – of identifications with homosexuality. Identifications, in the psychoanalytic sense, contain what to all external appearances has been given up or refused. Gender identifications contain the echoes and traces of desirous gender attachments that the self, the family and culture have prohibited. Following Freud closely, Butler initially argues that gender is acquired, at least in part, by repudiating homosexual attachments. To become heterosexual in our culture is to proclaim, 'I have never loved and I have never lost' someone of the same sex. Thus, for Butler, heterosexual gender is melancholic. It is haunted by the trace of the homosexual other. So in a culture of gender melancholy, masculinity and femininity become stronger only by repudiating (or denying) what they cannot grieve. Caroline Fusco (1999) considered melancholia in the sex/gender discourses surrounding the sexual abuse case in Canadian ice hockey involving Sheldon Kennedy and Graham James. By analyzing the discourses of the 'good homosexual' versus 'the pervert', she illustrated how the foreclosure of certain sexual subjectivities produced a culture of gender melancholia in sport. In *Gender Trouble* Butler (1990) also argues that, since all gender and sexed positions are performative imitations, even hegemonic heterosexuality is derived rather than being the 'natural' or originary form of human sexuality. Butler's notions of gender imitation and melancholic gender differ greatly from the notion of socially constructed gendered and sexual identities that express, or indeed constitute, a sense of self – even when these identities are constructed in relation to an 'other' social identity through discursive and material ways. 'In opposition to a conception of sexuality which is said to 'express' gender, gender itself is understood to be composed of precisely what remains inarticulate in sexuality' (Butler, 1997: 140).

Post-colonial studies and hybridity

In part, 'queer' initially attempted to address the exclusion of queers of color within the many areas of feminist, lesbian and gay movements (Seidman, 1994). de Lauretis envisioned queer theory as a new horizon for racial and sexual lives. One of the foci of queer theory has been the 'differential formation of homosexuality across racial boundaries, including the question of how racial and reproductive injunctions are articulated through one another' (Butler, 1993: 21). Scholars are gradually integrating queer theories and post-colonial theories[1]. In *Postcolonial, Queer* John Hawley (2001) draws on Michael Hardt and Antonio Negri's distinction between 'empire' and imperialism to link queer to globalization. They describe imperialism in the new world order as decentered and deterritorializing with hybrid identities, flexible hierarchies and plural exchanges. Hawley extrapolates that nation-states become irrelevant and borders become a blur such that 'globalization, in effect, becomes queer' (2000: 8). However, it is important to distinguish between the similarities, differences and specific meanings of concepts such as 'hybridity', 'diaspora' and 'nation' within post-colonial queer theories. Hybridity has been conceptualized within post-colonialism as, on the one hand, a colonializing strategy of miscegenation and extinction while it can also refer to the anti-colonial strategy of hybridity or *mestizaje* evoked by Roberto Fernández Retamar, Paul Gilroy and Gloria Anzaldúa (Brah and Coombes, 2000; Loomba, 1998). Kathy Jamieson (2003) uses a notion of hybridity derived from queer Chicana feminisms to conceptualize the diversity *and* sameness within the subjectivities of Latina softball players in the US college system. The notion of diasporic identification is used within post-colonial studies as a positive affirmation of hybridity (Ashcroft, *et al.*, 2002) and forms a central tenet in Gamal Abdel-Shehid's (2005) *Who Da Man*. Abdel-Shehid offers a feminist, queer analysis that interrogates ways that Black masculinities intersect with the dominant misogyny and homophobia in contemporary men's sporting cultures, such as football within a Black Atlantic context, Ben Johnson as a figure within Canadian nationalism and the Raptors pro basketball team within the Black publics of Toronto. Hybridity refers to the creation of new transcultural forms in the contact zone produced by colonization (Ashcroft, *et al.*, 2002) and is an example of what Robert Young called a double logic 'which goes against the convention of rational either/or choices' (cited in Ashcroft *et al.*, 2002) and has more to do with the relations within a field rather than the analysis of discrete objects. Homi Bhabha (1994) showed how cultural identities are produced within colonized/colonizer relations – what he calls the third space – and that these identities, far from being pure, one side or the other, purely colonizer or colonized, are always somewhat contradictory and ambivalent. He claims that recognizing this ambivalence may help overcome the exoticism of cultural diversity in favor of an empowering hybridity. Hybridization has been used by Carlos Alberto (1998) to examine the emergence of Brazillian gay/queer football teams in Rio de Janeiro and São Paulo.

Gloria Anzaldúa[2] wrote not only about what 'queer' as a hybridity meant to her but also about borderlands, entradas and reading practices. Anzaldúa was a central figure in Chicana lesbian writing, known for mixing genres, narrative and theoretical voices in her writing. She has been a very important figure in challenging racism within queer theory and second-wave white feminist theory. She has been using the word 'queer' since the early 1980s:

> We are the queer groups, the people that don't belong anywhere, not in the dominant world nor completely within our own respective cultures. Combined we cover so many oppressions. But the overwhelming oppression is the collective fact that we do not fit, and because we do not fit we are a threat. Not all of us have the same oppressions, but we empathize and identify with each other's oppressions. We do not have the same ideology, nor do we derive similar solutions. Some of us are leftists, some of us are practitioners of magic. Some of us are both.
>
> (Anzaldúa, 1983: 209)

Anzaldúa uses many metaphors and concepts derived from indigenous and Chicana knowledge, some of which predate similar ideas commonly attributed to Eurocentric post-structuralism and queer theory. For example she uses the notion of *entradas* as the 'doors and windows' through which we enter a text. Entradas into her writing differ according to our lived experiences, our identifications, hence she does not try to 'always spell things out' but leaves her writing, and the reader's process of identification, open. She wrote: 'I want the reader to deduce my conclusions or at least come up with her own' (Anzaldúa, 1998: 273). In her post-structural research about sexualities in Latina collegiate softball, Kathy Jamieson (2003) uses similar strategies to represent players' 'ongoing process of negotiating multiple identities that reflect an intersection of sexualities, physicalities, and cultural and family traditions' (2003: 21). Jamieson compiled the stories shared by women during interviews into fictional narratives that she intentionally aligned with 'Chicana feminisms, US, Third World feminisms, and innovations in interpretive representational tactics' (2003: 24). This decolonial queer approach to writing is profoundly similar to the shift in post-structuralism from pinpointing the intention of the author – structuralism – to the response of the reader – Barthes – to deconstruction which, if nothing else, relies on keeping meaning open to an extent. It resonates with Butler's reluctance to give concrete examples because she intends her philosophy to be taken up as a reading practice in localized, specific discursive political struggles. There is determined and extremely political openness in Anzaldúa's notion of queer. '...I fear a unity that leaves out parts of me, that colonizes me, that violates my integrity, my whole-ness, and chips away at my autonomy' (1998: 268). So queer simultaneously permits a wholeness and integrity while being open and refusing unity. This type of paradoxical thinking, way of identifying has similarities to Fuss' refusal of clear inside–outside boundaries, refusal of categorical clarity. The writing of queer edu-cation scholar Kevin Kumashiro (2001) also relies heavily on paradoxes. He asks for two seemingly contradictory things. On one hand, queers of color need to claim and assert their identities of difference – counter-identifications – to build community, name struggles, plan for action. At the same time, he demands that these identities and plans for action are 'constantly troubled so they don't close off possibilities for future change' (2001: 10), that 'dis-identifications' are used to disrupt the way identities function in new normalizing ways.

Psychoanalysis and queer theory

Another interdisciplinary strand in queer theory has been the reworking of psy-choanalytic theories. This allows different questions to be asked about sexualities and racialization within globalized, colonizing sporting practices and histories (Spivak, 1994). For instance, Deborah Britzman (1995) speculates how racial, gen-der and sexual dynamics might act as alibis for other psychic processes of exclusion and normalization. Britzman asked readers to consider whether the body can be without explanation. Using the narcissism of minor differences to disrupt the links between identity and oppression, race and racism, sexuality and homophobias, she asked if it is possible to 'think about the psychic structure of living without the alibi of gender, race and sex' (1995: 36). She argues that we are subject to the force of desires arguing with one another in a register beyond identity. Sport continually provides 'new editions of old conflicts' (Britzman, 1998: 35) and new exclusions emerge even as sport appears to become more inclusive. In the United States, twenty-five years have passed since Title IX was enacted to ensure equal access for girls and women into sport and education. Last year, the International Olympic Committee passed the Stockholm Consensus to allow transsexual athletes to com-pete at the Olympics (Cavanagh and Sykes 2005; Meyer, 2004; Sykes, 2005). Yet many of the anxieties about non-traditional, athletic femininities posing a threat to sport that were evoked twenty five years ago to oppose Title IX are now being repeated in relation to transsexual women athletes in elite sport (Sykes, 2005). These anxieties may be thought about in psychoanalytic terms. Sheila Cavanagh and myself (2005) recently argued that, while both transsexual and Olympic bod-ies have unique histories and vastly different experiences in the social and political realms, the presence of the transsexual body in sport reveals within the Olympic community a fascination with the athletic body which is, in part, about a voyeuris-tic engagement with bodies already transcending the boundaries of binary gender categories. Sex-testing and the Stockholm Consensus are, in essence, psychic attempts to manage muscularity and the illusions of binary gender in and between Olympic bodies, bodies that have already, by definition, transformed from the 'common' non-Olympic body. The difficulty managing gender in bodies that swell and enlarge is not unrelated to transphobia (the irrational fear or hatred of the gendered subject in transition). Sheila Cavanagh (2003) has argued elsewhere that transphobia is, in part, incited by the threat posed to stable body boundaries and genital configurations governing (and giving shape to) two bi-polar, gender positionalities. The hyperbolic concern about muscle mass, testosterone and chromosome counts (driving the discourses about male to female athletes having a physical advantage over female athletes and about drug testing in elite sport) are not only about gender. As Marica Ian suggests, 'muscle does not have gender' (2001: 75) and it can thus undermine the psychic defenses employed to cultivate the fantasy of gender. Thus, we argue that the psychic anxiety underpinning the fetishistic engagement with muscularity is about the problem of normative sexed embodiment; heterosexual bifurcations of gender; and ultimately about the body's mortality.

That sport is invested in boundary maintenance in so many ways indicates psychic anxiety. At the same time, sport operates as a complex site of pleasure and desire. Queer theorists informed by contemporary psychoanalytic theories are starting to examine these ambivalent, psychic dynamics across a range of sporting contexts, notably the Gay Games. Several studies have subjected the Gay Games to its own questions about inclusiveness, proposing psychic explanations why the Gay Games, emulating a western model of large-scale, meritocratic and commodified sporting competition, falls prey to reproducing familiar types of social exclusion. Both Judy Davidson (2004) and Elspeth Probyn (2000) have discussed how the trope of pride seemed to be a necessity in conceptualizing the Gay Games yet the insistence on pride hints at a shame that must be covered at all costs. This hints towards 'an ontology of gay life that cannot admit its other' (Probyn 2000: 19). This dread of admitting the Other is also manifest as a narcissistic heightened self-regard within the Gay Games community. The Pay Games protest at the Amsterdam Gay Games revealed how economic hardship and queerness had to be disavowed in order for the Games to become a global, Olympian event (Sykes, 2001). Thus, queer theories deploy psychoanalytic dynamics such as shame and narcissism to understand how even new gay sporting communities seem condemned to repeat the histories of exclusion that beleaguered earlier lesbian and gay identity politics.

In/Conclusion

Queering sport studies has the potential to alter how we think about sexualities, desires and bodies. Queer theories of sport take into account post-foundational assumptions about humanism, identity, social science and cultural practices. Some queer theoretical moves engage hybrid identifications as unruly, unconscious complications to sexual identity while others shine Foucaultian searchlights on how power/knowledge creates the possibility of desire and at the same time power acts to constrain desire and pleasure in sporting practices. Queer theorizing moves across interdisciplinary boundaries, employs deconstructive logics of paradox and contradiction while self-reflexively assessing its unpredictable yet necessary political and ethical commitments. Queer theory provides myriad, if temporary, capacities to re-signify and reroute oppressive forms of power/knowledge which is necessary given our global, cultural and academic context where uncertainty 'is a permanent condition of life' (Bauman, 1996: 36). Yet if queer theorizing in sport is to supersede the limits of previous queer, gender and feminist theories, José Esteban Muñoz (1999) warns 'it must be able to calculate multiple antagonisms that index issues of class, gender, and race, as well as sexuality' (1999: 22). Moreover, Rosaria Champagne (1998) declared that 'you cannot buy queer theory at Wal-Mart, and it's a good thing, too' (1998: 294) for if queer theory becomes commodified as identity politics it will lose the power to change and grow, becoming distorted by the same process that warps all liberatory paradigms. Thus de Lauretis' (1991) wish for theory that envisions another way of living the racial and sexual must be always remembered and deliberately invoked as sport studies engages with what Judith Butler (2004) calls the new gender politics forged in coalitions between queers, feminists, intersexual, transsexual and transgender movements. This is a belated call for scholarship, embodiment and politics that leans into and learns from *El Mundo Zurdo* or 'The Left-handed World' (Anzaldúa, 1983).

Notes

1   By the 1930s, colonies and ex-colonies covered 84.6% of the globe. Postcolonial theorist Ania Loomba (1998) argues that this vast sweep of colonialism makes any summary of postcolonialism reductive. Decolonization spanned three centuries, differing where white settlers formed independent nations such as Latin American, Australia and South Africa from where indigenous populations overthrew their colonizers. Postcolonial experience of diaspora, people displaced by colonialism, differs from people in colonized nations. Thus there can be no global 'whiteness' as there are important differences in power and history between Canada, the European metropolis and the United States metropolis (Loomba, 1998).
2   Sadly Gloria Anzaldúa passed away recently in 2004.

References

Abdel-Shehid, G. (2005) *Who Da Man? Black Masculinities and Sporting Cultures*. Toronto, ON: Canadian Scholars Press.

Adams, M. L. (1997) *The Trouble with Normal: Postwar Youth and the Making of Heterosexuality*. Toronto, ON: University of Toronto Press.

Alberto, C. (1998) 'Mapping gay culture in Brazil: The local experience of queer games', A paper presented at *Queer Games: An International Conference in Gay and Lesbian Studies*, Amsterdam, NL. July 29–31.

Andermahr, S., Lovell, T. and Wolkowitz, C. (2000) *A Glossary of Feminist Theory*. London: Arnold.

Anzaldúa, G. (1983) 'La Prieta', in G. Anzaldúa and C. Moraga (eds) *This Bridge Called My Back: Writings by Radical Women of Color*, 2nd edn. Watertown, MA: Persephone Press, 198–209.

Anzaldúa, G. (1998) 'To(o) queer the writer – Loca, escritora y chicana', in C. Trujullo (ed) *Living Chicana Theory*. Berkley, CA: Third Woman Press, pp. 263–76.

Ashcroft, B., Griffiths, G. and Tiffin, H. (2002) *Post-colonial Studies: The Key Concepts*. London: Routledge.

Bauman, Z. (1996) *Alone Again: Ethics after Certainty*. London: Demos.

Bhabha, H. K. (1994) *The Location of Culture*. London, New York: Routledge.

Brah, A. and Coombes, A. E. (2000) *Hybridity and its Discontents: Politics, Science and Culture*. London: Routledge.

Britzman, D. (1995) 'Is there a queer pedagogy? Or, stop reading straight', *Educational Theory*, 45(2): 151–65.

Britzman, D. (1998) *Lost Subjects, Contested Objects: Toward a Psychoanalytic Inquiry of Learning*. New York: State University of New York Press.

Broad, K. L. (2001) 'The gendered unapologetic: Queer resistance in women's sport', *Sociology of Sport Journal*, 18(2): 181–204.

Bunzl, M. (2000) 'Autocritique of 'Resistive play: Sports and the emergence of Jewish visibility in contemporary Vienna", *Journal of Sport and Social Issues*, 24(3): 321–23.

Butler, J. (1990) *Gender Trouble: Feminism and the Subversion of Identity*. New York: Routledge.

Butler, J. (1993). *Bodies that Matter: On the Discursive Limits of Sex*. New York: Routledge.

Butler, J. (1997) *The Psychic Life of Power: Theories in Subjection*. Stanford, CA: Stanford University Press.

Butler, J. (2004) *Undoing Gender*. New York: Routledge.

Caudwell, J. (1999) 'Women's football in the United Kingdom: Theorizing gender and unpacking the butch lesbian image', *Journal of Sport and Social Issues*. 23(4): 390–402.

Caudwell, J. (2004) 'The femme and football: Queering femininity, queering football?', Paper presented at the *North American Society for the Sociology of Sport*, Tuscon, AZ, November 3–6.

Caudwell, J. (2005) 'Queer in the sociology of sport', Paper presented in *The(e)ories: Advanced Seminars for Queer Research*, University College Dublin, Dublin, February 11.

Cavanagh, S. (2003) 'Teacher transsexuality: The illusion of sexual difference and the idea of adolescent trauma in the Dana Rivers Case,' *Sexualities* 6(3–4): 361–83.

Cavanagh, S. and Sykes, H. (2005) 'Transsexual bodies at the Olympics', Paper presented to *The(e)ories: Advanced Seminar in Queer Theory*. Dublin: University College Dublin. April 4.

Champagne, R. (1998) 'Queering the unconscious', *South Atlantic Quarterly*, 97(2): 281–96.

Clare, E. (2001) 'Stolen bodies, reclaimed bodies: Disability and queerness', *Public Culture*, 13(3), 359–65.

Cole, C. L. (1996) 'Containing AIDS: Magic Johnson and Post[Reagan] America', in S. Seidman (ed) *Queer Theory/Sociology*. Oxford: Blackwell, 280–310.

Cole, C. L., Giardina, M. and Andrews, D. (2004) 'Michel Foucault: Studies of power and sport', in R. Giullianotti (ed.) *Sport and Modern Social Theory*, Basingstoke: Palgrave, 207–23.

Connolly, M. (2003) 'Disability studies in physical education', in C. van Ingen and H. Sykes (eds) *AVANTE: Special Issue on Dis/placed Bodies*, 9(3): 44–51.

Crimp, D. (1988) *AIDS: Cultural Analysis/Cultural Activism*. Cambridge, MA: MIT Press.

Davidson, J. (2004) 'Olympic melancholia: Pride, shame and the emergence of the Gay Games', Paper presented at the *North America Society for the Sociology of Sport*, Tuscon, AZ. November.

de Lauretis, T. (1991) 'Queer theory: Lesbian and gay sexualities: An introduction', *Differences: A Journal of Feminist Cultural Studies*, 3(2): iii–xviii.

Duggan, Lisa. (1998). 'Queering the state', In P. Nardi & B. Schneider (eds.), *Social Perspectives in Lesbian and Gay Studies*, pp. 564–572. New York: Routledge.

Elliot, P. (2001) 'A psychoanalytic reading of transsexual embodiment', *Studies in Gender and Sexuality*, 2(4): 295–325.

Eng, D. (2001) *Racial Castration: Managing Masculinity in Asian America*. Durham, NC: Duke University Press.

Felski, R. (1998) 'Introduction', in L. Bland and L. Doan (eds) *Sexology in Culture: Labelling Bodies and Desires*, Chicago, IL: University of Chicago Press, 1–8.

Foucault, M. (1978) *The History of Sexuality, Volume 1: An Introduction*. (trans. R. Hurley). New York: Vintage Books.

Fusco, C. (1999) 'Gender melancholia and the organization of desire: Butler's 'Psychic Life of Power' and the sexual order of things in sport', Paper presented at the *North American Society for the Sociology of Sport, Cleveland*, OH. November.

Fuss, D. (1991) 'Inside/out', in D. Fuss (ed) *Inside/out: Lesbian Theories, Gay Theories*, New York: Routledge, 1–10.

Gibson-Graham, J. K. (2001) 'Queering globalization', in J. Hawley (ed.) *Post-colonial, Queer: Theoretical intersections*. Albany, NY; SUNY, 239–75.

Hawley, J. (ed.) (2001) *Postcolonial Queers: Theoretical Intersections*. Albany, NY: SUNY.

Hennessy, R. (1995) 'Queer visibility in commodity culture', *Cultural Critique*, 29, 31–76.

Hood-Williams, J. (1995) 'Sexing the athletes', *Sociology of Sport Journal*, 12(3), 290–305.

Ian, M. (2001) 'The primitive subject of female bodybuilding: Transgression and other postmodern myths', *Differences: A Journal of Feminist Cultural Studies* 12(3): 69–100.

Jagose, A. (1996) *Queer Theory: An Introduction*. New York: New York University Press.

Jamieson, K. (2003) 'Latina sexualities: What's sport got to do with it?', *AVANTE*, 9(3): 19–30.

Katz, J. (1995) *The Invention of Heterosexuality*. New York: Penguin.

King, S. (1993) 'The politics of the body and the body politic: Magic Johnson and the ideology of AIDS', *Sociology of Sport Journal*, 10(3), 270–85.

Kristeva, J. (1982) *Powers Of Horror: An Essay On Abjection*. New York: Columbia University Press.

Kumashiro, K. (2001) 'Queer students of color and antiracist, antiheterosexist education: Paradoxes of identity and activism', in K. Kumashiro (ed) *Troubling Intersections of Race and Sexuality: Queer Students of Color and Anti-oppressive Education*. Lanham, MD: Rowman and Littlefield, 1–25.

Latour, B. and Woolgar, S. (1986) *Laboratory life: The Construction of Scientific Facts*, 2nd edn. Princeton, NJ: Princeton University Press.

Laurendeau, J. (2004) 'The "crack choir" and the "cock chorus"': The intersection of gender and sexuality in skydiving texts. *Sociology Of Sport Journal*, 21(4): 397–417.

LeVay, S. and Harmer, S. (1994) 'Evidence for a biological influence in male homosexuality', *Scientific American*, May, 44–9.

Lock, R. (2003) 'The doping ban: Compulsory heterosexuality and lesbophobia', *International Review for the Sociology of Sport*, 38(4): 397–471.

Loomba, A. (1998) *Colonialism/post-colonialism*. New York: London.

Lourde, A. (1982) *Zami: A New Spelling of My Name*. Watertown, MA: Persephone.

Markula, P. (2004) '"Tuning into one's self": Foucault's technologies of the self and mindful fitness', *Sociology of Sport Journal*, 21(3): 302–21.

McGann, P. J. (2004) 'Of pucks and men: A queer female body in naturalized masculine terrain', Paper presented at the *North American Society for the Sociology of Sport Conference*, Tucson, AZ, November 3–6.

McRuer, R. and Wilerson, A. (2003) 'Introduction: Special Issue on Queerness and Disabilities', *glq: A Journal of Lesbian and Gay Studies*, 9 (1/2): 1–23.

Meyer, T. (2004) 'Trans/feminist sport sociology: Applying transgender theory to the sociology of sport', Paper presented at the *North American Society for the Sociology of Sport Conference*, Tucson, AZ, November 3–6.

Miller, T. (1998) 'Commodifying the male body, problematizing 'hegemonic masculinity'', *Journal of Sport and Social Issues*, 22(4): 431–47.

Mills, S. (2003) *Michel Foucault*. New York: Routledge.

Moraga, C. (1996) 'Queer Aztlán: The re-formation of the Chicano tribe', in D. Norton (ed.) *The Material Queer: A LesBiGay Cultural Studies Reader*, Boulder, CO: Westview Press, 297–304.

Morris, R. (1997) 'Educating desire: Thailand, transnationalism and transgression', Social Text 52/53: 53–79.

Muñoz, J. E. (1999) *Disidentifications: Queers of Color and the Performance of Politics*. Minneapolis, MN: University of Minnesota Press.

Namaste, K. (1994) 'The politics of inside/out: Queer theory, post-structuralism, and a sociological approach to sexuality', *Sociological Theory*, 12(2): 220–31.

Namaste, V. (2000) *Invisible Lives: The Erasure of Transsexual and Transgendered People*. Chicago, IL: University of Chicago Press.

Norton, D. (1996) *The Material Queer: A LesBiGay Cultural Studies Reader*, Boulder, CO: Westview Press.

Patton, C. (1990) *Inventing AIDS*. New York: Routledge.

Patton, C. (1994) *Last Served? Gendering the HIV Pandemic*. London: Taylor & Francis.

Patton, C. and Sanchez-Eppler, B. (2000) *Queer Diasporas*. Durham, NC: Duke University Press.

Penn, D. (1995) 'Queer: Theorizing politics and history', *Radical History Review*, 62(spring), 24–42.

Pérez, E. (2003) 'Queering the borderlands: The challenges of excavating the invisible and unheard', *Frontiers*, 24 (2/3): 122–31.

Pringle, R. (2001) 'Competing discourses: Narratives of a fragmented self, manliness and rugby union', *International Journal for the Sociology of Sport*, 36(4): 425–39.

Probyn, Elspeth. (2000) 'Sporting bodies: Dynamics of shame and pride', *Body and Society*, 6, no.1, 2000: 13–28.

Pronger, B. (1992) *The Arena of Masculinity: Sports, Homosexuality and the Meaning of Sex*, Toronto: University of Toronto Press.

Pronger, B. (1998). 'Post-sport: Trangressing boundaries in physical culture', in G. Rail (ed.) *Sport and Postmodern Times: Culture, Gender, Sexuality, the Body and Sport*. Buffalo, NY: SUNY.

Pronger, B. (2002) *Body Fascism: Salvation in the Technology of Physical Fitness*. Toronto: University of Toronto Press.

Prosser, J. (1998) *Second Skins: The Body Narratives of Transsexuality*. New York: Columbia University Press.

Rail, G. and Harvey, J. (1995) 'Body at work: Michel Foucault and the sociology of sport', *Sociology of Sport Journal*, 12(2): 164–79.

Sedgwick, E. K. (1990) *Epistemology of the closet*. Berkley, CA: University of California Press.

Seidman, S. (1993) 'Identity and politics in a 'postmodern' gay culture: Some historical and conceptual notes', in M. Warner (ed.) *Fear of a Queer Planet: Queer Politics and Social Theory*. Minneapolis, MN: University of Minnesota Press, 297–304.

Seidman, S. (1994) 'Symposium: Queer theory/sociology: A dialogue', *Sociological Theory*, 12(2):166–76.

Seidman, S. (1996) *Queer theory/Sociology*. Cambridge, MA: Blackwell.

Seitler, D. (2004) 'Queer physiognomies; Or, how many ways can we do the history of sexuality?', *Criticism*, 46(1): 71–102.

Semerjian, T. and Cohen, J. (2005) '"FTM means female to me": Negotiating identity and finding space in sport for transgender athletes', Paper presented at the *Women and Sport: Before, During and After Title IX Symposium*, Bowling Green State University, Bowling Green, OH. February 6.

Shildrick, M. (2002) *Embodying the Monster: Encounters with the Vulnerable Self*. Thousand Oaks, CA: SAGE.

Silverman, Debra (1993). 'Playing With Clothes', *Postmodern Culture*, Volume 3, Number 3, May.

Somerville, S. (1994) 'Scientific racism and the emergence of the homosexual body', *Journal of the History of Sexuality*, 5(2): 243–65.

Spivak, G. (1994) 'Psychoanalysis in left field and fieldworking: examples to fit the title', in S. Dasani and M. Munchow (eds) *Speculations After Freud*, New York: Routledge, 41–75.

Sullivan, Nikki. (2003). *A Critical Introduction to Queer Theory*. New York: New York University Press.

Sykes, H. (1998) 'Turning the closets inside/out: Towards a feminist-queer theory in physical education', *Journal of Sociology of Sport*, 15(2), 154–173.

Sykes, H. (2001) 'Understanding and overstanding: Feminist–post-structural life histories of physical education teachers', *International Journal of Qualitative Studies in Education*, 14(1):13–31.

Sykes, H. (2005) 'Transwomen and Sport: From Title IX to The Stockholm Consensus', Paper presented at the *Women and Sport: Before, During and After Title IX Symposium*, Bowling Green State University, Bowling Green, OH. February 6.

Talburt, S. and Steinberg, S. (2000) *Thinking Queer: Sexuality, Culture and Education*. New York: Peter Lang.

Treichler, P. A. (1999) *How to have Theory in an Epidemic: Cultural Chronicles of* AIDS. Durham: Duke University Press.

Van Ingen, C. (2003) 'Geographies of gender, sexuality and race: Reframing the focus on space in sport sociology', *International Review for the Sociology of Sport*, 38(2): 201–16.

Van Ingen, C. (2004) 'Therapuetic landscapes and the regulated body in the Toronto Front Runners', *Sociology of Sport Journal*, 21(3): 253–69.

Walters, S. (1996) 'From here to queer: Radical feminism, postmodernism, and the lesbian menace (or, why can't a woman be more like a fag?)', *Signs*, 21(4): 830–69.

Warner, M. (1993) *Fear of a Queer Planet: Queer Politics and Social Theory*. Minneapolis, MN: University of Minnesota.

Weeks, J. (1991) *Against Nature: Essays on History, Sexuality and Identity*. London: Rivers Oram Press.

Wesely, J. (2001) 'Negotiating gender: Bodybuilding and the natural/unnatural continuum', *Sociology of Sport Journal*, 18(2): 162–80.

Wikipedia. (2005) 'Social construction'. 23 January. <http://en.wikipedia.org>.

Wilchins, R. (2004) *Queer Theory, Gender Theory: An Instant Primer*. Los Angeles: Alyson Press.

Wright, J. and Clarke, G. (1999) 'Sport, the media and the construction of compulsory heterosexuality', *International Journal for the Sociology of Sport*, 34(3): 227–43.

2 Beyond the pale

The whiteness of sport studies and queer scholarship

Mary G. McDonald

Introduction

In his excellent book, *Disidentifications: Queers of Color and the Performance of Politics*, José Muñoz (1999) argues that too often queer theories and studies are interwoven with the dynamics of whiteness. He notes that 'most of the corner-stones of queer theory that are taught, cited, and canonized in gay and lesbian studies classrooms, publications, and conferences are decidedly directed toward analyzing white lesbians and gay men' (1999: 10). According to Muñoz the lack of inclusion does not signal the necessity of merely adding race to existing frameworks, a practice he calls a type of soft multiculturalism; but rather this omission and additive understanding of race points to the fact that something is seriously amiss in the 'vast majority of publications and conferences that fill out the discipline of queer theory' (1999: 11). As Yvonne Yarbo-Bejarano explains, too often this lack of explicit attention to interrogating race reinforces 'the belief that it is possible to talk about sexuality without talking about race, which in turn reaffirms the belief that it is necessary to talk about race and sexuality only when discussing people of color' (cited in Muñoz, 1999:10).

Laura Alexandra Harris is especially sceptical of those academic applications of queer which posit its 'political constituency as seductively fluid, unmarked, ambiguous and chosen' for this 'fluidity sounds dangerously like the status of white masculinity to me' (cited in Turner, 2000: 168). In particular, Harris alerts us to the hazards of always and everywhere seeing 'queer as free-floating signifier' as 'under the weight of historical precedent any 'unmarked' category might simply reinstall white, male subjectivity as normative' (Turner, 2000, p. 168).

In sum, these critiques of queer academic knowledge production, particularly with regard to the mutually constitutive and fragmented discursive character of race and sexuality are especially salient for those sport studies scholars now engaging with queer epistemologies. The writings of queers of color much like the multiple meanings implied by the first portion of this chapter's title 'Beyond the pale' suggest an alternative path for queer sport studies scholarship. First, those familiar with the etiology of this idiom will know that one tracing of its meaning dates back to the English Pale, the area of Ireland under English rule in the fourteenth century allegedly where 'civilization' reigned[1]. A common usage of the phrase 'beyond the pale' today suggests something unacceptable, out of bounds, outside the purview of common decency. Muñoz's work argues this sensibility and provides theoretical and epistemological justifications that queer sport scholars should embrace. That is Muñoz argues the need to move beyond what has become all too common; the reproduction of knowledges that rely upon a (queer) white subject and whiteness as the privileged and (often) unacknowledged universal referents.

The second meaning evoked by my title will be familiar to those of you who remember Vron Ware's 1992 book, *Beyond the Pale: White Women, Racism and History*. In that book Ware takes up the charge made by Black feminist thought to explore the intersectional character of raced, classed, sexed and nationalist discourses that mark bodies while also distributing resources and psychic (in)security unequally within the legacy of British colonialism. Ware's analysis is indebted to such feminist critiques as those offered in the 1970s and 1980s by Hazel Carby who argues for an epistemological shift among mainstream hegemonic feminist thought away from its preoccupation with white women's experiences as the alleged foundational standpoint of feminism. Indeed, Carby argues for a more relational, historical and intersectional focus than was common amongst white feminist analyses of the time. This is especially necessary, for as Carby (2000) sees it, history has constructed Black sexuality and femininity 'as deviating from those qualities with which white women, as the prize objects of the Western world have been endowed' (2000: 82).

These intersectional critiques continue and have been most persuasively and pervasively made by feminists of color, 'Third-World' feminists and post-colonial feminist critics. In my mind these writings also provide some of the most incisive critiques of feminist, and lesbian and gay scholarship available. Significantly these writings also make clear that politically proclaiming an uncontested racist (white) feminism in turn erases women of color's own critiques and intellectual contributions. In my view, the criticism produced by Black feminists, Chicana feminists, 'Third-World' feminists and post-colonial theorists including Hazel Carby, Chela Sandoval, Gloria Anzaldúa, Barbara Smith, Emma Pérez and Jasbir Kaur Puar, is not sufficiently given analytic due within queer scholarship, within sport studies scholarship or within so called 'whiteness studies' scholarship. As queer sport studies emerges, scholars must incorporate these and related critiques.

Siobhan Somerville (2002) suggests that fruitful engagements, critique and acknowledgement of forces of race and racialization such as those made both within and outside feminist circles must be ongoing for queer theory to realize its potential to 'not just reconceive the sexual, but the social in general' (Harper, *et al.* cited by Somerville, 2002: 788). That is, queer theory must be informed by and in dialogue with the theories and fields of race and ethnicity (including in the 'United States – Asian American Studies, Latino Studies, African–American/Black Studies, Native American Studies, as well as less institutionalized formulations including so-called whiteness studies') in ways which are beneficial in understanding that race and sexuality are mutually constitutive if not fragmented categories of analysis (Somerville, 2002: 788). Somerville concludes that the stakes of such engagement are 'potentially transformative theoretically, institutionally and otherwise' via the reconstitution of these 'fields' of knowledge (2002: 788).

As previously mentioned, while insufficiently cited, several scholars are now dealing with this very task of rethinking the relationships between race and sexuality[2]. What I am suggesting is that queer sport scholarship engages with the analytic lens of women of color feminism and queers of color/post-colonial queer critique. Such an engagement with these writings that are already moving beyond the pale, that is, already critiquing assumptions of whiteness, are also crucial for reconstituting the presumption of whiteness that often underlies analysis of gay and lesbian sexualities within existing sport studies scholarship.

In the remainder of this chapter, I first briefly discuss the ways whiteness often circulates within academic analyses of lesbian sexualities and sport in North America. Here I focus on writings about lesbian sexualities since until very recently this has been the central focus with regard to writings about the effects of homophobia, heterosexism and heteronormativity, while queer as descriptive of non-normative bodies, practices and epistemologies is only recently emerging in sport studies writings. In this, the first anthology that explicitly focuses on sexualities, queer theory and sport, the ultimate aim of my analysis is to interrogate existing scholarship on lesbian sexuality as instructive to emerging queer sport studies frameworks. Toward this end, I offer evidence to suggest that modernist assumptions of identity that reaffirm both whiteness and narrow understandings of sexuality need to be rethought as queer sport scholarship emerges. I conclude this chapter by very briefly drawing upon the writings of José Muñoz to make visible one existing queers of color analytic framework that he calls the practice of disidentification. Muñoz's insights offer queer sport scholars fresh ways of theorizing race, identity and resistance while exposing the complex cultural processes of normalization and difference. Thus the practice of disidentificaiton or 'reformulating the world through the politics of performance' (1999: xiv) is one way to help sport scholars reimagine what Somerville (2002) calls 'queer fictions of race'. In doing so, the practice of disidentification also provides another way to think differently about sport, the body, sexuality and the social.

Invisibility blues: critiquing normative assumptions in queer, gay and lesbian and sport scholarship

In '*Transnational configurations of desire: the nation and its white closets*' Jasbar Puar suggests that the 'whiteness of queer theory' can be loosely described as referring to the following tendencies: the Euro–American bias of queer theory, much of which lacks an analysis of ethnicity, race, nationalism, and citizenship issues while simultaneously effacing 'Third World' contexts; the emergence of queer theory from literary and psychoanalytic epistemologies supposedly lending to a lack of 'material' analysis; the positioning of subjects that utilize queer sexuality as the only axis of subordination, excluding other interpellations of identity (Puar, 2001: 179). Many of these critiques can be similarly applied to existing sport studies scholarship on gay and lesbian sexuality, although literary and psychoanalytic analyses are often ignored or marginalized within North American sport studies scholarship. Rather among the most applicable of Puar's critiques to North American scholarship on lesbian sexuality and sport is that with notable exceptions – here I would cite the work of Susan Cahn (1994) and Kathy Jamieson (2003) – this scholarship too frequently reaffirms only one axis of power around sexuality thereby assuming whiteness while effacing the complex processes that construct particular understandings of 'race,' nation and citizenship. Equally problematic are the broader assumptions and practices that bolster whiteness even when other axes of power are addressed. As Richard Dyer explains, whites 'are everywhere in representation. Yet precisely because of this and their placing as norm they seem not to be represented to themselves as whites but as people who are variously gendered, classed, sexualized and abled' (Dyer, 1997: 3)[3]. In a similar way, a substantial body of scholarship that crosses disciplinary lines also contributes to dominant constructions of 'white' as the normative point of reference.

Inattention to the normative workings of whiteness via focus on one relation of power can be seen in two works about the effects and consequences of homophobia and heterosexism in North American sport: Pat Griffin's 1998 text, *Strong Women. Deep Closets: Lesbians and Homophobia in Sport* and Helen Lenskyj's *Out on the Field: Gender, Sport and Sexualities*, a compilation of essays written between 1989 and 2002 that have been updated and excerpted in this 2003 book. My goal is to productively engage with these texts, for as Judith Butler (1997) reminds us:

> for intellectual movements to remain vital, expansive and self-critical, room must be made for the kind of immanent critique which shows how the presuppositions of one critical enterprise can operate to forestall the work of another. In many ways, the resistance to sympathetic or, indeed, immanent critique, symtomatizes the academic residue of an identity politics that thinks that critique only and always weakens a movement rather than understanding that the democratic and non-dogmatic future of any such movement depends precisely on its ability to incorporate, without domesticating, challenges from its own alterities.
>
> (Butler, 1997:1)

Indeed, it would be impossible to imagine an anthology about sexualities, queer theory and sport without the significant contributions by both Griffin and Lenskyj in exposing the systematic debilitating effects of homophobia on some lesbians in sport. Both books seek to offer, in Griffin's words

> an affirmation, a breaking of silence, and a collective coming out that challenge the despised sexual predator image that has forced too many of us into the shadows of the closet out of fear: fear of loosing our jobs, our place on the team roster, our families, our friends, our credibility.
>
> (Griffin, 1998: xi)

Strong Women, Deep Closets provides a way 'for young lesbian and bisexual athletes in particular to understand their experiences and learn to challenge the
self-hatred and fear that live inside so many of them' (xi).

The historical breadth that each author engages with and the variety of
themes that each explores, including a focus on the history of the 'muscle moll,'
Olympic industry, sport media, same sex love in the locker room and narratives
recounted by a diverse group of lesbians, might suggest the possibility of reading
a queer sensibility into these chapters by inferring lesbian to be a contingent and
unstable historically produced, embodied category. Both books offer, as Lenskyj
suggests, a type of 'historical record that reflects the state of play from the late
1980s to the early years of the 21st century—a chronicle of changing times,
emerging insights and evolving political strategies' (Lenskyj, 2003: xiv).

Each of Lenskyj's chapters chronicle a particular type of political struggle and
both Lenskyj's and Griffin's work is imbued with a worldview that has been foundational to hegemonic white feminist and lesbian thought. Griffin includes
narratives from women of color in her work, several of whom note the interrela-
tionships between homophobia and racism. And when discussing the complex
process of coming out, Griffin makes clear that 'white lesbians often do not
understand what a privilege it is to assume that they will be welcomed into a primarily white lesbian subculture if their families withdraw their support' (Griffin,
1998: 164). In doing so Griffin makes clear the racialized discourses that impact
discussion about lesbian visibility in and out of sport, suggesting that we all must:

> take into account the complexities and differences between the experiences
> of White lesbians and lesbians of color. The color of our skin and our access
> to economic resources can have a huge impact on how we choose to present
> our lesbian identity to others.
>
> (Griffin, 1998: 164)

Lenskyj acknowledges that the choice whether to be oneself or to 'pass' as a
member of the dominant group is not available, for example, to lesbians and gays
who are Black, or to those who have disabilities.

> Liberal individualistic notions of self-discovery and self-expression are insuf-
> ficient for authentic, universal empowerment because they overlook the
> double or triple oppressions suffered by minority members of lesbian and gay
> communities. Furthermore they simply bring together diverse groups of les-
> bians and gay men in sport which does not in itself guarantee 'love for each
> other,' and it is naïve to hope that sexism, racism and ableism and other
> entrenched forms of discrimination that divide communities will simply
> evaporate.
>
> (Lenskyj 2003: 139)

Still, the promising and powerful analytic insights provided in these two specific
citations never fully materialize in subsequent analysis. Rather, the majority of

topics engaged with rely upon unproblematic acceptance of an unquestioned core sexual identity with very little specific analysis provided about articulations of race and class. Thus, while both Lenskyj and Griffin mention the significance of race and class to their analysis they mostly appear to engage in the type of soft multiculturalism that Muñoz is so critical of with regard to queer theory. At times both books infer race as an additive quality to sexuality, which is positioned as the most important feature of individual core or essential identity. This is visible, for example, in Lenskyj's chapters devoted to the Gay Games, sexual harassment in sport and woman-centered alternatives to mainstream sport. In short, while mentioning the importance of an intersectional focus, this work fails to explicitly take up and delineate complex articulations of 'race,' sexuality, class and nation that manifest themselves both historically and in contemporary times.

Writing about a different context, Puar (2001) notes that absent in popular discussions 'are questions of relations to the state vis-à-vis who can and cannot afford to participate' in such public visibilities based upon an 'uninterrogated assumption of queer citizenship' (2001: 172). This critique is not merely to suggest class privilege underlies who gets to play sport in the first place, but also exposes the presumption of whiteness and a homogenized nation, which frequently limits analytic perspectives. The result is that (sport) scholars repeatedly fail to account for the ways in which immigrants are often absent from public actions and activities such as sport and indeed, in an ideological sense, for the ways in which 'immigration functions to keep the nation-state in crises' (Puar, 2001: 172).

Consistent with a larger body of scholarship related to critical analysis of sport, Griffin's and Lenskyj's arguments rely upon certain strands of identity politics, that queer, 'Third-World' feminists and (feminist) post-structuralists also critique. Ultimately underlying this body of scholarship is the often unspoken claim of a singular focus on sexuality (or gender or social class, etc.) that infers whiteness and problematic modernist understandings that individual identity is a simple reflection of uniform group membership. Similar modernist assumptions circulate in popular Western consciousness although within this conceptualization identity is not just merely singular, but also static, ahistorical, and apolitical (Mohanty, 2004).

Thus when difference is engaged, a significant drawback in these understandings is an all too frequent concurrent reproduction of group homogeneity. Analysis, for example, that does speak to Black lesbian experiences regularly reproduces commonsense understanding of similarity. This is indeed the case when speaking of the experiences of 'the black lesbian without attention to or acknowledgement of a multiplicity of identities or subject positions for black women' (Hammonds, 1997: 136). While modernist understandings of identity have no doubt allowed activists to mobilize identity in the service of political gains, and this sensibility habitually arises within mainstream gay and lesbian civil rights organizing especially visible in the United States, a singular aspect of identity such as sexual orientation, simultaneously 'deemphasizes other aspects of identity' while ignoring the historical production of identity and group membership as powerful effects of discourses that greatly shape life changes (McLaren, 2002: 119).

When race is relegated in scholarship and political action to an additive category of identification this wrongly infers that gays and lesbians of color have more in common with their white gay and lesbian counterparts than with communities of color, thus dismissing the racism that disproportionately limits opportunities for people of color within a dominant knowledge system that continuously seeks to privilege a binary racial logic. Counter-evidence suggests that the interactions of racism and heteronormativity have produced a variety of diffuse, contradictory consequences suggesting the need for varied responses. One such response is the necessity of exploring ways in which construction of the 'closet' articulates with and diverges from a broader historical legacy, what Evelyn Hammonds calls a 'politics of silence' that renders aspects of both Black female sexuality in general and Black lesbian sexuality in particular 'as dangerous, for individuals and for the collectivity' (Hammonds, 1997: 147). And while Black feminists are exploring 'the restrictive, repressive, and dangerous aspects … the pleasure, exploration and agency' of Black sexuality 'have gone underanalyzed' (Hammonds: 145).

Simply stated, race is at least as important as sexuality in shaping life changes, personal identifications, erotic sensibilities and political struggles. This sensibility in turn radically destabilizes the notion of a unitary gay identity and by extension a unitary gay politics that underlie traditional understandings of sexuality including that within sport studies scholarship (Jagose, 1996: 63). Most notably, in discussions of the often unaligned disruptive couplings of gender and sex regularly enacted through sport, on the whole, both books (by Lenskyj and Griffin) not only serve to uncritically accept dominant understandings of a mostly unitary gay identity but by extension, a unitary gay politics as well.

This unitary focus ultimately privileges whiteness by downplaying the material impact of racialized discourses. And there is more at play within existing sport studies sexuality scholarship. What is also assumed to be self evident, even logical in commonsense understanding of sexuality is the current normative understanding that 'sexual orientation is determined principally or even solely by the gender of one sexual object choice' (Jagose, 1996: 63). Sedgwick (1990) is among many queer critics who argue against normalizing such a historically specific classification system of sexuality that, I would add, also operates within sport studies scholarship:

> It is a rather amazing fact that, of the very many dimensions along which genital activity of one person can be differentiated from that of another (dimensions that include preference for certain acts, certain zones of sensations, certain physical types, a certain frequency, certain symbolic investments, certain relations of age or power, certain species, certain numbers of participants, etc., etc., etc.) precisely one, the gender of object choice, emerged from the turn of the century, and has remained the dimension, denoted by the now ubiquitous category of sexual orientation.
>
> (Sedgwick, 1990: 8)

Concurrent with the ubiquitous understanding of sexual orientation within both popular culture and existing mainstream scholarship, where the gender of one's object choice is determined to be pre-eminent, is the persistent process that reifies rather than problematizes the binary logic of Western culture in structuring hierarchical oppositions among such categories as heterosexual vs. homosexual, man vs. women, masculinity vs. femininity, normal vs. deviant. Furthermore, the racialized hetero–homo binary is not an innocent coupling, but rather serves political aims in that the dominant notion of heterosexuality relies upon a homogenized homosexuality for its meanings and authority. Many queer theorists have thus shifted attention away from what appears to be the explicit focus of much of the existing writings on sport and sexuality, that is 'an exclusive preoccupation with the oppression and liberation of the homosexual subject' (Seidman 1997: 93). More frequently, queer sensibilities seek to expose, interrogate, indeed, question 'the institutional practices and discourses producing sexual knowledges and the ways that they organize social life with particular attention to the ways these knowledges and social practices repress difference' (1997: 93).

This queer sensibility to shift the focus away from modern understandings of identity toward knowledge production can be found in certain strands of critical race theory and post-colonial scholarship as well (McDonald, 2002; McDonald, 2005). For example, critical race theorists argue that contemporary racial classification systems that rely upon appeals to skin color and phenotypes continuously produce raced bodies. This is a historically contingent development as questions of skin color did not seem to draw the attention of Europeans before the sixteenth century. This brief historical example additionally reveals that the phenomenon of whiteness is not just about racism *per se* but about socially created worldviews, forms of representation, meaning and knowledge systems, 'which are capable of being re-worked, subverted and undermined through cultural and institutional practices outside the confines of' traditional 'anti-racist politics' (Gabriel, 1998: 6). Just as importantly, if queer sport discourse is to 'supersede the limits' of white hegemonic feminism and lesbian scholarship and the limits of sport studies writings about sexuality 'it must be able to calculate multiple antagonisms that index issues of class, and race, as well as sexuality' (Muñoz: 22). And yet as Muñoz reminds us, too frequently in mainstream and in queer scholarship – and I would add in writings about gay and lesbian sexualities in sport – dominant understanding suggests that 'queer is a white thing.' This misunderstanding suggests the need to both interrogate continuing articulation of white supremacy with heteronormativity and to make intelligible subjugated knowledges, particularly in the form of existing critiques by racially and sexually marginalized queers of color in order to move toward more politically progressive ends.

Muñoz offers one strategy to meet this end, the practice of disidentification – a tactic that moves away from scholarly and popular conceptualizations of core, essential and singular identities to recognize the complex performativity of subjectivities. That is, building upon the work of feminists of color, particularly Chicana feminists, and postmodern theories of subjectivity, Muñoz argues that the phobic normative assumptions and dominant ideologies historically inscribed on bodies of minority subjects can be worked on and against with a difference. Instead of surrendering to

> the pressures of dominant ideology (identification, assimilation) or attempting to break free of its inescapable sphere (counteridentification, utopianism), this 'working on and against' is a strategy that tries to transform a cultural logic from within, always laboring to enact permanent structural change while at the same time valuing the importance of local and everyday struggles of resistance.
>
> (Muñoz, 1999: 11)

In this way the practice of disidentification exists as 'a hermeneutic, a process of production, and a mode of performance' (1999: 25) that also serves as a 'survival strategy' of minoritized subjects and as an analytic lens that can be used by queers of all races and hybridities 'to resist and confound socially prescriptive patterns of identification' (1999: 28). Indeed this new sensibility understands identities and identifications as the effects of socially produced embodied narratives that misrecognize, hierarchically organize and individuate bodies. Too often bodies that are naturalized through dominant processes erroneously appear as coherent fixed identities labeled as normal and deviant, as apparently white and straight vs. of color and gay. This means that minoritized subjects have to constantly navigate and remake 'a phobic majoritarian public sphere that continuously elides or punishes the existence of subjects who do not conform to the phantasm of normative citizenship' (1999: 4). Counter to dominant proclivity that seeks to fix narrative coherence on bodies, disidentification offers a different strategy, a new way of viewing the world that does not reproduce singular, binary understandings but rather, values the 'recycling and rethinking' of 'encoded meanings' (1999: 31). It recognizes that this dominant process of fixing truth within bodies is always full of slippages and failures, never seamless, but far more queer than it first appears. Read from this perspective, whiteness and heteronormativity are not naturalized identities or simply inevitable sets of politicized knowledges but are frequently used to marginalize non-normative bodies through 'performative projects.' In contrast to this dominant process, Muñoz offers 'disidentification' as 'counterperformativity'.

> That is, the process of disidentification scrambles and recodes the encoded message of a cultural text in a fashion that both exposes the encoded message's universalizing and exclusionary machinations and recircuits its workings to account for, include and empower minority identities and identifications. Thus disidentification is a step further than cracking open the code of the majority; it proceeds to use this code as raw material for representing a disempowered politics or positionality that has been rendered unthinkable by the dominant culture.
>
> (Muñoz, 1999: 31)

In this way 'disidentificatory performances opt to do more than simply tear down the majoritarian public sphere. They disassemble that sphere of publicity and use its parts to build an alternative reality. Disidentification uses the majoritarian culture as raw material to make a new world' (1999: 196).

Muñoz offers numerous examples of this process from the performance art of Vaginal Davis and Carmalita Tropicana to the public pedagogy offered by Pedro Zamora's stint as an AIDS activist on MTV's reality based show *The Real World*. For example, in a chapter titled, 'The white to be angry? Vaginal Crème Davis's terrorist drag,' Muñoz argues that Davis demonstrates 'a strategy of resisting the normalizing discourse of dominant ideology' thus countering the 'sanitized and desexed queer' drag subject now offered for mass consumption (1999: 99). Davis offers cultural critique that both works through and against normative sensibilities with the ultimate aim to encourage all to break free from the constraints of the social body. That is against mainstream gay and lesbian proclivity to eschew negative images, in contrast Davis' political drag seeks to 'create an uneasiness in desire' in an effort to trouble and subvert the broader social fabric. For example, Davis does not just perform femininity but she also takes on such character roles as a white, straight military militiaman, and also parodies the famous serial killer Jeffrey Dahmer. In doing so Davis embodies the nation's most dangerous citizens thus performing the nation's internal terrors around race, gender and sexuality (1999: 108). And yet, this desire for a 'bad' subject draws upon parody in such a way as to suggest 'an active disidentification with strictures against cross-racial desire in communities of color and the spectres of miscegenation that haunt white sexuality' (1999: 105).

Muñoz's notion of disidentification offers a way to think differently about sporting performances. Muñoz points toward such a focus on sport through critical appraisal of sporting images produced by painter Jean-Michel Basquiat. Indeed, the *Famous Negro Athlete* is an image meant to provoke both the spectre of black idolization and 'the problematic of being a famous black image that is immediately coded as a trademark by a white entertainment industry' (1999: 49). The simply drawn lines of Basquiat's art stand for incompleteness while evoking drawings of childhood where a child's simple visual grammar creates a beloved image. Basquiat makes this sensibility visible in the simplicity of images of a crown and a ball with the words *Famous Negro Athletes* drawn plainly in between these objects. In doing so, this painting also demonstrates the powerful ways in which 'both lack and desire are negotiated' (1999: 52). That is, this work focuses on idolization just as it hails the spectre of the white imaginary where black men are reduced to their physicality, as alluringly sensual, ever hypersexual, and in the case of athletes, as naturally athletic. *Famous Negro Athlete* thus also recodes commonsense interpretations to reveal both transcendent possibilities via beloved figures and realization that even celebrity status fails to insulate Black athletes from the historical legacies of white normativity and sexualized racism as indexed via the word negro. As with the artist's larger body of work, this sport-inspired painting displays contradictory and complex impulses to honour as well as to 'mourn, remember and flesh out' (1999: 52).

A second work examined by Muñoz features a similar unadorned image that provokes multiple sensibilities. This Basquiat sketch features the name of the famous boxer, Sugar Ray Robinson, and a coarsely drawn crown above an equally crudely sketched face. The simplicity of these images hails the legacies of a prior era 'when black representations were only the distorted images of athletes and the occasional performer that the white media deemed permissible' (1999: 52). The plain lettering of Sugar Ray Robinson and the half-formed, crude lines of the drawing additionally stand in for the idolization of Black athletes and the loss of childhood itself. On the whole, the painting works at the level of disidentification, in recoding and reordering commonsense understandings of identity especially that of race and athlete. No longer a biological entity, or merely an athletic performer, the painting is meant to infer that subjectivities are always in process while also exposing the complex dynamic of being both celebrated and racially categorized in the United States (Muñoz, 1999).

Moving beyond the pale in queer sport studies scholarship

In sum I have argued that modernist assumptions of identity that reaffirm whiteness in sport sexuality scholarship must be radically rethought and challenged as queer sport studies scholarship progresses. To do so, those deploying queer must give up the primacy of sexuality, that is, exclusively anchoring analysis within the domain of the hetero–homo binary, as this framing ignores complex processes of racialization, a process always and already interacting with this binary. Furthermore, movement away from an exclusive preoccupation with the sexual is an especially important endeavour given that queer sensibilities seek to challenge liberal assumptions by interrogating, questioning and destabilizing grounds upon which any claim to identity is made (Somerville, 2002: 787). There are numerous ways to both critique and move away from modern assumptions of identity that underlie gay and lesbian studies, and queer models of inquiry infused with assumptions of normative whiteness. One such strategy involves the active process of disidentification, a shift in worldview toward recoding and reordering commonsense understanding. This sensibility further encourages numerous queer scholars to disidentify with the normative whiteness of queer scholarship and scholars of sexualities and sport to disidentify with their modernist understandings of identity and identifications to join those labouring differently for change. The ultimate aim of such an inquiry is to productively imagine knowledges about bodies and desires apart from the white hetero–homo binary as privileged referent beyond the pale.

Notes

1   The case of the British colonialism and the Irish is instructive in demonstrating that the production of raced bodies is historically and geopolitically specific. That questions of skin color and phenotype did not concern the British during this particular process of colonization is ably explained by George Fredrickson (1981) who writes that:

> The rationale for expropriating [Irish] land and removing them from it was that the Celtic Irish were savages, so wild and rebellious that they could only be controlled by a constant and ruthless exercise of brute force. The application of the concept of savagery to the Celtic Irish may strike a modern reader as very peculiar since they were both white and Christian. But in the sixteenth century, savagery was not yet associated with pigmentation or physical type
>
> (p. 15)

2   For examples of such engagements, see Pérez (1999), Sandoval (2000), Weed and Schor (1997), Bergmann and Smith (1995), Eng and Hom (1998), Rodriguez (2003). Earlier interventions can be found in Smith (1977), Moraga and Anzaldúa (1981) and Anzaldúa (1987). Eng *et al.'s* (2005) recent overview on the current state of queer studies notes the contributions of women of color feminism to queer theory.

3   Just as Puar is critical of queer scholarship and I have extended this critique to sport scholarship on sexuality, similar criticism has been applied to gay and lesbian sexuality scholarship. For example, in discussing the classic, *The Lesbian and Gay Studies Reader* (Abelove *et al.*, 1993), Hammonds (1997: 138) argues that the canonical terms and categories of the field: 'lesbian,' 'gay,' 'butch,' 'femme,' 'sexuality,' and 'subjectivity' are each 'defined with white as the normative state of existence.'

Acknowledgements

Thanks to Jayne Caudwell for her support of this project. Thanks also to Susan Birrell and Madelyn Detloff for reading and commenting on earlier versions of this chapter. Any errors that remain are mine.

References

Abelove, H., Barale, M. and Halperin, D. (eds) (1993) *The Lesbian and Gay Studies Reader*. New York: Routledge.

Anzaldúa, G. (1987) *Borderlands/La Frontera: The New Mestiza*. San Francisco: Spinsters/Aunt Lute.

Bergmann, E. and Smith, P. (eds) (1995) *Entiendes? Queer Readings, Hispanic Writings*. Durham: Duke University.

Butler, J. (1997) 'Against proper objects', in E. Weed and N. Schor (eds), *Feminism Meets Queer Theory*. Bloomington: Indiana University, (1–30).

Cahn, S. (1994) *Coming on strong : Gender and Sexuality in Twentieth-century Women's Sport*. New York: Free Press.

Carby, H. (2000) 'White woman listen! Black feminism and the boundaries of sisterhood', in K. Owusu, (ed.), *Black British Culture and Society: A Text-reader*. London: Routledge, (82–8).

Dyer, R. (1997) *White*. London: Routledge.

Eng, D. and Hom, A. (eds) (1998) *Q&A: Queer in Asian America*. Philadelphia: Temple University.

Eng, D., Halberstam, J. and Muñoz, J. (2005) 'Introduction: What's queer about queer-studies now?' *Social Text* (Special Issue), 23(3–4): 1–18.

Fredrickson, G. (1981) *White Supremacy: A Comparative Study in American and South African History*. Oxford: Oxford University.

Gabriel, J. (1998) *Whitewash: Racialized Politics and the Media*. London: Routledge.

Griffin, P. (1998). *Strong Women, Deep Closets: Lesbians and Homophobia in Sport*. Champaign, IL: Human Kinetics.

Hammonds, E. (1997) 'Black (w)holes and the geometry of black female sexuality', in E. Weed and N. Schor (eds), *Feminism meets queer theory*. Bloomington: Indiana University, (136–156).

Harper, P. B., McClintock, A., Muñoz J. and Rosen, T. (1997). 'Introduction: Queer transexions of race, nation, and gender.' *Social Text*, 52–53, (1–4).

Jagose, A. (1996) *Queer Theory: An Introduction*. New York: New York University.

Jamieson, K. (2003) 'Occupying a middle space: Toward a mestiza sport studies'. *Sociology of Sport Journal*, 20(1): 1–16.

Lenskyj, H. (2003) *Out on the Field: Gender, Sport and Sexualities*. Toronto: Women's Press.

McDonald, M. G. (2002) 'Queering whiteness: The peculiar case of the WNBA'. *Sociological Perspectives*, 45(4): 379–96.

McDonald, M. G. (2005) 'Mapping whiteness and sport: An introduction. *Sociology of Sport Journal* (Special Issue: 'Whiteness and Sport'). 22(3): 245–255.

McLaren, M. (2002) *Feminism, Foucault and Embodied Subjectivity*. Albany: State University of New York.

Mohanty, C. (2004) *Feminism without Borders: Decolonizing Theory, Practicing Solidarity*. Durham: Duke University.

Moraga, C. and Anzaldúa, G. (1981). *This Bridge Called My Back: Writings by Radical Women of Color*. Albany: Kitchen Table.

Muñoz, J. (1999) *Disidentifications: Queers of color and the Performance of Politics*. Minneapolis: University of Minnesota.

Pérez, E. (1999) *The Decolonial Imaginary: Writing Chicanas into History*. Bloomington: Indiana University.

Puar, J. (2001) 'Transnational configurations of desire: The nation and its white closets'. in B. Rasmussen, E. Klinenberg, I. Nexica and M. Wray (eds), *The Making and Unmaking of Whiteness*. Durham, NC: Duke University, (167–83).

Rodriguez, J. (2003) *Queer Latinidad: Identity Practices, Discursive Spaces*. New York: New York University.

Sandoval, C. (2000) *Methodology of the Oppressed*. Minneapolis: University of Minnesota.

Sedgwick, E. (1990) *Epistemology of the Closet*. Berkeley, CA: University of California.

Seidman, S. (1997) *Difference Troubles: Queering Social Theory and Sexual Politics*. Cambridge: Cambridge University.

Smith, B. (1977) *Toward a Black Feminist Criticism*. Trumansburg, NY: Out & Out Books.

Somerville, S. (2002) 'Introduction: Queer fictions of race', *Modern Fiction Studies* 48(4): 787–94.

Turner, W. (2000) *A Genealogy of Queer Theory*. Philadelphia: Temple.

Ware, V. (1992) *Beyond the Pale: White Women, Racism and History*. London: Versco.

Weed, E. and Schor, N. (eds) (1997) *Feminism Meets Queer Theory*. Bloomington: Indiana University.

Part II

Sports' practices and communities

Disrupting heteronormativity?

3 Queer athletes and queering in sport

Heidi Eng

Introduction

S: Eh... of course I peeped, particularly at those I got interested in. But, you might put it this way, heterosexual boys, they measure each other up and down, and it is a fact that the boys have measured before... they are... what has been a bit difficult for me, of course, is the fact that there were those 'things', the playing in the shower and stuff like that. I found that uncomfortable. I kept away from that.

H (Heidi): Why?

S: Because to me it meant something! For them it didn't mean anything. The game that they played might hurt me more than it might do me good. I became like this – 'No, no.' And it... I got too shy, kind of. I kept away from it all. I never joined in. Eh... and there was never anyone who... you heard of those guys that jerk off together and stuff like that... And that is a typical hetero thing to do without there being anything homosexual to it, kind of, and eh... none of my friends have done that together. At least not with me! (laughs).

The purpose of this chapter is to examine how Norwegian athletes living as lesbians, gays or bisexuals experience doing sex/gender and sexuality in sport. On this basis I discuss the effects of queer visibility in sport, and in particular look at how the concepts of *queer* and *queering* can highlight the potential for change (into less homophobic environments). The chapter focuses on theoretical issues surrounding the use of queer theory, and on 'data' from a study on how sex/gender and sexuality are acted out in Norwegian sport contexts.

The concepts of queer and queering are useful analytical tools for interrogating hegemonic and powerful 'laws' about how to act and speak. Sport highlights processes of the social construction of sex/gender, sexuality and the body (Eng, 2003; Coakley, 2001). In this chapter I explore the phenomenon of queering, which I explain more fully below, and whether queering occurs in sport. I make use of the concept of *sex/uality*, inspired by the work of Jennifer Harding (1998) in her book *Sex Acts: Practices of Femininity and Masculinity*. Her rationale for writing sex/uality in one word is to deconstruct 'the culturally and historically entrenched idea that an *a priori sex* is expressed through a gender and then through sexuality' (1998:55).

Gay and lesbian sport clubs can be described as constituting a queer alternative to mainstream sport today, but the question remains – does such queer existence have an effect on the dominant heteronormative discourses of sexuality, sex/gender and the body in sports in general? The athletes I present in this chapter participate in mainstream sport (intermediate and elite). It is therefore the effect of different queer practices inside mainstream sport that are the focus of the chapter.

Queer theory and core concepts

The emergence of queer theory has parallels with the development of feminist theory. Queer theory is, like feminist theory, an interdisciplinary perspective of critical inquiry more than a clearly defined theory. Theory is actually quite a misleading term in the same way as 'queer' is not a regular academic term. Hence, some scholars take on the use of queer perspective, or methodology or a queer lens on academic work. As a rather young theoretical movement with equally young political counterparts, it is in constant flux and development. While philosophy, history and literature criticism were essential in its early phases, the social sciences and cultural criticism have become more central to it during the last few years (Jorde 2005).

The development of queer academic work expanded as part of the emergence of poststructural theory, which emerged from a critique of structuralism (Jones, 1997)[1]. Contained in both postmodernism and post-structuralism is the critique of 'grand narratives' of enlightenment, the emphasis on language as something that shapes reality rather than reflecting reality (including power relations), and the use of deconstruction as a reading technique to capture language as a process of play and deferral of meaning (Davies 1997). Post-structuralism claims that structures do not exist in an objective sense, but are discursive/historical constructions. A focus on how power exists in the structures of meaning is crucial to understand how 'truth' and 'reality' are produced through discursive practice. At the same time, discursive practice also accentuates the instability, heterogeneity and fluidity about the structures of meaning, because meaning is always constructed for our consciousness through language, hence constantly set in motion each time it is practised. Knowledge (and hence discourse) is being produced in a process of power and dominance where individual acts, and social groups in interaction with each other, have the potential to destabilise hegemonic discourses.

Within the field of post-structuralism we find different theoretical perspectives or empirical focuses where certain aspects are emphasised, instead of the attempt to establish another 'grand theory'. Queer theory is an example of such theoretical contribution to post-structural research, where issues concerning sexuality are brought into the foreground of the analysis of knowledge and the social practises that organise society (Seidman 1996: 13). Again we can draw a parallel between the development of feminist theory and queer theory: in the same way as feminists started to use the analytical concept of gender as an absolute filter to understand aspects that did not immediately appear gender-specific, queer theory brings forward a focus on sexuality that is useful in almost all fields of research. By bringing in sexuality, and focusing on heterosexuality as the dominant system in our culture, new knowledge might be generated, new knowledge about sex as an important sign that carries meaning in our culture.

Feminist theory and research can be criticised for having a heterosexual presupposition in the understanding of gender, a presupposition that is not questioned, and therefore makes the term 'gender' ineffectual as an analytical tool in research in general (Ingraham, 1996). Addressing 'heterogender' in feminist theory and gender studies is one contribution from queer theory. The other is addressing how traditional gay/lesbian studies re-establish binaries of heterosexual – homosexual, normal – not normal, or centre – periphery. The focus on the phenomenon of homosexuality and homosexual ways of living in gay/lesbian studies, run the risk of repeating the dualistic categorisation of homo–hetero when doing research on a group of people identified by a certain linguistic category. The critique of knowledge production that reproduces well established categories of sexuality (and sex/gender) is a central aspect of queer theory. Such a critique refuses a majority–minority model, questions the taken-for-given normality position of heterosexuality, and asks for theoretical and empirical investigations where heterosexuality has to explain itself.

Last to be mentioned about queer theory is its contribution as a methodological approach. I argue it is much the same as a post-structuralist approach in its concern with the unseen, the taboo, acts/practices/language that is 'not spoken' – outside known language, or seen as problematic speech acts. Since queer theory is focused on sexuality issues, unquestioned/presupposed heterosexuality has been highlighted as a powerful discourse, which silences sexual practices that could challenge heterosexuality as the hegemonic norm.

Normalised heterosexuality is part of a definition of *heteronormativity*, which is a core concept in queer theory. Heteronormativity does not equal heterosexuality, although it is strongly associated with it. Heteronormativity is expressed, for example, through the fact that many of our social rituals are built around heterosexuality, manifested in pictures, cultural signs, and symbols, and through concrete acts in the social 'game': the social game that is formed around the two-sex model – the couple comprised of him and her. In a heteronormative culture heterosexuality is not only the expected and the dominant way of living, it has the status as the norm, and is often referred to as what is 'natural'. In a worst case scenario, heteronormativity might therefore breed homophobia or homonegativism and lead to violence, harassment, social stigmatising and negative sanctions against marginalised sexualities.

In the article 'Sex in Public', Berlant and Warner (2000) present a clear definition of heteronormativity as structures of understanding that makes heterosexuality coherent and privileged in a culture. At the same time, they argue for an understanding of heteronormativity as not equal to heterosexuality. Such a distinction is necessary to open the way for a view on heterosexual practice as not always heteronormative. Such clarification allows for an understanding of heterosexuality as *not* heteronormative, which means that some forms of heterosexual ways of living might be stigmatised and suppressed in a heteronormative culture (for example heterosexual non-monogamy, or heterosexual couples choosing not to have children).

To return to two concepts mentioned earlier in the introduction; *queer* and *queering*. I see queer as practices, as acts, or as speech, and as representations, bodies that do not signify 'the normal' or the 'wanted'. It is a collective term for what can be seen as 'unnatural'/'not normal' in a dominantly heterosexual culture, for example one's body, behaviour, values, appearance and sexual orientation. A crucial point in queer theory is to make visible a queer existence within normality. Such queer existence can take on two forms; either as the visible abjected or postponed, that forms the understanding of the opposite (the 'deviant') of the normal, straight and not-queer, or as a queer existence inside of normality, as (silenced) practices that often are subject to discursive muteness:

> Silence itself – the things one declines to say, or is forbidden to name, the discretion that is required between different speakers – is less the absolute limit of discourse, the other side from which it is separated by a strict boundary, than an element that functions alongside the things said, with them and in relation to them within over-all strategies. [...] There is not one but many silences, and they are an integral part of the strategies that underlie and permeate discourses.
>
> (Foucault, 1990: 27)

Homoerotic desire and practice in the changing rooms, as knowledge that is not spoken/out (outspoken), might be examples of what Foucault describes as silences underlying and permeating discourses of normality in sports. Exposing queerness in a certain arena that is expected to be 'straight' and 'purely normal' is conceptualised as 'queering' in the field of queer theory (Roseneil, 2000). The very recognition of what is seen as queer appearance in a social space can lead to queering of that context in general. Queering is used as a noun to describe a process where queer existence in a certain context challenges and effects heteronormative structures and/or acts, speech and identities, so that the heteronormative context, the culture, the discourses change over time.

Doing sex/uality in sport

The discussions now turn to the Norwegian sports context and I present some research findings taken from qualitative interviews with 18 athletes living as lesbians, gays or bisexuals. The research participants were intermediate and elite athletes involved in 13 different sports. They were asked about their experience of the conditions provided, in their sports, for *doing* sex/uality – that is how they were able to make visible, communicate and embody sex/uality through, for example, flirtation, falling in love, and sexual and erotic interaction. Results from the study show that locker room culture is based on the view that homosocial spaces are nonsexual. For example, how the locker rooms as sex segregated – one for female athletes and one for male athletes – are supposed to eliminate sexual acts (such as voyeurism, sexual harassment, or sexual/erotic intercourse). This is a striking example of what is called heteronormative thinking, where homosexuality does not come to mind – or more precisely, exists as silences underlying and permeating discourses of normality.

The specificity of sport as a context for doing sex/uality was found to be dependent upon several aspects. Here I discuss three:

1 Assumptions of different sports as masculine or feminine sports activities

Stigmatization of masculinity and femininity and homosexuality, and assumptions of what are masculine and feminine sports, was found to have a positive effect on the informants' participation in sports, since the hegemonic position of heteronormativity in these sports settings can be weakened. Hence, queer elements are to a greater extent made possible, such as homosexual appearances and homoeroticism. One of the women research participants is actively involved in a sport that is traditionally understood as masculine and she identifies, and passes, as masculine (when she was younger she successfully passed as a boy). Her sport allows masculine enactments and because of this she feels it provides a refuge for her and other like-minded women:

C-A: It's like this, (in her sport) you've got to have some aggression and be a bit rough and a bit... maybe the things that sort of can be found on the masculine scale of personal qualities, in a way. [...] Like when I was little, then I wanted to be a boy. But I don't as an adult, but sometimes the sports setting and things like that make it all right to be just who you are. Because there you're all the same, and this makes it a place of your own where you can create your own identity [...].

H: Is this true for the tomboys in particular?

C-A: Yes, especially for them, they probably find eh... I was about to say... a kind of... refuge, or somewhere where they are appreciated and can be themselves. Appreciated for what they are. [...] And that probably wouldn't have been as easy in the standard man–woman society...

Foucault (1986: 24) established, in his work on space, a notion of 'heterotopia', a word that is to be associated with heterogeneous (as opposed to homogeneous) space, and must not be confused with heterosexual or heteronormative (spaces). Foucault used heterotopia in order to name what he saw as counter-sites to utopias, the latter being sites with no real place, as fundamentally unreal spaces. Heterotopias however, are real places that exist and are formed in the founding of society, and he argues:

> [...] there is probably not a single culture in the world that fails to constitute heterotopias. That is a constant of every human group. But the heterotopias

obviously take quite varied forms and perhaps no one absolutely universal form of heterotopia would be found.

(Foucault, 1986: 24)

The sports arena as a site for leisure and physical activity might contain counter-sites; effectively enacted heterotopias of deviation. That is to say, if the athletes enact deviation instead of obeying the 'law' of heteronormativity; the 'law' being to act heterosexually or non-sexually in the sports context, and to enact traditional gendered norms concerning femininity and masculinity. Some of the research participants in the study did act openly as gay/lesbian. In the case of C-A and her sports friends this involves acting sex/gender as 'tomboys' and masculine athletes, and the acting of sexuality, mentioned by C-A as contrasting 'the standard man–woman society'. C-A met her girlfriend in the sports club, as several of the research participants did. I argue that the refuge established by C-A and some others is an example of queer visibility effectuating a queer alternative, a queer space inside mainstream sport. However, according to queering and how I explain the concept earlier, I argue that this queer space does not effectuate queering of the heteronormative context in general. On the contrary, it can run the danger of strengthening heteronormative existence as the 'normal' by constituting a queer refuge as an alternative for the 'deviants' and hence articulating what is not normal in the context.

Turning to the male informants in the study, it is clear that gay men in sport (even those living openly as gays) *do not find each other* in the same way as those living as lesbian appeared to. Therefore, in this research, they do not seem to create alternative, social sites and queer communities in the same way. It was reported as something some of the men wanted. Some of the research participants reported a lack of knowledge on how to spot others living homosexually:

O: Okay, there are other gays, but they go to bars. They don't do sports. Gradually, though, I've come to understand that they can be found in sport too. Well, everywhere! You just can't see them. It's something hidden...

H: Yes. And didn't you sometimes feel that you could make out some...secret codes, something that made you think: 'He looks gay'?

O: No. What is there to look for? I didn't know the code, what sort of codes are there to look for in sport? The code you have in sport is not the same as the one that can be found in gay bars.[2]

Creating heterotopias or queer spaces and queer alternatives in sport (intermediate and elite) appeared to happen among the women, the men, on the other hand, report attempts to queer their sport setting by acting in ways that disrupt hegemonic beliefs of how homosexual men behave:

E: [...] Well, I think it's a bit... eh... to some extent I can enjoy it, the fact that I have a rather rough way of playing. [...] earlier I used it to get some elbow-room, I had this hetero-image, now I use it to... I enjoy using it to tackle the heterosexual players (that I play against) hard. For that reason I become a sort of... eh... well, I think it's important to demonstrate there and then, that homosexuals aren't necessarily small and queer and running around on high heels! [...] I think it's important to demonstrate that homosexuality has other sides to it than those that people in general already know about. And I enjoy making use of that.

Living as a heterosexual previously, E learned how to perform traditional masculinity, in order to survive. He even got some freedom inside heteronormativity to very carefully explore homosexual acts. E preferred a 'masculine enactment' for two different reasons: one; to help him survive living closeted as gay and to pass as heterosexual. Secondly, because he now wants to act masculine as openly gay, he finds that it gives him the possibility to challenge, in front of other athletes, the strong myths about gay men as effeminate. One can say that the masculine behaviour of E has not changed during his shift from acting heterosexual to an open homosexual enactment. However, the effects of his acts have changed. When E makes a shift from heterosexual to a 'language' of homosexuality, he brings in the potentiality of a deconstruction of heterosexuality as an absolute basis for masculine behaviour, and a potentiality for queering a heteronormative masculine sport context.

2 The existence of homosocial spaces in sport

The sport arena as one which is distinctly sexed, by this I mean sport participation in general is organised by the contestants' sex, was found to result in both heteronormativity and homophobia. A focus on sex as a binary opposition, that organises difference, creates what Ingraham (1996: 169) calls 'heterogender'. When there are conceptualisations of sex and gender as opposite, defined as woman or man, sex/gender is inextricably bound up with heterosexuality as a 'natural' state. Ingraham calls the connection between gender and heterosexuality 'the heterosexual imaginary':

> Ask students how they learned to be heterosexual, and they will consistently respond with stories about how they learned to be boys or girls, women or men, through the various social institutions in their lives. Heterosexuality serves as the unexamined organizing institution and ideology (the heterosexual imaginary) for gender.
>
> (Ingraham, 1996: 186–87)

Sport can work as a social institution and one research participant (B) said that she thought of sport as very heterosexual. When I asked her why, she started to talk about the centrality on the body that exists in sport. Such a focus increases the actual awareness of the two sexes: men's bodies and women's bodies. B finds that the sexual dichotomy used to materialise the body in the sport leads to both heteronormativity and less tolerance for homosexuality:

H: Why do you think of sport as heterosexual?

B: Well, because in sport there is, at least in the sport I have been doing, there is a great focus on the body. And then there are... well, you have the male body and the female body and in a way sex. And... that is when the norms quite clearly can be seen, I mean, it is not as if you sing in a choir or do something which has less focus on the body. And at least when it comes to the sport that I have been doing... (laughs) there I have definitely not experienced great open-mindedness and tolerance when it comes to homosexuality.

Heterosexual enacting is also described by the research participants to be present in the social spaces that make up the sporting arena.

M: It is always like this: the boys are supposed to choose the sexiest woman during the tournament. There are plenty of those kinds of silly things. And sometimes it has been the case that the girls are supposed to vote for a boy, and then they match the two into some stupid couple or something.

When heterosexuality is prompted in this way it leads to what I argue as a lack of language or discourses for love scripts for same-sex love relations. Heterosexuals are taken by the hand, so to speak, and guided into coupling and dating, while same-sex coupling remains silenced or closeted and hence is script-less in a heteronormative culture. That said, sport often provides homosocial spaces because many activities are separated by sex. This is particularly apparent in team sports, but also in individual sports that are dominated by male or female participation. Therefore, the possibility of homoeroticism and homosocial diversions may be cultivated.

Homophobia is often more clearly expressed when the research participants openly communicate sexuality through love, flirtation and other sexual advances. On the contrary, if the sport setting expresses little fear and contempt towards lesbians/gays, the potential for romance and sexual confirmation, which can be found in homosocial arenas with a great deal of body intimacy, is experienced as positive and attractive. The latter was only found among some of the lesbian research participants who created queer spaces inside their mainstream sport context, described above as heterotopias in sport. These research participants were open as lesbians in their sport context. Those (female and male athletes) who were closeted about their homosexual experiences in sport, seemed to be left with few available discourses when approaching someone romantically in the sport context. However, some research participants made use of what I call a script-less, but homosocial situation to realise love stories in secret. I will argue that they managed to draw benefits out of a heteronormative and homosocial context and made use of the script-less situation as a reticent position for initiating an approach towards the one they fell in love with. Here is their story written in the voice of a female athlete:[3]

'Babes'

To be honest: girls have always turned me on. I know what I like best. The real feminine ones: soft, compassionate, sweet, with feminine curves; hips, tits and soft skin. The sweet smell of a woman's soft belly-skin. Muscles are OK, but I don't fancy a 'six-pack-belly', not the androgynous female with strong biceps and unisex-perfume. That's not for me. When I am together with my woman, I love having her on my lap. I want to hold her hard, wrap my arms around her, protect her, and do everything to make her happy. But, maybe hard to believe: often, I feel shy and embarrassed towards the woman that I fancy. I blush, and wonder if she understands my thoughts, my fantasies, when I look at her. There are so many beautiful women where I exercise. I often watch other classes than my own. But I can't say that I flirt with women. I never take the active part in that game towards women, that's too dangerous. I hate the thought of being turned down by women who think a woman who is wild about her is disgusting. I could never show my face there again. But the women flirt with me!

I flirt only with men, and I flirt a lot. People see me as a big flirt, especially where I exercise, because I play around with my coach. There are not many men around us, in fact he is almost the only one, and he is married and well off. But I like those men best; it is the most fun to flirt with them. Very safe, because you don't have them on the door two days after, you know!

What the others don't know is that my closest friend is also my secret lover. We have been together like that for years now. It's easy to keep the relationship secret; everybody sees us as sisters. Living together on tournaments; training – competing, always a double room in the hotel for us. We can be really close, hugging, holding hands, almost kissing when all the other team-mates are around; you know – that's not unusual for close girl-friends. I love having her on my knee when we sit around chatting with the other girls. Sometimes it's almost like foreplay, you know; sitting there together touching each other cautiously, and hiding a tremendous secret in the face of all the others.

There is one thing to remember: they must never get to know about this! She would break down completely. She says that she is not like that – not even bisexual, and that it would be very unfair to the whole sport community if we should announce openly what we have been sharing all the time. Think of the sponsors. And the media. We are supposed to do our best, also when it comes to representing our sport and Norway abroad. Our feelings for each other should not be exposed like that. It has nothing to do with sport. And she has her boyfriend too, of course. I know I have to be 100 per cent loyal to our secret, or else I'll lose her, for sure. But I feel good when we are together. I can be fine with that. It's more complicated when we are back home, where she lives with her boyfriend. But we really travel a lot with the team, you know, spending a lot of time together away from her boyfriend.

Actually, I think it is a bit tiring that I fancy women that much. I don't want to become like that – I mean like those lesbians. I am also going to find me a man eventually. I want kids, and a normal decent life. I don't want to be different. Think of my parents, my whole family – I would be an outcast there! I am lucky really, that I am bisexual. I know how to flirt with men! I am able to choose what I find the best. So why should I choose a life full of problems?

3 *Locker room culture*

Body intimacy, and the fact that athletes are naked together in locker rooms and saunas, is an aspect of sport that makes it extraordinary as an arena in relation to sexuality. The social relations in the locker room exist in an atmosphere of nakedness, close body contact, and focus on the body, often in small, hot, steamy and clammy rooms. Heteronormativity effectuates a paradoxical sensitivity towards homosexuality – this can make the small rooms even clammier. Homosexuality is often exaggerated and ridiculed by others and 'extra visible' in contrast to heterosexuality because heterosexual is recognised as normality, while homosexuality is characterised by rumours, myths and taboos. This can lead to an extremely low level of tolerance towards the open presence of lesbian and gay athletes. As the quotation at the start of the chapter illustrates, the feeling of being perceived as an unwanted voyeur in the showers is reported among the research participants to be unpleasant, and consequently they often kept a low homosexual profile in the changing room.

Nevertheless, homophobia in the sport context does not prohibit sexual activity among the athletes in the changing room. One research participant told me about what happened between some adult men and a few younger athletes, in the sauna after finishing training. Rules of sexual behaviour were established and lasted for many years, teaching the research participant both the language of a homosexual erotic love script and homophobia at the same time. I found Pronger's (1990) notion of the homoerotic paradox easy to read out of the experiences of pain and pleasure linked to locker-room behaviour:

C: Well... we were... we learned... we were taught never to touch each other because then we were gay, you see. [...] So we never ever were to do that. We'd take a shower together, we could masturbate in the sauna while watching each other, and it was extremely exciting. [...] And when I was about 16 or 17 years old, and wanted to lie close to someone, to caress, right? When I felt these desires... And you're not supposed to do that. Because then you're gay, right? And then... then this strange idea gets into your head, that you mustn't touch another person because then you're gay!

The pleasure of sexual activity in the sauna transforms slowly into frustration for C as he admits to himself that he wants 'something more', but that 'something more' is strongly forbidden since anything associated with romantic feelings, or personal interest would bring homosexual discourses to the sauna culture. Hence, the language learned in this context, is based on a shared non-spoken agreement: You are not allowed to touch each other, or to hug, or initiate sexual contact that is associated with flirtation and being romantic. The activity in the sauna that C talks about could go on for many years (it started when he was around 13 years). Sexual activity outside discourses of romantic love is acceptable in male hetero-sexual sport contexts. This is an example of how mainstream sport culture can exist alongside gay, cruising culture. Cruising culture, acted out by straight ath-letes, young athletes questioning their sexuality, and possible closeted adult homosexuals, makes the context queer. However, as long as a sexual non-roman-tic script is in use, hiding any homosexual desire under a cover of secrecy, straightness and homophobia, I argue that queer existence in these cases does not contribute to a queering of the sports context in general. The border between what is acceptable and not acceptable body intimacy and sexual contact between boys or men fits a logic that supposes that if nobody is gay, then the sexual acts going on are not homosexual or forbidden. As long as C accepts the 'rules', he becomes obedient instead of trying to extend or break the law. As such, C is not what is called a hybrid agent (Søndergaard, 1996) with the potentiality of queer-ing a specific space. The existence of such an agent will often have great impact on discourse production. The result might be queering of a practice, which until then has been viewed as entirely 'normal', or quite acceptable. But C cannot be described as queering the context, since he never opposed the law of not touch-ing another person in the sauna, or expressed his romantic desire, since that would signify the forbidden: 'being gay'.

Conclusion

Mainstream sport culture seems to exist through an understanding of homosex-ual love/desire as taboo, and/or a naïve blindness for the potential presence of homoeroticism and homosexual/lesbian desire. At the same time, findings from the study show that the interpretation of sport as heterosexual and empty of homoerotic elements, is a mere illusion that rebuilds itself based on lack of com-municated knowledge about homosexual practice. Hence, homoerotic desire and practice in sport, as knowledge that is not outspoken, is an example of what Foucault (1990) describes as silences underlying and permeating discourses of normality.

Discourses of heteronormativity in sport have great impact on the research participants. The female participants are affected differently compared with the male participants. Let me again take the locker room culture as an example: The study shows that discourses of normality, established in the female locker room are based on a homosocial intimacy *without sexuality:* The female participants describe the locker room as a friendly and playful space for women, but not loaded with sexuality/desire in the same way as male locker rooms seem to be. For men, comments, jokes, bragging about heterosexual experiences and posing physical potency fill the air. On the contrary, among women, hugging, physical contact and caressing are common, and allowed to an extent that girls and women can develop physical, intimate and loving relations. Importantly, the acceptance of such an intimate and potential 'sexy' bodily atmosphere is also vulnerable to queering. In addition, it can also be quite homophobic, as is the case for the men's locker room where the male research participants saw danger in displaying aspects of intimacy. Some women in the study did manage to provoke and challenge the atmosphere of non-sexuality in the locker room, by being open as lesbian (but not having sexual play/intercourse as with some of the men's experiences).

Most of what was found in the study, is, I argue, queer existence or queerness in sport. It appears as something deviant and alternative, without the potential for transcending heteronormative dominance. Women were sometimes found to operate as queer agents, either by individually sexualising the locker room (being openly lesbian), or when lesbian athletes appear together in the same sports clubs and act love-scripts or erotic sexual desire that challenge and violate the discourse of non-sexual female intimacy in sport.

Notes

1 Post-structuralism is also strongly connected to postmodernism since it is part of the postmodern debate in the US, where French academics' theoretical contributions are called post-structuralism. French theorists saw postmodernism and post-structuralism as American constructions, and often denied the labels; postmodernist and/or post-structuralist, which led to some unexpected statements, e.g. Foucault's remark in an interview that he did not know what postmodernism actually referred to (Raulet 1985).

2 Other sites for sports and physical activity that are labelled feminine, such as ballet or other forms of dance might contain heterotopias of deviation for some homosexual men. These, however, are not among the activities represented in the study.

3 This story is developed and written by me, but contained and based solely on information I got from female participants in the study. The story is based on interviews with three of the informants. Several researchers have started to experiment with new forms of writing offered by postmodernism. The effect is, among others, a violation of prescribed conventions and a transgression of traditional social science writing genres (Bruce 1998:3).

References

Berlant, L. and Warner, M. (2000) 'Sex in public', in: L. Berlant (ed) *Intimacy*. Chicago: Chicago University Press.

Bruce, T. (1998) 'Postmodernism and the possibilities for writing 'vital' sports texts, in: G. Rail (ed.) *Sport and Postmodern Times*. New York: State University of New York press.

Coakley, J. (2001) *Sport in Society: Issues and Controversies*, 7th edn. Boston: McGraw-Hill.

Davies, B. (1997) 'The subject of post-structuralism: a reply to Alison Jones', *Gender and Education*, 9(1): 271–83.

Eng, H. (2003) 'Sporting Sex/uality: Doing Sex and Sexuality in a Norwegian Context', Doctoral thesis, Oslo: Norwegian School of Sport Sciences.

Foucault, M. [1976] (1990) *The History of Sexuality, Volume 1*. New York: Vintage.

Foucault, M. (1986) 'Of other spaces', *Diacritics*, Spring, 22–27.

Harding, J. (1998) *Sex Acts: Practises of Femininity and Masculinity.* London: Sage Publications Ltd.

Ingraham, C. (1996) 'The heterosexual imaginary: feminist sociology and theories of gender', in: S. Seidman (ed.) *Queer Theory/Sociology.* Cambridge: Blackwell Publishers Inc.

Jones, A. (1997) 'Teaching post-structuralist feminist theory in education: student resistances', *Gender and Education*, 9(3): 261–69.

Jorde, B. (2005) 'Queering in the Urban Sphere', Master thesis, Oslo: Oslo School of Architecture.

Pronger, B. (1990) *The Arena of Masculinity: Sports, Homosexuality, and the Meaning of Sex.* London: GMP Publishers Ltd

Raulet, G. (1985) Structuralism och poststructuralism. *Res Publica*, 3.

Roseneil, S. (2000) Queer frameworks and queer tendencies: towards an understanding of postmodern transformations of sexuality, *Sociological Research Online*, 5(3), <http://www.socresonline.org.uk/5/3/roseneil.html>.

Seidman, S. (ed.) (1996) *Queer Theory/Sociology.* Cambridge: Blackwell Publishers Inc.

Søndergaard, D. M. (1996) *Tegnet på kroppen. Køn: Koder og konstruktioner blant unge voksne i akademia.* København: Museum Tusculanums Forlag.

4 Ten men out

Gay sporting masculinities in softball

Nigel Jarvis

Introduction

The purpose of this chapter is to explore subordinated masculinities, namely those of gay men participating in a softball team in Toronto, Canada, and to relate the research results to wider theoretical issues and debates. The chapter begins by presenting an overview of past research on gay men and sport, first focusing on key issues centred around the construction of masculinity. It then explores literature related to the role and politics of gay men participating in sport. The softball site under examination and how ethnographic research was carried out are described. Finally, the findings will be debated as to how they contribute to an understanding of the queer sociology of sport before offering ways forward to comprehend gay men participating in sport.

Before progressing, the use of the term *queer* needs to be clarified. While much of queer theory is grounded in the instability and indeterminacy of all gendered and sexed identities (Salih, 2002), and on the deconstruction of the heterosexual/homosexual binary (Sedgwick, 1990), Morland and Willox (2005) point out that the politics of queer have moved beyond identities and are about actions and ways of living. An important sense of queer politics is about shared lifestyles, and how these can challenge notions of fixed identities (Butler, 1990; 1993; Gauntlett, 2004) such as those hegemonic masculinities found in the world of sport. Thus queer is used in terms of whether gay men participating in softball are potentially resisting dominant sporting norms, which are centred around the concept of heteronormativity.

Gay men and sport – an overview of issues and past research

There is growing concern over issues of identity in modern globalized society, and more specifically debates over fragmentation and homogenization of identity. Vertinsky (2004: 8) points out that globalization raises questions about how people relate to their sporting experiences as part of their personal and/or professional lives and whether, in the face of massive global movements and increasing homogenization, people can retain any sense of local places and their particularities. The flow of gay men's sporting lifestyles, customs and practices from one part of the world to another and participation in global events such as the Gay Games, are examples of a small-scale globalization process at work. Houlihan (2003) and Maguire (2000) both see that while globalization processes lead to greater interdependence and increased awareness of a sense of the world as a whole, there is also a concomitant resurgence of the local/national. Coakley (Coakley and Dunning, 2000: xxviii) argues that at the start of the twenty-first century, 'sport and societies are most accurately conceptualized as the unplanned products of the interaction over time of pluralities of conscious, interdependent, differentially powerful, emotional as well as rational embodied human beings who make choices.' It is these precise products, patterns and choices that need to be studied empirically as suggested by Maguire (2000).

According to Horne *et al.* (1999) the globalized postmodern world is fragmented, with surface appearances having become central and authenticity impossible to identify. There is growing self-consciousness and self-reflexivity permeating all areas of cultural and social life, by pastiche, parody, irony and playfulness. In this context sports, and more specifically gay sporting settings, can be seen as another form of cultural playfulness. Sport's place and meaning in everyday life is negotiable and culturally created, and is not simply socially imposed. It has social meanings and is itself a social product and not merely a reflection of a society. The fragmentation and inequalities that exist in sport in modern society continue to create tensions and conflicts. Contestations of space and meaning, and aspirations and desire to acquire or provide space for new types of cultural expression, such as gay sporting experiences, is one key theme that has emerged in the sociological and cultural analysis of modern sport (Horne *et al.*, 1999).

Another key issue is the gendered nature of sport. More specifically, feminist literature on gender and sport has raised issues of concern about the relationship between masculinity and sport (Robertson, 2003). Sports, and games in particular, primarily celebrate male space, male physicality, and male dominance (Bryson, 1990; Kay, 2003; Robertson, 2003; Vertinsky, 2004). What is crucial about the contribution of sport to the construction of gender is that sport provides an image and forum of idealized or culturally exalted masculinity (Connell, 1995), which tends to be the most dominant or powerful image within sport cultures. Thus many men actively attempt to preserve, defend and promote this dominant version of masculinity. Griffin (1998: 20) argues that sport serves five social functions that ensure the gender order supporting presumed hegemonic masculinity and male superiority. These functions are: 1) defining and reinforcing traditional conceptions of masculinity; 2) providing an acceptable and safe context for male bonding and intimacy; 3) reinforcing male privilege and female subordination; 4) establishing status among other males; and 5) reinforcing heterosexuality.

Pronger (1990) highlights that male athletes are generally assumed to be heterosexual. A gay male athlete violates the image that male athletes are strong, virile, tough, and competitive. It also calls into question the image that gay men are effeminate. Many heterosexual male athletes and coaches consider it important to keep gay men marginalized and not to welcome them into their sporting spheres. As Hekma (1998: 2) states 'gay men who are seen as queer or effeminate are granted no space whatsoever in what is generally considered to be a masculine preserve and a macho enterprise.'

Connell (1995) has noted that a common theme in sociology in the 1990s was to examine the differences among masculinities. However, Connell (1995: 37–41) has stated that to identify diversities in masculinities is not enough, that research must also explore and recognize the *relations* between the different kinds of masculinity: relations of alliance, dominance and subordination. Nardi (2000) and Theberge (2000) also identify the need to research how gay men engage in, contest, reproduce, and modify hegemonic masculinity. Connell (1995), mentions that much of the important academic discourse on masculinity is the outcome of analysis by gay and feminist oppositional movements. Connell points out that gay men's collective knowledge should examine and explore gender ambiguity, tension between bodies and identities, and contradictions in and around masculinity. Indeed, Robertson (2003: 711) believes that sport represents an arena where masculinities can become unstable, evoking contradictory emotions for individual men. Here, even men who are predominantly marginalized or subordinated by hegemonic displays in sport can find momentary pleasure in complying with dominant masculine ideologies.

The history of formal organized gay sport is a rather recent phenomenon. Organized lesbian and gay sport occurs within a complex and increasingly sophisticated network of individuals, teams, clubs and leagues operating on a local, regional, national and/or international level. Since gay men and lesbians tend to migrate to urban areas (Adam, 1985; Levine, 1979; Murray, 1979), the vast majority of their sporting experiences take place in cities. Gay sport tends to be minimally integrated with the majority of sport in mainstream[1] places as gay men and lesbians tend to practise a degree of self-organization through their own sport leagues and/or competitions such as the Gay World Series, Eurogames, and most notably, the Gay Games which have been held every four years since 1986. Some competitive integration occurs where a few openly gay teams compete in mainstream leagues (Price and Parker, 2003). Additionally, some inverse integration occurs as some heterosexuals play on gay teams (Elling *et al.*, 2001).

Messner (1992) cites that since the outset of the gay liberation movement in the early 1970s, organized sport has become an integral part of developing lesbian and gay communities. Gay sport offers the opportunity for many gay men and lesbians to experience pride and a sense of belonging to the larger gay community (Elling *et al.*, 2001). Sport for gay persons is seen as part of a general celebration of gay culture with a marked emphasis on making conspicuous lifestyle statements (Hargreaves, 2000). Many sports participated in by lesbian and gay athletes reflect what Messner (1992) identifies as a value system and vision based on feminist and gay liberationist ideals of equality and universal participation. The emphasis in lesbian and gay sporting clubs and organizations seems to be on bridging differences and building relationships within the gay community, and perhaps overcoming prejudices. However, Messner (1992) states that whilst the Gay Games represent a radical break from past conceptions of the role of sport in society, they do not represent a major challenge to sport as an institution. Alternative sport events like the Gay World Series or the Gay Games may not necessarily confront or change the dominant structure of sport because they largely occur in spaces outside dominant sports institutions (Elling and de Knop, 2003). Still, McKay *et al.* (2000) note that gay sport can provide a nuanced opportunity for gender play, disruption or even resistance to hegemonic traditional conservative masculinity.

Pronger (2000) further debates some problematic issues with gay sport. While he appreciates the growth of gay sporting cultures over the past few decades as signifying progress for sexual minorities in the arena of physical activity, Pronger sees lesbian and gay cultural embrace of sport as part of a liberal strategy of legitimation, that is liberals are essentially satisfied with the fundamentals of sport as a bodily practice and do not seek basic changes to the practices and rules of sport. Gay community sports have not pursued a radical strategy of liberation that would see gay engagement with sport as an opportunity to transform sport's cultural conservatism. He argues that gay sport has not taken an opportunity to refigure the construction of sport as a conservative culture of desire, which can in turn contribute to the critique and transformation of oppressions that are perpetuated by conservative political cultures more generally. Many gay sports groups have gone out of their way to stress inclusiveness, regardless of ability, age, gender, race, class and sexual orientation. Indeed, some gay sport events like the Gay Games have stressed friendship over sexuality; thus this could be seen as the erasure of lesbian and gay difference in the pursuit of sporting legitimation. Pronger (2000: 232) states that 'gay sports proves the normality of lesbians and gay men.' Many gay sport events are sanctioned by mainstream sport governing bodies, conducted under the rules of the particular sport. This is seen as important as it legitimizes the events as sport. Certainly gay men meet each other in gay sport settings and pursue sexual liaisons, but this is peripheral to the practise of the sport itself. Pronger (2000: 241) concludes that gay sport is 'inclusive of gay identities but continues to marginalize homosexuality from the activity'.

Pronger (2000) is a leading critic and questions the political nature of gay sport, stating that the goal of gay sporting movements should be to challenge, resist, undermine and transform existing traditional hegemonic sporting cultures. This can be considered to be part of a queer political strategy. However, he does not identify any new structures or figurations once this transformation begins to take place. Indeed, he also does not offer any future suggestions as to what sport will look like after gays 'undermine and transform' existing sporting cultures. Further, Pronger (1990; 2000) seems to offer a phenomenological interpretation of gay men in sport but his research lacks empirical understanding of men's participation in sport.

The majority of research on gay men and/or sexuality and sport has been limited to mainstream sporting locations (Anderson, 2002; Griffin, 1998; Hekma, 1998; Janssens, 2003; Price and Parker, 2003; Pronger, 1990, 2000) or has tended to focus on large global events such as the Gay Games (Krane, 2002; Waitt,

2003). Little research has been undertaken focusing upon the everyday experiences of gay men within gay community sporting places. In contrast, this chapter presents research at this local level, namely a gay men's softball team. The nature and structure of the interaction of gay athletes will be related to key wider political issues largely focusing on the potential of gay men's sport to challenge dominant hegemonic masculine sporting cultures and practices.

Methodology

Research for this study focused on softball, one of the more popular sports among gay men in Canada. It was chosen because the researcher was familiar with the gay sport scene in Toronto. However, softball may not be typical of gay men's sport participation, that is, it may be difficult or inaccurate to base generalizations derived from the data onto other gay sporting experiences. While a popular mainstream sport in participation and spectatorship, softball does not receive significant media coverage. Still, it is a very recognizable sport and occupies a significant space within contemporary sporting cultures, and thus can be understood in relation to broader political and social contexts which can be applied to many aspects of mainstream sport. In this setting, softball is a team sport that allows men to participate and compete in an organized framework. Also, softball may be considered by some gay men as a more traditional 'masculine' sport compared to other team sports such as volleyball or badminton which are also popular with gay men. Indeed, as Maxwell (1996: 73) states, there is increasing agreement that cultural groups incorporate substantial diversity and that homogeneity cannot be assumed. Still, it was deemed that research on a gay men's softball team would provide valid insight into gay men and their experiences in sport and how this relates to wider political issues about the role of gay sport.

Since the 1970s gay softball in Toronto has been organized through the Cabbagetown Gay Softball League (CGSL). Games are held on City of Toronto permitted softball diamonds. Play is open to lesbians and gay men, as well as heterosexuals, of all skill levels. The League is divided into men's competitive and recreational divisions, as well as a women's division. The CGSL had approximately 400 members during the 2002 season, making up 18 teams consisting of about 13–16 players. The 2002 season lasted some 20 games between May and September, which provided an ample opportunity to collect ethnographic data.

The researcher played with a team called the 5ive (*sic*) Star Generals. All participants were informed of the nature and implications of the research from the start of the season. They consented to the research, which is an important ethical consideration (Christians 2000). Ethnographic data was collected through field notes taken during the season, starting with pre-season practices during April, and continuing with the regular season. All respondents allowed their names to be used in publication of any data. A variety of men were observed, although the majority was considered to be from a white, middle-class background. They ranged in age from 29–57, although most were in their early

30s. All can be considered 'out', in participating openly as gay men within a gay sport setting, although there was some variation among participants concerning the disclosure of their sexuality in other spheres of their lives, such as workplace and family.

The ethnographic approach, concentrating on observing interactions between players, was used to investigate the variety of masculinities that exist within the softball setting. It is envisioned that through analysis of the data, theoretical explanations related to hegemonic dominance and the potential for queer political resistance to mainstream sporting cultures could be explored.

Research findings

The findings highlight how the softball players demonstrated their gay sporting masculinities, and how this may challenge or conform to traditional hegemonic sporting masculinities (Connell, 1995) found in mainstream sport settings. This was largely explored by employing Brake's (1985) analysis of subcultural styles, namely language or argot, demeanour, and image.

Language

Much of the argot or jargon used during games was similar to that of mainstream softball (*'Let's get some hits boys'*, *'Nice poke'*, *'Way to use your power'* and *'Line it into the gap'*), but in some instances these were shouted out in mocked lisping voices (*'Let's get some hit, hits, hits!'*). Many examples of sexual innuendo were used throughout the games to subvert the argot. Tim stated to Steve, *'Alright Steve! you hit it into the hole'*, then Steve commented, *'Oooh, you bet I like it like that.'* Brian called to Steve to bend his legs more to stop some of the ground balls hit his way, *'Hey, I only bend down for a few things in life'*, Steve responded jokingly. Dennis said to another player who had just made a tough defensive catch in the outfield, *'Nice catch on your knees, but then again you're probably used to being on your knees.'* Steve S., a part time player, commented during a pre-game warm-up, *'Alright these guys get hard on each other if they get behind and take it out on each other.'* *'Oooh, we don't want that much detail'*, Paul joked as the rest of the team laughed. Craig, resting on the sidelines, and nearly hit by two stray balls joked, *'Balls coming from everywhere, now normally I wouldn't mind this.'* Steve commented on his batting average being '10 for 16' providing a twist on a key hitting statistic in softball, *'Yeah, I have had sex the last ten days out of 16.'* The team name provided an opportunity to link to sexual connotations. The team chant at the end of one game, *'Way to go Generals!'*, was subverted to *'Genitals!'* by Les. *'Hey I like that cheer better'*, commented some other players.

Other language used during games was related to gender roles with many instances of calling players by female or feminine names: Steve to Chris, *'Nice catch Christina'*; Tim shouted out to Dennis after he fell to the ground just missing a line drive, *'Give that girl an Oscar!'*; Arnold greeted the team upon arrival, *'Morning ladies'*; and when the umpire asked what was the name of the player wearing number 7, Nigel responded '*Miss*'. The use of '*bitch*' was very common throughout the season. '*Nice play (or throw), bitch*' would be heard in most games. Other expressions such as, '*Thanks dear*' or, '*Come on honey*' were widely used. Craig commented after one dropped ball in practice, '*I could have caught that if I had my dress on.*' Many catches or plays were accompanied by high pitch screams. Players that were due to bat next, generally referred to as being 'on deck', were sometimes told '*(player's name)… you're in makeup next*'.

Further examples cited made gentle fun of players by calling them lesbians. Tim said to Tim F. as he curled his jersey sleeves up over his shoulders, '*Wow, Tim, you have lesbian shoulders*'. In another game, Steve (laughing) stated to Dennis after Dennis dropped an easy catch, '*You looked like a lesbian when you called for the ball, but you certainly were a gay boy when you dropped it.*' In another match, Steve commented to Dennis, '*You're the second best looking lesbian on the team*', after which Dennis gave a faint mock of disgust and then tossed his hair back and said with a limp wrist, '*Well!*' One game during a tournament provided the opportunity to question whether one player from a team in Atlanta was actually a male or female player since the player had a very feminine appearance (and since some female players participate on men's teams). Chris commented, '*Is that a guy or a girl?… He runs like a girl or else he's a butch lesbian… Nigel go close to him or her to find out.*' Some of the umpires in the league were lesbians and the ribbing with 5ive players was lighthearted and centred around sexuality. Tim jokingly referred to the lesbian umpire after a ball was tipped and hit her in the groin, '*Well, that's the closest a ball will get to that area.*' A few plays later the umpire made a comment about '*girl on girl sex*', and Jeff, a player from the opposition, joked, '*Ewww, please I was just ready to bat. You've made me lose concentration. I feel like I am going to be sick.*'

Much of the talk and language was directly related to gay sexuality and same sex attraction. Many players commented on the bodies or looks of other players. Chris said of one player on another team, '*Nice catch, but it would have been better if he had no clothes on him.*' He also remarked to a player on a Toronto team, '*James is so hot. Nice little body, look at that chest.*' Many observations about other players occurred especially during a tournament when teams from all over North America were playing, providing the opportunity to see many men for the first time. Talk centred around expressions such as, '*Look at that ass*' or '*crotch*'. Many players from 5ive cheered on a team from Chicago, '*Oh my God, these guys are all gorgeous, they are the best looking team here*', noted Chris.

Condoms were distributed in the registration packages for the tournament, which provided the opportunity for some players to engage in sex with other men visiting Toronto. Sean, a registration official, stated, '*Nigel, here's some condoms in case you want to meet an American boy tonight.*' Pre-game practice talk was often based around discussion of who (usually the same five or six players) had gone out the night before and who had slept with other men. Just before an early morning game in July, Craig stated upon his arrival, '*Guys I am dedicated. I just threw out the hottest guy from my bed 30 minutes ago so I could play today… I hope you appreciate my dedication.*' Many players talked about sleeping with other men in the league or who they would like to sleep with.

Demeanour

Demeanour constitutes the body language and behaviour of players. Many exhibited the same traditional patterns of aggressive and competitive behaviour that would be found in mainstream male sport settings. Numerous instances of shouting and yelling between players were noted throughout the season. One player on another team was suspended from the league for yelling at an umpire, while another was fined for arguing. There was noticeable animosity between several league teams, including the 5ive Star Generals against the SX Express team. Brian, the 5ive team manager, stated to the team before a game that, '*We want to beat these guys (SX Express) because we used to play with half of them from last year… and some of us didn't get along with them.*'

During a match with time close to being called, one of 5ive's batters stepped out of the batter's box to slow down the pace of the game. The pitcher on the opposing team noticing this stalling tactic yelled out, '*Fuck, get up to the plate will you!*' Subsequently, the pitcher threw down his glove at his team's bench, obviously irate with events during the game. Other games were filled with tension with many disputed calls made by both teams. Arguments between managers were noted in some games, but were not common. Opposing teams had many instances where team members were yelling at each other for mistakes made during the game, and some crossed into shoving matches with other players stepping in to divide and calm down players. Angry throwing of gloves to the ground or the kicking of the bats was noticeable among a few opposition players.

No major examples of yelling and/or fighting took place among the 5ive Star Generals; however, there were some tensions within the team on certain days. Some players would throw their gloves to the ground in disgust or be visibly angry with themselves. Sometimes this anger lashed out against team members especially during key plays where errors occurred, allowing the opposition to score runs and/or advance base runners. Brian shouted out to Tim during a May match, '*Jesus fucking Christ Tim why did you call Arnold to come in, the guy hit the ball way over his head.*' During a game, some team members were yelling at outfielders to catch some of the balls but at the same time were making their own defensive errors. '*Can you believe they are telling us how to play? They should learn how to fucking catch the ball themselves*', Chris said whilst watching the game. Still, the overall atmosphere on the team was supportive throughout the year, even when the Generals were initially losing and despite the few examples of hostility and tension. Team cheers and encouragement for individual batters were common during all games. Shouts of, '*Let's go Generals!*' or, '*Let's rally!*' were always used, as well as 'high fiving' players who made outstanding catches or plays. Anxiousness or tensions during games or poor play were often immediately eased by humour and ribbing. Brian noted in an email to the team after a game, '*Guys, we played great this weekend. Thanks to myself and Dennis for the tosses to first base, perfect if Steve had been twelve feet tall to get them.*' Steve shouted out to Dennis in another game while laughing, '*You could have got the guy out if the ground hadn't got in the way of your throw to me!*'

While most team members appeared to play seriously during matches, running hard to make defensive catches, or trying to run for extra bases, some team members would behave in a way that would likely be different from those in more traditional mainstream settings. Paul would sing in the outfield and dance, waving his hands and wrists singing, 'La, la, la'. Instead of running normally, some players would skip to second base from first if they had automatically advanced because of a walked batter. Some on-field behaviour obviously differed compared to mainstream sites. There were numerous instances of players hugging and kissing each other on the lips at the conclusion of a game during the team handshakes and congratulations. Indeed, some players would spontaneously kiss an opposition player during the game if they were standing on the same base.

Playing with injury was a common theme with regard to the behaviour of team members. While the importance of stretching and warming up before and during games was stressed to all players in order to reduce risk of injury, six team members played despite injury during some games. This helped to demonstrate that players were committed to the team, but can be interpreted as 'toughness', exhibiting a similar attribute related to more traditional sporting masculinities. Tim played through a shoulder injury even though he was scheduled for surgery in the autumn. Three players cut their legs during games and were bleeding; however, they continued to play after covering the wounds with bandages according to league rules. Other players were hit by balls during the game and continued despite heavy bruising. Paul played the entire season suffering from colitis. One player on another Toronto-based team broke a leg during a match in a tournament as he attempted to slide into second base. While many players continued through injury, they also made light of the situation at the same time. After being hit in the back and chest during two consecutive plays by the opposition while running bases, Dennis commented (while in serious pain), '*I'm bruising but they (Boston) were such sweet girls for asking if I was okay.*' When a line drive hit the pitcher Les in the chest, a team mate shouted out, '*Oh, the silicone[2] helped cushion the ball. He'll be alright!*'

A further key theme related to the demeanour of players was the desire to compete and win. While the atmosphere during most games was filled with encouragement and humour, as well as some tensions, the goal of defeating opponents and playing to a competitive level was apparent. Desire to win was shown in the practices between games as some other teams did not practise between games. Practices included drills to develop and sharpen skills such as hitting and catching. Coaching sessions were held to improve batting techniques. Les tried to coach Quinn, a quiet player, '*You're too nice. You need to be aggressive. Call for the ball out there, otherwise you may crash into other players and injure yourself.*' Some players commented that one of the motivations for playing softball was the chance to develop and hone their skills. Discussions on strategies before games were presented by the two managers.

Pressure to win was apparent throughout the season, especially after a poor start. The manager's talk before games stressed the need to start winning some games. The importance of winning was identified by Les after an error filled game, 'Who cares how we won, we won, that's the most important thing.' During a tournament, the importance of placing second in the C division was noted, 'We won silver medals. We played great defence, and hit well… We really competed well today', Brian concluded. Still, while winning was deemed important, both managers continually pointed out that the team should have fun.

Image

Image is related to the appearance of players. Team and league members had to conform to league rules. 5ive Star General team members wore two different jerseys (one black, one white) for all games as players were required to wear a number and the name of their team, according to CGSL rules. All players would either wear shorts or long sport trousers for all games, as well as cleated footwear. The uniforms of players were no different from those worn by mainstream softball players, and they did not display any overtly gay images.

The CGSL conformed to American Softball Association governing rules, including that any player wearing jewellery would be called out automatically. This rule was in place to reduce the chance of injury and the threat of lawsuits. Several players in the league wore jewellery such as earrings which had to be removed. Tim told Quinn at the beginning of the season, 'You have to take it (earring) out. If the umpire sees you like that you will be called out. No jewellery.' Steve joked immediately, 'You mean I cannot even wear my cock ring.'

Discussion

Ethnographic data provided valuable insights into the gay sporting masculinities of the softball players and show that their patterns of behaviour are complex and diverse. Clearly the observations demonstrate that the softball players conform to what Connell (1995) refers to as traditional hegemonic masculinities found within mainstream sport, but at the same time challenge or undermine these same masculinities. Thus there were many contradictions apparent. McKay *et al.* (2000) identify that gay sport can provide a nuanced opportunity for gender play, disruption and even resistance to hegemonic masculinity. Some results, especially those centred on the argot used, indicate that indeed the softball players participate in gender play with prominent use of feminine names or sexualizing common sporting expressions. Much talk between players is centred around same sexual attraction between players. Pronger (2000) states that the gay sport movement has tried to erase sexual desire, but here research indicates it was an open and integral aspect of the cultural practices of many players.

Some body language of the players represents a very gay sporting masculinity (dancing in the field, skipping between bases, kissing other players on the lips). This would support Horne *et al.*'s (1999) point that there is much playfulness and irony in the actions of players which is common in increasingly fragmented sport sites. This demonstrates that some disruption was occurring within the gay softball setting compared to a mainstream site. These actions occur openly in front of some of the heterosexual players participating in the league who do not seem to mind. Thus there appears to be some queer potential to challenge and subvert existing notions of dominant sporting masculinities. Indeed there seems to be a diversity of sporting masculinities on display among the softball players. Morland and Willox (2005) state that *queerness* is about celebration of a range of identities. Generally though, the softball occurred in temporary gay settings, that is, public permitted fields. Unless passers-by stop to watch games and observe closely the interactions between players and their range of identities, they would likely not conclude the game was being played by gay men. The image of players with their traditional uniforms was not overtly gay. While style can be an integral part of other subcultures resisting dominant norms, it is not a crucial aspect in this setting. Because gay sport tends to be self-organized and played largely within gay contexts (Elling and de Knop, 2003; Elling *et al.*, 2001), there seems little opportunity to publicly challenge or resist traditional hegemonic masculinity if these sporting experiences are not integrated into mainstream sport. Indeed the CGSL is a gay league and teams only play other teams in this organization or other gay teams in tournaments. Thus the queer potential of this gay softball team is largely lost.

Further, many softball players exhibit characteristics associated with more traditional hegemonic sporting masculinities (team fighting, swearing, disputing calls, competitiveness, typical sporting jargon, desire to win, toughness, playing through injury, traditional uniforms). The players and league rigidly follow existing mainstream softball rules, which could be seen as what Pronger (2000) refers to as part of a liberal strategy of legitimation. Players on the softball team appear to be satisfied with their participation in the game and its rules and practices. The men seem to have no problem in complying with existing hegemonic displays of masculinity (Robertson, 2003).

Whilst some players obviously outwardly play with their masculinities, the politics of the gay men researched does not indicate that they have explicit interest in subverting or transforming wider sporting cultures. Pronger (2000) states that gay sport has not pursued a radical strategy of liberation that would provide the opportunity to alter sport's cultural conservatism. While Pronger may desire this as a goal for gay sport, it may not reflect the everyday experiences of current participants.

Conclusion

The research shows that participating in gay softball for the players is a liberating experience (Pronger, 2000). It allows many players to get away from the gay bar scene (Young, 1995) and shows them a wider, more diverse gay community (Messner, 1992). Players seem satisfied with their participation in gay sport and its setting. Thus while the politics of this gay sport site may not obviously support Pronger's (2000) queer strategy of challenging and transforming existing conservative sporting cultures, the research has shown how gay men can engage in, contest, reproduce, and modify hegemonic masculinity. The very fact that these gay men are participating openly in a sport setting can be seen as subtly challenging hegemonic sporting masculinities. Perhaps then, a way forward, would be to frame this research employing Antonio Gramsci's (1891–1937) concept of hegemony which is fruitful in examining power relationships between dominant and subordinate groups. All groups in sport, either dominant or subordinate, compete with each other and negotiate and contest their aims, cultural values and norms, social functions, organizational and material framework. These processes are social conflicts in which dominant/subordinate ideologies, that are economically, politically and culturally founded, take on central functions. Key themes within these conflicts have generally centred around issues such as gender relations (Butler, 1990; 1993), class, race, sport consumption, globalization, the organization of sport, and nationalism (Rigauer, 2000: 43). However, issues related to sexuality and sexual orientation and sport, while part of gender relations, have largely been ignored within a hegemonic theoretical framework.

This research demonstrates that gay men have the potential to challenge pervasive views about sport. Subordinate groups like gay men are able to translate their material and ideological aims and values into action with the assistance of their own organizations and structures. Sport has indeed played an integral part in developing gay and lesbian communities. The increasing number of gay sport organizations like the softball league in Toronto, and the popularity of global events such as the Gay Games clearly show that sport does not fully overcome social differences but provides a forum for reinforcement and resistance. The softball research reveals that for gay men, gay sport activities and clubs provide an opportunity to relax from wider societal pressures and to mix with other men largely of the same sexual orientation. In addition, one of the most significant social functions of these organizations is their ability both to provide members and supporters with a distinct identity and to represent their community publicly. Sporting success and/or participation can significantly contribute to a general process of de-stigmatization, particularly if the represented group is usually considered to be inferior or subordinate.

Notes

1 Mainstream sport places refer to settings not geared toward any subculture. Typical mainstream sport sites would include schools, work-related groups, adult community volunteer-led sport organizations, and the world of professional sport. Heterosexuality, especially among male participants, is assumed in most of these settings.
2 Silicone in this quote refers to breast implants; however, the player in question did not have actual breast implants.

References

Adam, B. (1985) 'Structural foundations of the gay world', in P. Nardi and B. Schneider (eds) (1998) *Social Perspectives in Lesbian and Gay Studies: A Reader.* London: Routledge 220–29.

Anderson, E. (2002) 'Openly Gay Athletes: Contesting Hegemonic Masculinity in a Homophobic Environment', *Gender and Society*, 16 (6): 860–77.

Brake, M. (1985) *Comparative Youth Culture: The Sociology of Youth Cultures in America, Britain and Canada*. London: Routledge.

Bryson, L. (1990) 'Challenges to Male Hegemony in Sport', in M. Messner and D. Sabo (eds) (1990) *Sport, Men and the Gender Order: Critical Feminist Perspectives*. Champaign, IL: Human Kinetics 173-184.

Butler, J. (1990) *Gender Trouble: Feminisim and the Subversion of Identity*. London: Routledge.

Butler, J. (1993) *Bodies That Matter: On The Discursive Limits of 'Sex'*. London: Routledge.

Christians, C. G. (2000) 'Ethics and politics in qualitative research', in N. K. Denzin and Y. S. Lincoln (eds) (2000) *Handbook of Qualitative Research*. Thousand Oaks, CA: Sage Publications, 133–55.

Coakley, J. and Dunning, E. (eds) (2000) *Handbook of Sports Studies*. London: Sage Publications.

Connell, R. W. (1995) *Masculinities*. Cambridge: Polity Press.

Elling, A. and de Knop, P. (2003) 'Gay/Lesbian sport clubs and events: places of homo-social bonding and cultural resistance?' *International Review for the Sociology of Sport*, 38 (4): 441–56.

Elling, A., Knoppers, A., and de Knop, P. (2001) 'The social integrative meaning of sport: a critical and comparative analysis of policy and practice in the Netherlands', *Sociology of Sport Journal*, 18 (4): 414–34.

Gauntlett, D. (2004). 'Queer Theory' [online]. Available at <www.theory.org.uk> [Accessed November 16, 2004].

Griffin, P. (1998) *Strong Women, Deep Closets*. Champaign, IL: Human Kinetics

Hargreaves, J. (2000) *Heroines of Sport: The Politics of Difference and Identity*. London: Routledge.

Hekma, Gert. (1998) 'As long as they don't make an issue of it...: gay men and lesbians in organized sports in the Netherlands'. *Journal of Homosexuality*, 35 (1): 1–23.

Horne, J., Tomlinson, A. and Whannel, G. (1999) *Understanding Sport: An Introduction to the Sociological and Cultural Analysis of Sport*. London: E & FN Spon.

Houlihan, B. (2003). 'Sport agnd lobalisation', in B. Houlihan, (ed.) *Sport & Society*. London: SAGE Publications Ltd, 345–63.

Janssens, J. (2003) 'It's the sport that counts: participation in sports by lesbians and gays'. Paper presented at the *2nd World Congress of Sociology of Sport*, Cologne, June 18–21.

Kay, T. (2003). 'Sport and gender', in B. Houlihan (ed.) *Sport & Society*. London: SAGE Publications Ltd, 89–124.

Krane, V. (2002) 'Social pyschological benefits of gay games participation: a social identity theory explanation', *Journal of Applied Sports Psychology*, 14 (1): 27–42.

Levine, M. (1979). 'Gay ghetto', in P. Nardi and B. Schneider, (eds) (1998), *Social Perspectives in Lesbian and Gay Studies: A Reader*. London: Routledge, 194–206.

Maguire, J. (2000) 'Sport and globalization', in J. Coakley and E. Dunning (eds) *Handbook of Sports Studies*. London: Sage Publications, 356–69.

Maxwell, J.A. (1996) *Qualitative Research Design: An Interactive Approach.* Applied Social Research Method Series. Volume 41. Thousand Oaks, CA: Sage Publications.

McKay, J., Messner, M. and Sabo, D. (eds) (2000) *Masculinities, Gender Relations, and Sport.* London: Sage.

Messner, M., (1992) *Power at Play: Sports and the Problem of Masculinity.* Boston: Beacon Press.

Morland, I. and Willox, A. (eds) (2005) *Queer Theory.* Basingstoke: Palgrave MacMillan.

Murray, S. (1979) 'The institutional elaboration of a quasi-ethnic community', in P. Nardi and B. Schneider (eds) (1998) *Social Perspectives in Lesbian and Gay Studies: A Reader.* London: Routledge, 207–14.

Nardi, P. (ed.) (2000) *Gay Masculinities.* London: Sage Publications.

Price, M. and Parker, A. (2003) 'Sport, sexuality, and the gender order: amateur rugby union, gay men, and social exclusion', *Sociology of Sport Journal*, 20 (2): 108–26.

Pronger, B. (1990) *The Arena of Masculinity.* Toronto: University of Toronto Press.

Pronger, B. (2000) 'Homosexuality and sport: who's winning?' in J. McKay, M. Messner and D. Sabo (eds) *Masculinities, Gender Relations, and Sport.* London: Sage, 222–44.

Rigauer, B. (2000) 'Marxist theories', in J. Coakley & E. Dunning (eds) *Handbook of Sport Studies.* London: Sage Publishers, 28–47.

Robertson, S. (2003) 'If I let a goal in, I'll get beat up: contradictions in masculinity, sport and health'. *Health Education Research*, 18 (6): 706–16.

Salih, S. (2002) *Judith Butler.* London: Routledge.

Sedgwick, E. (1990) *Epistemology of the Closet.* London: Penguin.

Theberge, N. (2000) 'Gender and Sport', in J. Coakley and E. Dunning (eds) *Handbook of Sports Studies.* London: Sage Publications, 322–33.

Vertinsky, P. (2004) 'Locating a "sense of place": space, place and gender in the gymnasium', in P. Vertinsky and J. Bale (eds) *Sites of Sport: Space, Place, Experience.* London: Routledge, 8–24.

Waitt, G. (2003) 'Gay Games: performing 'community' out from the closet of the locker room'. *Social & Cultural Geography*, 4 (2): 167–83.

Young, P. D, (1995) *Lesbians and Gays and Sports.* New York: Chelsea House Publishers.

5 Exploring the limits of queer and sport

Gay men playing tennis

Ian Wellard

Introduction

I was first introduced to queer theory after drawing upon Butler's (1993) concept of performativity whilst exploring performances of masculinity within the context of mainstream (heteronormative) and gay sports within the UK.[1] In this research, I had initially expected the emergence of gay sports to provide some form of challenge to mainstream sports, where hegemonic masculinity (Connell, 1995, 2000) continues to prevail. According to Butler (1993), the main exercise of queer theory is to expose 'queer acts' which may disrupt the formulation of normative gender. If this is the case, then it could be claimed that the initial establishment of a group set up for gay men and women to play sport may be considered a queer act. However, Butler goes on to suggest that queer acts need to make people renegotiate the way in which they read public signs.

'Queer' as a theoretical movement has developed, in a short space of time, a voice for not only sexual minorities but also a broad range of other subordinated groups. In doing so, it has provided a means to challenge normative understandings of, for instance, gender and race. However, some of the issues raised within these debates become more problematic when applied to the arena of sport, for it is within this context that the body is foregrounded and specific bodily performances are prioritised. Queer theory has been successful in highlighting the tensions which exist within normative understandings of categories such as sexuality, gender and race. However, within the context of sport, although these tensions remain, they are preceded by the prominence of bodily performances which dictate the level of entry or participation, which, in turn, highlights the dominance of heteronormativity. Much of queer theory has been inspired by the personal experiences of 'outsiders' to the normative, often through the insight of a writer who is gay, female or non-white. But queer experiences framed through and within the specific context of sport have, until recently, been rare. Pronger (1990; 2000) has been an exception and provides more of an insider account which is often absent in much critical analysis of sport. He suggests that although gay sport has provided lesbian and gay people the opportunity to enjoy sports in an inclusive and safe environment, ultimately it has made these people conform to the established norms, particularly those based on oppressive male heterosexual practices. Thus, the initial possibilities which arise to challenge established understandings of gender, sexuality and sporting participation can be lost in the effort to adopt (hetero)normative performances of mainstream sport.

In his more recent work, Pronger (2002), drawing upon Drucilla Cornell's (1992) 'philosophy of limit', describes the potential, or 'puissance' (2002: 66) to be found in bodily pleasures which exist 'outside' the boundaries of conventional thinking. Within the limits of mainstream sports, though, alternative forms of bodily expression are restricted or not even allowed. Queer acts, then, could be considered as a means of 'bringing to light' alternative ways of contemplating the body, particularly in relation to sexuality. However, the theoretical underpinning of queer theory[2], grounded as it is in 'post-event' textual analysis and elite cultural texts (Edwards, 1998), risks understating the influence of everyday lived practices and the rituals associated with taking part in an activity such as sport. Often, the transformative potential of queer is held in check by the gay participants themselves.

I attempt to explore the conflicts which arise when applying 'queer' to sport by considering these theoretical implications within the context of actual lived practice, in this case participant observations of a gay tennis club and interviews with some of the men who took part in it. I argue that it is important to recognise the social processes and rituals which inform general understandings of how sport 'should' be performed and the extent to which these modes of behaviour are shaped by heteronormative assumptions.

Methods

Reflecting upon aspects of my own identity, such as gender, sexuality and bodily performances, not only influences my personal life history, but also the whole research process. I have always enjoyed physical activity. My parents were both enthusiastic sports players and sporting activity was a big part of my family life. Looking back now, I can see that my abilities in some sports enabled me to negotiate, relatively successfully, my childhood, and especially my schooldays, in ways that others were unable to do. Sexuality was not an issue then, but I can remember that performances of what were considered appropriate masculinity were important.

Recognising the reflexive processes at play means that research can be located within social, historical and political processes and, at the same time, take into account the effect that these have on the research procedure (Bourdieu and Waquant, 1992; Hammersley and Atkinson, 1995). In this particular case, the context is located within the dynamics of a cultural system of sport based in the United Kingdom.[3] I mention this, as I believe it is an important aspect which needs to be taken into consideration as much of queer theory has been generated within a North American context.

Getting 'inside' the research site is a major strength of observational ethnography. In more recent years there have been many studies which address masculinity and the body and incorporate participant observation (for example: Aycock, 1992; Fussell, 1992; Klein, 1993; De Garis, 2000). I adopted similar approaches and incorporated participant observation and interviews with a range of men (gay and straight) who participated at several sports clubs. Consequently, I was able to gain an understanding of the relevance of bodily performances in relation to the men's everyday practices. I was also able to assess the significance placed on various issues relating to the men's experiences of their bodies, for example, whether the gay men articulated their own sexuality as being a significant factor in their ability to participate in sport in comparison to heterosexual men (Wellard, 2002).

In all, I spent over three years taking part in the sports clubs. I eventually concentrated the research on two tennis clubs, one mainstream, predominantly straight[4] club and a gay tennis club, both based in the South East of England. I took an active part in all aspects of the clubs' activities and maintained a research diary. I also conducted twenty interviews in the form of sporting life histories (ten men from each club). These were tape-recorded, transcribed and analysed. For the purposes of this paper, I have drawn upon the data collected at the gay tennis club, but also reflect upon my experiences as an active participant and observer in a variety of sports settings.

Rituals and processes: forming a gay tennis club

The gay tennis club had its origins in a smaller gay tennis group which had formed at the start of the 1980s. This group was informally established by a few gay men who wanted to play tennis together on a regular basis. In the 1990s, this tennis group continued to play and attract new members. Many of the new players would meet at the tennis session on Sunday mornings and then arrange to play with others from the group in the afternoon at various public parks. There were also some newer members who played at a high level and had played competitively in mainstream (straight) clubs throughout their lives. Several continued to play for their straight clubs in local leagues and competitions. This eventually led to a group of these players setting up another session on Sunday evenings at a different location which meant that tennis could be played all day on Sundays. Initially, in 1995, three courts were booked for three hours every Sunday at an indoor tennis centre and this formed the focus for a new gay tennis club. The club grew to the stage where, at the time of the research, it had a regular booking of six courts for four hours and a membership of about 150 players. At the same time, the competitive nature of the players who formed the new group meant that there was a demand for orthodox competitive play. There were also a number of players who were flight attendants and some of these had previously taken part in competitive gay tennis tournaments in America. These were gay tennis tournaments held throughout the year in various cities, organised by a governing body called the Gay and Lesbian Tennis Alliance (GLTA). At that stage there was only one other gay tournament outside America and that was in Amsterdam. In 1996, the group decided to hold a tournament in the UK and became affiliated to the GLTA. This led to a need for greater organisation and the formation of a tennis club committee with additional subcommittees for running the tournament and other matters.

Although no formal mission statement was drafted when the club was first established, the original intention was to provide a setting for gay men and women to play tennis in a safe non-threatening environment, without the fear of harassment from heterosexual men (and women) and also free from the prejudices prevalent in traditional sports, not only to gays, but to women in general. Ironically, although initially aiming to provide an alternative environment for gay and lesbian sports players, the more successful it became the more it began to adopt traditionally established sporting codes. For example, playing sessions were based on competitive doubles games and in order to accommodate players with differing abilities, they were divided into categories according to playing standards. As such, there were four groups: red, blue, green and yellow, with red the more advanced.

The success of the club in terms of its ability to establish itself as a legitimate tennis club meant that any 'alternativeness' to mainstream sports clubs was downplayed. The more informal and social atmosphere found in the original Sunday morning tennis group was replaced by an emphasis on competitive play. It also meant that traditional, male, heterosexual-based sporting values became more evident. An example of some of these conflicting ideals can be seen in an observation at the club. A new member had started attending regularly. He was a reasonable player and extremely competitive. He also had a great liking for the professional tennis player, Monica Seles, in that he had modelled his style of play on hers (double-fisted forehand and backhand and accompanying grunt). The new player was immediately given the nickname 'Monica' with the effect that most people at the club used this name when either addressing him or referring to him. The association with the real Monica Seles developed to such an extent that he started to wear similar tennis outfits to her during the club sessions. Consequently, this caused some consternation amongst some of the other members and several complained that it made a mockery of the club's efforts to be a 'legitimate' sporting club, whilst others complained that it was not 'manly' or merely looked silly. It was only after discussion by the committee that it was remembered that the original policy of the club was to provide an alternative space for men and women to play tennis and express their sexuality without the prejudice so often found in traditional heterosexual sports clubs. Therefore, to make an issue out of a player wearing a particular style of clothing and enforce some form of sanction was, in effect, to reinforce some of the oppressive codes found in other mainstream sports clubs. As such, 'Monica' was allowed to continue playing in the way that he wanted. However, shortly afterwards he stopped attending altogether.

Queer competition?

The levels of competitiveness found in the gay tennis club were also similar to those found in the other mainstream tennis clubs I took part in. The structure of social play in clubs where the tennis was based around competitive matches placed greater emphasis upon playing ability. In these situations, social identity was based mainly on playing performance and capital was gained from demonstrating this to others. For example, in the straight clubs where I participated there was a 'pecking order' in terms of the priority given to those who were deemed good players even though, with the exception of juniors, membership rates were equal. In the straight clubs greater prestige or rank was awarded to the men who played in the first or 'A' team and similar prestige was granted to those who held a red card in the gay tennis club.

The failure of the gay tennis club to acknowledge the problems of traditional competitive sporting practices, particularly in terms of the focus on ability, meant that forms of discrimination based on bodily performance were often practised. Probyn (2000) describes how the organisers of the Gay Games faced similar problems when they attempted to ignore the social aspects of competitiveness by focusing on the notion of 'personal best'. The liberating aspects of performing to one's own level within a particular sport and, consequently, only competing with oneself were overshadowed by the structure of competitions which in many cases pitted one individual against another. Medals, in the manner of the Olympic Games, were awarded for winning performances, with little recognition for losing performances. Similar problems were experienced at the gay tennis club where competitive games ultimately produced a focus upon winning performances. They also provide a possible reason for the steady decline of women taking part and the prevalence of more able players in comparison to novices.

Any attempts to emphasise personal best were further undermined by the club's introduction of a competitive singles ladder and the affiliation to the American-based GLTA so that it could stage an annual tournament. The various tournaments provided for singles and doubles competitions and were divided into playing categories ranging from the highest level of Open, then A, B, C, D and Novice divisions. Points were awarded to participants within their category for a win and these were compiled by the GLTA and displayed on its own website. Players could compete in any number of tournaments held throughout the year, with the idea that more wins would mean more points and if a threshold was reached, the player would move up into the next division. Most of the members of the club took part in the tournament which meant that they all had rankings which became a main source of social capital. The following is part of an entry I made in my diary after playing a tournament which took place towards the end of the first year of the research.

> I have experienced more competitive play than at any other time (maybe more than when I played rankings tournaments in my youth). It seems that I have had to 'put myself on the line' in that I have had to contemplate my body in the physical sense and also take into account the emotional factors involved when playing competitive matches. On occasions, the primary motive for taking part (having fun and in my case, the research) has been forgotten in the pursuit of winning and beating the other person. I did not

enjoy the tournament on a personal level and have to try to assess why I did not. For some reason, the competition seemed fierce, not just in playing standard, but in the general approach to the games. Winning did appear to be everything.

(Diary entry July 2000)

Participation in GLTA tournaments and the focus on competitive play appeared to deflect the initial intentions of the club. On one hand, the GLTA was an organisation established for gay men and women, but on the other it merely replicated the traditional forms of competitive sport and this was probably an influence in the evident gender imbalance. It may also be significant that the GLTA, as an American-based organisation, adopted a sporting ethos evident in mainstream American sport where elite male-based, heterosexual participation is dominant and aggressive competitiveness is considered an integral aspect of playing (Messner, 1992, McKay *et al.*, 2000). Jagose (1996) has pointed out that a problem with queer as a social movement is that in terms of its global aspirations it often combines American ideology with queer. The consequence of this is that competitiveness derived from heterosexual male practice, an integral part of accepted mainstream ideology, is not questioned. This may provide a possible explanation for why the tournament held by the gay tennis club in its first year had a strong entry of women, presumably expecting something different, but in subsequent years the numbers of women taking part declined significantly.

'You'd never know it was a gay tennis club'

The focus on the social and the possibility that a gay tennis group would provide a 'safe' haven or alternative space for gay men and women was a reason for joining given by all the gay respondents in the interviews and was a common theme in the many informal conversations I had throughout the research. van Ingen (2004), in her study of gay and lesbian participants in a Toronto-based running club, found similar reasons given for attending a gay sports club as opposed to a mainstream (heterosexual) one.

The men in the tennis clubs I observed appeared to have developed their understandings of traditional sport through their wider social experiences gained at school and, to varying degrees, through organised sports clubs. Their experiences were not uniform in that there were some who had participated successfully, whereas others had either found difficulty fitting in or had little opportunity in the first place because of their inability to perform hegemonic masculinity (Connell, 1995). What is important, though, is the realisation by each of the men that their sexuality was considered a 'problem' in that it was something which either precluded participation or needed to be masked or managed.

I think what I started to do is that I'd been 'out' for a while. I'd had one long term relationship and that had ended quite badly and then I think I wanted to go out, but felt that it wasn't really me. I found it quite difficult to pick men up because I didn't really want casual sex and then I found it quite difficult in a (night)club environment cos either I'd get drunk and then not know what I was doing, so I would, I was probably quite, I wasn't very confident about doing it. And then, so I thought, oh well what I'll do, I'll join one of the social groups that I saw at the back of 'Gay Times' ... at least then I'll start playing tennis and you'll start doing it like that ... So I did primarily come to tennis to get a boyfriend (laughs).

(Peter, 33)

But the thing about going to the (gay tennis) club was that, erm, there was that element of, 'wouldn't it be nice to meet someone who played tennis that I could have a relationship with'.

(Matthew, 38)

The initial attraction of a gay tennis club was, therefore, the prospect of attending a social sporting activity where acceptance was not based on one's sexuality or determined by performing a particular version of masculinity. However, these original motivations for going along to a gay tennis club did not always match up to the experiences once there.

Oh there are differences, it's a different, it's much more, funnily enough it's much more straight the (gay) tennis club.

(Keith, 46)

Oh yeah definitely, Yeah ... I mean that remains a big difference. It shouldn't do, but you know it's the same in any sort of sporting club. The better you are, the more respect, in a way, you get. You know, as long as you're not an idiot.

(Peter, 33)

Much of the emphasis in mainstream heterosexual sport is on playing skills and the ability to perform in a particular manner (Messner, 1992). This has led to many men and women (gay and straight) to feel anxious about their own abilities and also to be aware of the constant scrutiny of others. For many of the members, part of the initial appeal of a gay tennis club was to escape this form of discrimination, but the structure of the club and the focus on bodily performance made it difficult to achieve. Playing ability and bodily performances were the indicators of successful participation. The criteria for determining appropriate behaviour were based upon hegemonic heterosexual distinctions between masculine and feminine bodily performances where masculine equated with strength and feats of power and feminine equated with weakness and passivity. The discursive binary distinctions between men and women evident within heterosexual hegemony appeared to be reproduced in the gay club between men through gendered bodily performances. Matthew was also in a similar position to Peter in that he continued to take part in mainstream sport. One of the main reasons for attending the gay tennis club was that it would provide the opportunity to display his tennis abilities without the fear of being found out that he experienced in straight sport. However, Matthew did not appear to grasp fully the conflicting ideals found in mainstream heterosexual sport and a gay tennis club, but related participation to his own needs. The gay club offered, for him, the chance to experience the sport that he was accustomed to without the need to hide his sexuality. He did not appear to consider that having to act in an appropriate way within the environment of a mainstream sports club was problematic. Homosexuality was, therefore, clearly considered an embarrassment within the confines of mainstream sport and something which needed to be hidden. As he was able to operate successfully in both settings, he had failed to recognise the importance of an alternative 'gay' space for those who had been excluded from mainstream sport and take into account the reasons for sexual discrimination in the first place.

For another member, Jamie, the discovery of gay sport and in particular a gay tennis club did not provide the smooth path to participation which he may have expected. Peter and Matthew were able to negotiate sport during their childhood successfully that had created an association of sporting activity with enjoyment. In contrast, Jamie's experiences of sport as a child were similar to those of several other men in the gay tennis club and these had created a more cautious approach to it. Sport, for Jamie, had involved a constant struggle based on his own sense of inappropriate masculine performance and although the gay tennis club was initially regarded as a means to escape these fears, there was a sense that he was still constantly trying to prove himself.

> You go to (the evening gay tennis club) and you're feeling paranoid, I think, you know heterosexual interpretation of gay people is that we're all happy together, having a great time and it's not true. I mean we're not one big happy family living in a gay ghetto. We are vile to each other. We are all each other's enemies.
>
> (Jamie, 28)

When questioned why he had such an opinion, Jamie related it to the negative experiences gay people have in their childhood and the development of defence mechanisms developed to deal with these. Jamie's previous experiences of sport, when he had been constantly judged on his own physical performances, had made him acutely sensitive to how others saw him. His initial expectation of the gay tennis club was that it would focus less upon sporting performance as an indication of worth. However, the contrasting experiences of the other gay members and the focus on traditional competitive forms of sporting practice meant that those who were able to display hegemonic forms of masculinity were generally more able to participate effectively.

Although the social aspect was a general reason for joining a gay tennis club, the expectations of how this was to be achieved varied depending upon previous experiences of sport. The research revealed that those who were previously able to take part successfully in mainstream heterosexual sport unconsciously (or consciously) continued the same practices. Competition and sporting performance remained the central factors for participation and there was often little realisation by those who took part that discrimination was more likely to be experienced by those without the appropriate sporting capital. Therefore, the members of the gay tennis club who were less able to perform hegemonic masculinity shared similar experiences to non-macho heterosexual men, women, elderly people and the disabled in mainstream heterosexual sport. The established practices found in contemporary sports provided the focus for the gay tennis club but ultimately, rendered the 'fluidity', so often described as a part of queer identity, more static.

Pronger (1990) suggests that part of being gay is the ability to recognise the irony of existing within a heterosexual world. In gay sport there appears to be the possibility to challenge some of the orthodox views of sport as a masculine arena. Some of the members of the original Sunday morning tennis group had started staging a mock 'Federation Cup' which was based on the professional women's tournament where different countries would compete against each other. The gay version provided the chance for the players to represent different countries and take part as a female player from that country. The idea was for a camp, fun tournament where the players could dress up as their favourite player and also bring along traditional food from their chosen country. The Fed Cup ran for several years before the competitive gay tennis club was formed, but when it was taken over by the club it immediately lost a large part of the camp element and although teams still represented a country, the attraction became that groups of friends could play as a team with the objective of winning. Dressing up and any other subversive behaviour were eventually 'straightened' out so that it merely became another competitive tennis tournament.

The cultural understanding of sport as expressed through hegemonic heterosexual male practices provided the mainstay of sporting practice within the gay tennis club. The members who were able to display evidence of established sporting practices were also able to wield the most power to the extent that their previous experiences of mainstream sport were merely replicated within the environment of the gay tennis club. Consequently, issues relating to gay politics, broader discriminatory gender practices and inclusive participation were overlooked in favour of established mainstream sports practices.

On several occasions during the course of the fieldwork, there were comments from members of the gay tennis club about how similar the club was to other 'straight' clubs. This was not, however, a criticism, but meant as praise and an affirmation that the club was successful in terms of its ability to be the same as other straight clubs. There was often a sense of pride displayed when there was evidence to suggest that the club was just like any other (straight) tennis club. On one occasion, I was with a group of other members waiting for the next available court and watching the players on court finishing their game. One of the men commented, 'You'd never know it was a gay tennis club.' The remark was made as a compliment and demonstrated how the gay club, and gay sports, were considered as inferior to mainstream (heterosexual) sport. A mark of success was the ability to appear like mainstream sport rather than contest it.

Can sport be queered?

From the observations and accounts revealed during the research, 'queering' sport was not a priority and it appeared difficult to contest the discriminatory practices evident within mainstream sport. Similar conflicts of interest were found in recent UK-based studies of a gay rugby club (Price and Parker, 2003) and a gay rowing club (Owen, 2002). In these, the practices inherent within traditional sports restricted much of the focus upon 'gayness', often to the extent that hegemonic masculinities were reinforced at the expense of subordinate ones. Consequently, the emphasis within gay sports is generally placed upon activities and practices established within the context of traditional sport. The location of sport within the discourse of gendered and heterosexual practices means that it is often difficult to confront or replace the forms of social conduct which predominate. One of the central insights of queer theory is that the privileging of heterosexual intercourse is a social construction which gives rise to a binary division of gender (Ostenfeld *et al.* 2004). The binary of heterosexual and homosexual also implies that queer is a political and cultural strategy aiming to destabilise contemporary configurations of gender, sexuality and sex, thereby allowing something more capacious (and less occupied with sex as an indication of identity) to emerge. The 'queer acts' which Butler (1993) describes are supposed to disrupt the formulation of normative gender and make people reinterpret public signs. Positioning gay and lesbian space as 'alternative' is initially problematic since it reinforces the heterosexual/homosexual binary rather than exposing their constructed characters. In addition, the evidence collected during the research suggests that the gay tennis club continued to produce more signs of 'straight acts' than queer ones.

In terms of a collective identity, the gay tennis club had conflicting ideals. On the one hand, it had been set up to provide an environment away from the often oppressive heterosexuality found in mainstream sports clubs, whilst, on the other hand, the club was based around competitive sport and adopted traditional sporting procedures. My research supports the claims made by Pronger (2000) when he suggests that the emancipatory power which appeared initially within the gay and lesbian community, particularly in its approach to sport, has been quelled in recent years through the attempts to 'normalise' and become part of mainstream sport. This is not to say that the gay tennis club has 'failed' as it has been successful in providing the opportunity for some gay men to play tennis in a relatively safe environment and that, similar to the wider achievements of the lesbian and gay movement, it has contributed to making gay sport more visible. However, those who are granted greater opportunities to participate freely in gay sport are more likely to have had less traumatic experiences of mainstream sport as children. The evidence in this research suggests that amateur sporting practices in gay sport continue to reinforce discriminatory practices based on bodily performance and heterosexual configurations of gender.

In the research I found that consciousness of gayness as a political issue was more often than not displaced by orthodox understandings of how sport 'should' be played. At the same time, gay sport in general has adopted a liberal approach which seeks to provide access for lesbians and gays to the mainstream rather than confront or challenge the core ideals. The Gay Games could be seen as a prime example of an inclusion approach (Pronger, 2000). Consequently, it is a very popular form of mainstream gay culture and expresses dominant gay liberal philosophy that lesbians and gays are just like anybody else. Gay sport, it follows from this line of reasoning, proves normality in the same way that being a successful business person or doctor proves gay normality. Because of this many gay sports organisations seek legitimation from traditional sports authorities. For example, the gay tennis group in my research adhered to the rules of conduct laid down by the British Lawn Tennis Association. Also, affiliation to the Gay and Lesbian Tennis Alliance could be seen as another factor in negating potential opportunities to be queer. Prioritising winning, ranking points and competitive tournament play established a more individual-based mentality rather than that of a group with a collective sense of identity.

Muñoz (1999) suggests disidentification as a means to resist and challenge generalised understandings of identification. However, within the process of taking part in sports, the individual is more likely to attempt to identify *with* established practices, rather than contest them. Pronger (1990) suggests that gay sport irony is a step towards challenging heterosexual sensibilities. There was evidence of this within the gay tennis club, but it was not significantly acted upon. As mentioned above, there were attempts to stage a mock Federation Cup, based upon the women's professional tennis circuit, which had developed out of a general interest among many members in the women's professional tennis circuit rather than the men's. This aspect was more confined to off-court activities which appeared to provide more opportunities for gay sport irony or queer acts. The identification with women's tennis presented further evidence to suggest that issues relating to sexuality were not completely forgotten. However, the practice of sport and the on-court performances of the men where greater capital was conferred upon hegemonic masculine displays appeared to diffuse many further opportunities for queerness during the off-court activities.

I have spoken of 'potential' throughout this chapter in terms of the possibilities which may be revealed within the context of an apparently subversive activity such as gay sports. I have already mentioned the potential which Pronger (2002) describes, where the social restrictions which limit the full possibilities of bodily experience can be challenged. However, it is also worth considering the potential for radical forms of social praxis, found within subordinated groups which may impose 'new categories of perception and appreciation' (Bourdieu, 2001: 123) and, ultimately, provide a challenge to accepted heterosexual masculine dominance.

These forms of symbolic destruction could be expressed through queer bodily acts which highlight the divisiveness of mainstream sport practices. Gay sport that aims to be queer, or, at least, 'gay' in that it is able to contest the discriminatory practices found in mainstream sport, should promote activities which have the potential to cater for those with a variety of bodies and not place specific hetero-normative bodily performances as the prerequisite for participation. To this extent, queering should be a verb, a 'doing' thing, which disrupts or extends the boundaries of existing sporting practices.

I was interested in the potential of 'queer' when applied to sport as a means of challenging many of the prevalent attitudes found within it. However, as the research progressed, it did appear that there was a wide gulf between the theoretical claims of academic queer theory and the 'real' or lived practices of those who took part in sport. However, there were instances of performances which could be considered 'queer'. The example of 'Monica' wearing a dress to play tennis with other gay men did cause reflection upon the normative understanding of sport. For a brief period, many of the gay men had to reflect upon their own understanding of masculinity within the context of an alternative social space. Thus, it is here, on a positive note, that I want to conclude. Much of the research I conducted during my time with the tennis clubs chronicled instances of discriminatory practices within the field of sport and the continued dominance of a heterosexual-based hegemonic masculinity. However, given that gay sport is a relatively recent phenomenon and that little research has been conducted within this field, I take the more optimistic view that continued investigation will reveal more instances of transformative acts. At the same time, more research which focuses upon sporting bodily experiences, pleasures and performances that occur outside mainstream sporting conventions will highlight the fact that sport does not necessarily have to be the domain of exclusive masculinity.

Notes

1 The research was conducted as part of a PhD investigation into masculinities, the body and sport. The research was funded by the Pavis Centre at the Open University between the period of 1999 and 2003 (see Wellard, 2003).

2 Jagose (1996) provides a comprehensive overview of the emergence of 'queer theory'.

3 See Hargreaves (1986) for a concise account of the emergence of traditional sport within the UK. This is particularly important in relation to the specific cultural climate in which sport is experienced in comparison to other countries. As suggested, the ideological foundation upon which much of traditional sport in the UK is based draws upon a historical legacy in many ways different from the US and other continents.

4 I use the term 'straight' as a generalisation for sports clubs that are based upon traditional, heterosexual practices. It is in contrast to a 'gay' sports club, which has been established as a result of a need to provide a social space where assumptions about heterosexuality are taken for granted. This does not imply that all those who take part in 'straight' clubs are necessarily heterosexual. Many of the gay respondents in the research also played in straight clubs.

References

Aycock, A. (1992) 'The confession of the flesh: disciplinary gaze in casual bodybuilding', *Play and Culture*, 5 (4): 338–57.

Bourdieu, P. (2001) *Masculine Domination*. Cambridge: Polity Press.

Bourdieu, P. and Wacquant, L. (1992) *An Invitation to Reflexive Sociology*. Cambridge: Polity Press.

Butler, J. (1993) *Bodies that Matter*. New York: Routledge.

Connell, R. (1995) *Masculinities*. Cambridge: Polity.

Connell, R. (2000) *The Men and the Boys*. Cambridge: Polity.

Cornell, D. (1992) *The Philosophy of the Limit*. New York: Routledge.

De Garis, L. (2000) '"Be a buddy to your buddy": male identity, aggression and intimacy in a boxing gym' in J. McKay, M. Messner and D. Sabo, *Masculinities, Gender Relations and Sport*. London; Sage.

Edwards, T. (1998) 'Queer fears: against the cultural turn', *Sexualities*, 1 (4): 471–84.

Fussell, S. (1992) *Muscle*. London: Abacus.

Hammersley, M. and Atkinson, P. (1995) *Ethnography, Principles in Practice*. London: Tavistock.

Hargreaves, J. (1986) *Sport, Power and Culture*. London: Polity.

Jagose, A. (1996) *Queer Theory*. Melbourne: Melbourne University Press.

Klein, A. (1993) *Little Big Men:Bodybuilding Subculture and Gender Construction*. Albany: State University of New York Press.

McKay, J., Messner, M.A. and Sabo, D. (2000) *Masculinities, Gender Relations, and Sport*. London: Sage.

Messner, M. (1992) *Power at Play: Sports and the Problem of Masculinity*. Boston: Beacon.

Muñoz, J. (1999) *Disidentifications: Queers of Color and the Performance of Politics*. Minneapolis: University of Minnesota.

Ostenfeld, S., Woodgate, K., and Wafer, J. (2004) 'Queer studies: where but here?', *Inter-Cultural Studies*, 4 (1): 9–18.

Owen, G. (2002) 'Catching Crabs: sport, masculinity and gay identities'. Paper presented at the *Queer Studies: Out from the Centre Conference*, University of Newcastle, Australia, November 2002.

Price, N. and Parker, A. (2003) 'Sport, sexuality, and the gender order: amateur rugby union, gay men and social exclusion' *Sociology of Sport Journal*, 20 (2): 108–26.

Probyn, E. (2000) 'Sporting bodies: dynamics of shame and pride', *Body and Society*, 6 (1): 13–28.

Pronger, B. (1990) *The Arena of Masculinity*. London: GMP Publishers.

Pronger, B. (2000) 'Homosexuality and sport – who's winning?' in J. McKay, M. Messner and D. Sabo (2000) *Masculinities, Gender Relations and Sport*. London: Sage, 222–244.

Pronger, B. (2002) *Body Fascism: Savaltion in the Technology of Physical Fitness*. Toronto: University of Toronto Press.

van Ingen, C. (2004) 'Therapeutic landscapes and the regulated body in the Toronto front runners', *Sociology of Sport Journal*, 21 (3): 253–69.

Wellard, I. (2002) 'Men, sport, body performance and the maintenance of "exclusive masculinity"', *Leisure Studies Journal*, 2 (3/4): 235–47.

Wellard, I. (2003) 'Game, set and match to exclusive masculinity: men, body practices, sport and the making and remaking of hegemonic masculinity', Unpublished PhD Thesis, Open University.

6 The necessity of queer shame for gay pride

The Gay Games and Cultural Events[1]

Judy Davidson

Introduction

> A certain place for psychoanalysis is secured in that any mobilization against subjection will take subjection as its resource, and that attachment to an injurious interpellation will, by way of a necessarily alienated narcissism, become the condition under which resignifying that interpellation becomes possible. This will not be an unconscious outside of power, but rather something like the unconscious of power itself, in its traumatic and productive iterability.
>
> (Butler, 1997: 104)

The Gay Games and Cultural Events have become the best recognized, lesbigay amateur sporting competition and multi-day athletic and cultural festival in the world (Krane and Waldron, 2000). It is now a mega amateur sporting and cultural event with a multimillion dollar budget, upwards of 15,000 participants and hundreds of thousands of spectators. The Games have been held every four years since 1982 in the US, Canada, Europe, and Australia. Their main message, which is trumpeted loudly and proudly, is gay pride through involvement in the Gay Games. They encapsulate the fervent desire of their founder (Dr Thomas Waddell) to have gays and lesbians welcomed as full human beings into athletic contexts and society at large.

The spectacle emulates the modern day Olympics in size and grandeur. The Gay Games' founding vision was to provide opportunities where 'athletes could openly celebrate both their athletic and sexual identities in ways not currently possible in most mainstream sporting events' (Griffin, 1998: 190). As might seem appropriate, San Francisco was the site for the first two Games (in 1982 and 1986) and Celebration 90 was staged in Vancouver. These Games were the largest sporting event of its kind held in the world that year. New York City hosted Unity '94, which included the marking of the 25th Anniversary of the Stonewall Riots (often heralded as the 'birth' of the gay rights movement). Over ten thousand people participated in 1994. Gay Games V were held in Amsterdam in August, 1998. Fifteen thousand athletes competed in 30 events in the Netherlands with 250,000 spectators involved in cheering them on. Gay

Games VI were hosted in Sydney, Australia, in November 2002, utilizing the Homebush Olympic Park for many of the events. Gay Games VII will be held in Chicago in 2006. The Federation of Gay Games (FGG) is the international governing body for the organization of the Games which claims to be the most inclusive major sporting event in the world (Davidson, 2003).

In this chapter, I argue that the metonymic relationships between Tom Waddell, his death, homophobic shame, and juridical Olympic prohibitions that changed the naming from the Gay Olympics to the Gay Games underpin and motivate the production of a frenzied athletic event of urgent gay pride. When the United States Olympic Committee (USOC) was granted a court injunction to stop the first Gay Olympic Games from using the word Olympic in 1982, the ceaseless haunting of the Gay Games by discourses of Olympism and queer shame was secured. It is my argument that the (sometimes unconscious) identifications with things Olympic and with gay pride discourses have both enabled and constrained the success and viability of the Gay Games through the past 25 years. To make this argument, I briefly outline the historical events leading up to the loss of the word Olympic in a US Supreme Court decision and the death of Tom Waddell shortly after that decision. I then read the Games' complicated processes of melancholic incorporation, where shame and pride are important parts of a particular identification, which produces the fraught relationship between Olympism and the Gay Games. I use Judith Butler's argument about gender melancholia (1990; 1997) and rework that heuristic to consider how loss has operated in the discursive production of the Gay Games. I suggest that loss of a founder, and prohibition of an Olympic ideal, have made homophobia a seemingly contradictory form of motivation for the success of the Gay Games. I end with a queer disruption by suggesting that the Gay Games must give up their reliance on conventional sporting practices to interrupt their necessary complicity with a melancholic identification with a shaming Olympism. In short, I will argue that the psychic domain is a condition of possibility for the social domain of the Gay Games.

Some history concerning a lost object and a lost ideal

Dr Tom Waddell was the founder and obsessive organizer of the Gay Games. He literally single-handedly put together the first Games against massive odds, including serious legal challenges, lack of financial support, no experience in organizing large events, and a gay community reluctant to embrace the idea. Nonetheless, Gay Games I occurred in late summer 1982 in San Francisco and were considered a raging success, attracting about 1700 athletes from around the world who competed in 17 athletic events. The event was consciously styled after the modern international Olympics, combining athletic and cultural events for an international competition with a gay inflection. There were active outreach programs to attract 'minorities' such as women, people of color and gays and lesbians from small town America as well as other countries. A trans-America torch run started in New York at the site of the Stonewall Inn, and was used to light the flame of the Gay Games during the Opening Ceremonies. To a large extent, Tom Waddell influenced and created many of these 'Olympic-style' touches for his event. His history and experiences inform not only the emancipatory thrust of the Gay Games, but much of its conservatism as well (Davidson, 2003).

Tom Waddell's life, in many ways, reads like the stereotypical American dream come true. He was born into poverty and a broken home, escaped it to spend his adolescence with liberal artists who nurtured in him a love for the finer things in life. He attended college, chose to pursue a medical degree, and became 'radicalized' through a job at a socialist summer camp. He was also an all round athlete in high school and college, competing on the football, gymnastics, and track and field teams. During his medical training, he competed nationally in track and field and, as a member of the US Track and Field team, traveled to developing countries, extolling the virtues of Americanized athleticism to the colonized. Waddell also got very involved in the civil rights movement, volunteering his time and medical expertise (Waddell and Schaap, 1996). Throughout his formal athletic career, Waddell managed his sexuality carefully, keeping it well hidden. His full-blown love for the Olympics emerged in and through that closeted athletic identity. As he became more politicized in his early twenties, his homosexuality (particularly its public expression) was sublimated through his civil rights efforts.

In 1966, Waddell was drafted for the Vietnam War, and trained and qualified for the 1968 Olympic team while in the army. He placed sixth in the decathlon at the Mexico City Games after speaking out against the racism that had Tommy Smith and John Carlos thrown off the US Olympic Team for raising their defiant fists in the black power salute on the medal podium. After the '68 Olympics, Waddell left the army and serious sporting competition. He worked for an international medical conglomerate and came out as a gay man (Waddell and Schaap, 1996). His next serious political battle was to be with the United States Olympic Committee.

Waddell had wanted the first Games in 1982 to be called the Gay Olympics. The appropriation of the Olympic ethos of friendship, athletic achievement, and international participation was strategically paired with the invocation of gay identity. It was Waddell's mission to create space where gays and lesbians could be fully who they were in athletic and cultural contexts. The Gay Olympics would be a public space where everyone, regardless of sexual orientation, gender, race, age, or ability would be welcome. Tom Waddell fervently believed in the 'higher' ideals of Olympism[2] (often figured as education, equal opportunity, fair play, excellence, and international goodwill) and wanted his Gay Olympics to embody those virtues (Segrave, 1988). Waddell individualized the pursuit of excellence through athletics to become the mainstay mantra of the most current Gay Games, exhorting gay and lesbian athletes to individualistically excel 'despite' their sexuality. Waddell hoped that the ideals of Olympism would transcend the petty squabbling of the scandal-ridden 'real' Olympics and that true athletic competition could thrive. As Rikki Streicher (1988), an SFAA[3] board member for Gay Games II, suggested, 'Sports are the great social equalizer. It is possibly the only time that it does not matter who you are but only how you play the game' (1988: 6). Athletes from around the world paraded behind city team signs in highly regulated uniforms (no corporate advertising, no Olympic logos) at highly choreographed opening and closing ceremonies ('Athletes package', 1982; Herkenhoff and Lewinstein, 1986). Athletic events were organized according to set rules and regulations with teams competing and crowds available for cheerleading. Medal ceremonies were ritual affairs. Waddell endeavoured to combine the allure of the Olympics with the beauty of sport in a vibrant gay community.

Apparently, however, the allure of the event was *too* Olympic for the American Olympic organization. The USOC reacted to what they considered to be an infringement on their trademark. Seven months before the event, the USOC had contacted Waddell, warning that they should drop from the title of the event – Gay Olympics. The threat had been leveled against similar organizations (the Police Olympics for example) but the USOC had never followed through. For the Gay Olympics it was to be a different story.

Days before the start of the first Gay Games, the USOC was successfully granted a court injunction forbidding the word Olympic from appearing on any Gay Games materials. Volunteers scrambled to literally scrape the offending word off the medals, change souvenirs and T-shirts; posters and signs were destroyed all at considerable expense. As one archival document graphically demonstrates, a promotional article for the first Games had appeared in the gay magazine, *Coming Up!* It had been included in the press kits to be handed out to media personnel at the start of Gay Games I. Each copy of the article had to be removed and reinserted with all instances of the word Olympic crossed out with thick black marker, including, most prominently, the large title Gay Olympiad I (April, 1982; Coe, 1986; Gildersleeve and Wardlaw,1982; Peterson and Kennedy, 1994). Until the changes could be made, button and t-shirt sales were suspended (White, 1982). According to the court injunction, the event had to be referred to as the Gay Athletic Games or the Gay Bleep Games by the organizers. A note on the inside of the Official Program read:

> Due to the last minute court action taken by the U.S. Olympic Committee concerning the use of the word 'Olympic', all references to that term had to be deleted from this program. The judge's decision on the permanent injunction had not been made by publication deadline. We apologize to the writers and advertisers whose articles and ads we had to change to comply with the court's original temporary restraining order.
>
> (Gay Athletic Games I, 1982: 2)

The only fundraising tactic left to the event was to sell tickets to the Opening and Closing Ceremonies. Estimates of the losses due to the last minute court order ranged between $15,000 and $30,000, substantial sums for the fledgling organization (Coe, 1986; Salter, 1982). This was the beginning of a protracted legal conflict, upon which Waddell's home had a substantial lien placed by the USOC, constant harassment by this athletic organization, and huge amounts of work done *pro bono* by Gay Games' attorneys. The court battle went on for another five years, resulting in a decision just weeks before Tom Waddell's death from AIDS-related complications in 1987.

Hoping to make the USOC's claim obviously unfair, Waddell had tried to articulate an anti-homophobia argument early in the battle with the USOC:

> There is a discriminatory action on the part of the USOC which has sanctioned the 'Junior Olympics' and the 'Special Olympics' but has looked the other way on the Armenian Olympics, the Xerox Olympics, the Crab-Cooking Olympics, the Diaper Olympics, the Rat Olympics, and the Dog Olympics, while at the same time takes exception to the term 'Gay Olympic Games'.
>
> (Waddell in Lorch, 1982: 9)

Over the next five years, this litany of not sanctioned, yet sanctioned, Olympic events was to become the most oft-quoted and popularly used lament to illustrate what gay activists believed would be apparent – that the USOC was a homophobic and nasty behemoth, unreasonably targeting the Gay Olympics. It was to no avail. While other 'Olympic' groups who borrowed the word remained untouched by the USOC, in 1987 the US Supreme Court deemed there was no discriminatory action against the Gay Games, and granted the USOC exclusive and proprietary right to use of the word Olympic. The USOC and the American legal system effectively controlled all uses of the word Olympic through commercial trademark law.

It was after piecing together this story from archival documents that I started to consider how the Games came to be, and to ask what were the conditions of their possibility? Rather than being satisfied with describing *what* happened, I wanted to understand *how* the Gay Games may continue to be motivated and structured by the original refusal of an Olympic designation. What I came to discover was that the archival discourse about the Gay Games was absolutely rife with over-the-top invocations of gay pride. The individual and organizational investments in lesbian and gay pride were almost overwhelming, and too insistent to ignore. In what ways might this pride be linked to the original shaming?

Subjectivating the Gay Games: incorporation and melancholic gay pride

Elspeth Probyn (2000), in an article in *Body and Society*, forayed into the world of sport and considered how shame and pride might function within that enterprise, particularly focusing on the Gay Games as a place where shame, pride, and sport converge. While Probyn used the Gay Games in her discussion, it was with a focus on the 'visceral nature of the capacities of the body' (2000:14). I want to push Probyn's ideas about shame at the Gay Games in a different direction by focusing on a particular reading of how shame and pride were inaugurated through loss in the formation of the Gay Games. Probyn, though, provides an interesting starting point for my analysis. She writes, 'One of the most striking features of the narratives of gay pride... is the way in which pride operates as a necessity, an ontology of gay life that cannot admit its other' (Probyn, 2000: 19). The Gay Games are a narrative of gay pride and the 'other' that Probyn refers to is shame, queer shame that must be prohibited, but which is absolutely necessary for proud, gay life to operate.

I think the Gay Games may be read as complicated processes of melancholic incorporation, where shame and pride are important parts of a particular dynamic, which produces the fraught relationship between Olympism and the Gay Games. As one of my favourite theorists, Judith Butler, puts it:

> The account of melancholy is an account of how psychic and social domains are produced in relation to one another. As such, melancholy offers potential insight into how the boundaries of the social are instituted and maintained, not only at the expense of psychic life, but through binding psychic life into forms of melancholic ambivalence.
>
> (Butler, 1997:167–68)

Melancholia is an effect of loss and prohibition, and I want to understand how these psychic processes materialize socially and organizationally. In the story of the emergence of the Gay Games, prohibition and loss occurred profoundly and quickly. Prohibition occurred when the Games were never allowed to formally occur as the Gay Olympics. The 'Gay Games' were founded through the ban on the word 'Olympic', and hence the Gay Olympics *per se* were foreclosed. The USOC maintained from start to finish, that their complaint with the Gay Olympics was about fundraising and protecting trademarks. Olympic virtue could not be diluted. What remained unsaid, disavowed, was the USOC's homophobia. The unsaid implication was that the purity of the Olympic ideal would be badly tarnished by the homosexual; in this reading, the queer threat hovered and would likely scare away potential financial sponsors and donors.

Although the case for discrimination (and a particular kind of gay rights discourse) was given the legal space to be uttered (by the Gay Games attorney Mary Dunlap at the Supreme Court hearing in 1987), it was never acknowledged nor legitimated by the Supreme Court justices. Within an Althusserian framework, the hail must be responded to in order for the subject to be subjectivated into being (Butler, 1997). The Supreme Court did not accord gays and lesbians subject status as it did not recognize their claims, despite Mary Dunlap's exhortations to the contrary. Homosexuals were denied sanction and blessing by the Supreme Court decision which resedimented homophobic shame yet again. Approximately three weeks after this denial of legal legitimation, the most visible and public hero of that shaming Olympic ban, Dr Thomas Waddell, died of AIDS-related causes.

Since 1982, the organizers of the Games have consistently and completely complied with the court orders and have not and do not use any references to Olympics, Olympiad, or the patented five-ring symbol. The most powerful aspect of that forced prohibition is the shame that is implicit in the Supreme Court decision. Unavoidably, the success of the USOC's claim sanctions the culturally prevalent notion that homosexuals are lesser, shameful, and that they do not deserve legitimation. The lesbian and gay community of San Francisco spent five years protesting the USOC's legal action, denouncing it at all turns as homophobically motivated. That the USOC then won the court case, legitimized the homophobia that the protesters were decrying. Perhaps the best encapsulation of the impotence of the protest (and the potency of the concurrent shaming) was summed up by a palliative, bedridden Waddell, who responded plaintively to the Supreme Court decision just weeks before his death. He asked, 'Why are gay people the only people in the world who can't use it [the word "Olympic"]?' (Repa, 1987: 20).

The Gay Games lost Tom Waddell and his Olympic dreams. However, the organization keeps Waddell's memory alive by still invoking his philosophy of inclusion and emulating Olympic-style ideals. On these terms, the Gay Games can be read as not having given up their lost object (Waddell) or their lost ideal (the Olympics). Instead, they have melancholically incorporated them. As I understand psychoanalysis, melancholic incorporation is one of the processes that occur with the experience of loss. An object or ideal is lost in the world. In incorporation, the attachment to that lost object or ideal is not let go. What occurs is that the attachment continues, but now it is psychically enacted, and its effects are split, expressed as both love and hate for the lost object or ideal (Butler, 1990; 1997). The Gay Games lost both an object and an ideal. They lost the idealism of Olympism through the prohibition on the word 'Olympic', and they lost their founder to AIDS, a founder very committed to Olympic ideals. The Gay Games acts out its love and hate for the lost homophobic Olympics in an egoic identification, in and through an organization identity.

So it is shame (and its metonymic relationship to Olympic) that comes to be the uneasy site of identification for the Gay Games. But in the rejection of Olympic (and the attendant shaming within it), the desire for the Gay Games becomes queer shame's opposite – gay pride – however ambivalent that desire is. I return to Elspeth Probyn. 'Pride operates as a necessity, an ontology of gay life that cannot admit its other.' Shame has been lost (with the word Olympic) to the external world in which the organization expressed itself, only to be internalized and preserved psychically within the Gay Games phenomena. 'In melancholia, the presence of ambivalence in relation to the [lost] object ... [is evidenced in] countless separate struggles [which] are carried on over the object, in which love and hate contend with each other' (Butler, 1997: 173). The love/hate relationship with the incorporated lost object (the shaming Olympics) plays out in interesting ways for the Gay Games. These material and social effects are the cathectic manifestations of melancholic psychic traces.

The incorporated 'love' for the Olympics

Even in its snub from the Olympic movement, the Gay Games continue to style themselves in Olympic fashion. Each quadrennial event continues to get larger, involving more money and organization. Whenever and wherever possible, the Games use sanctioned international sporting rules and regulations including officiating and recording of world records. Mike Mealiffe broke world records in the 1990 Gay Games for Masters swimming competition (Forzley and Hughes, 1990). There was a skirmish with the International Skating Union (ISU) in 1998 when the ISU refused to sanction the Gay Games V figure skating competition in Amsterdam. Rumor had it that this decision was made because the Gay Games insisted on same-sex partner dance competitions. In fact, the event was not sanctioned because the Amsterdam organizing committee did not file organizational documents soon enough with the ISU for them to officially sanction the event (Dermody, 1998).

The Gay Games and Cultural Events have a bureaucratic organizing structure that echoes the international Olympic movement. The Federation of Gay Games (or the FGG) was formed in 1989 and is an analogous body to the IOC (International Olympic Committee). Like the IOC, it grapples with the prohibited use of performance enhancers. This is interestingly complicated at the Gay Games as they openly encourage HIV positive people and those with AIDS, who are often on steroids for their medical conditions, to participate. The FGG struggles with bidding scandals for site selection (potential host cities are carefully restricted about how much they can spend on various trinkets like hats, flags and pins for each FGG delegate) and the organization contends with accusations that they are elitist and secretive (Davidson, 2003).

In addition, the Rainbow Run has become the Gay Games' version of the Olympic torch run. It has commemorated and remembered all those lost to AIDS and, since 1998 to breast cancer as well. The Gay Games Torch Run had, after Gay Games I in 1982, become an AIDS awareness and fundraising tool. The International Rainbow Memorial Run started in 1990 with a run between San Francisco and Vancouver for Gay Games III. A rainbow flag stood in for the torch, and started to represent not only the Gay Games but also a host of social issues affecting lesbigay and trans communities. By 1998, the symbolic 'torch' left San Francisco, the 'Athens' of the Gay Games, and the run was incorporated into the European tour of the AIDS memorial quilt, which coincided with Gay Games V. As part of the push for gender equity, the FGG recognised that the prevalence of breast cancer among lesbians was a major health concern and breast cancer prevention was twinned with AIDS in the 1998 International Rainbow Memorial Run (American Run, 1998). The sad story is that so many giving and talented people involved with the Gay Games have succumbed to one or the other of these diseases.

A notable feature of gay pride at the Gay Games is the expressions of love and almost idolatry for the dead Tom Waddell. There are awards, bursaries, commemorative coins and trophies all in his honour. One of the criteria for the

Waddell Cup is 'someone who personifies the standards of selflessness, devotion, humility, dignity and love of humanity set by the late Dr Tom Waddell' (Farrell, 1990: 2). The Waddell Cup winner symbolized for a short time at each Gay Games the lost Tom Waddell, a hopeful but ultimately ineffective replacement, a mournful substitute that was to be revived every four years. Echoing the constant references to the founder of the modern Olympics, Pierre de Coubertin, Tom Waddell is still invoked in Gay Games' promotional discourse. Segments from speeches he gave have become mantras of gay pride for Gay Games' organizers. For example, Waddell's claim that 'To do one's best is the ultimate goal of human achievement' opened the beginning of the glossy, coffee table book produced for the 1994 New York Games (Waddell in Labrecque1994: i).

Along with such expressions of similitude, differences from the Olympics are also expressed. There are, for example, protestations about how the Gay Games are absolutely NOT the Olympics and many distinctions between the two are made.[4] Waddell's dream of inclusion is invoked. Passionate claims point to the recreational categories for all athletic events, no minimum performance standards, a wide range of age categories, and an absolutely joyous atmosphere of gay camaraderie that pervades the event. Stories abound from each of the Gay Games as to the altruistic, sportsperson-like actions that differentiate them from the performance-driven Olympics. The emphasis is on participation and doing one's best.

Paradoxically, even when differences from the International Olympics are emphasized, this keeps in play the reification of the Olympics. While Waddell and fellow Gay Games' organizers were talking up a more enlightened, progressive 'gay' Olympism, they were also capitalizing on the powerful draw the International Olympics generate:

> There is no other event to match the drama, spectacle, and pageantry of the games or the moments of elation when the world unites to cheer on the victorious Olympians... Images from the games remain etched in our collective memories. We carry the dramatic moments with us as intimate aspects of our own experience.
>
> (Schaffer and Smith, 2000: 2–3)

Depending on which 'we' is inhabited, a whole host of stories from the Gay Games produce the 'dramatic moments [that comprise the] intimate aspects of a (lesbigay) experience'. Gay Games I and II provided many poignant, metaphorical gay empowerment moments that relentless personal testimonial confessions reiterate over and over again in Gay Games literature. The Opening and Closing Ceremonies contributed to the pageantry, pride and affirmation of a beleaguered gay community. At Gay Games I, people in the stands wept openly as over 1300 gay and lesbian athletes from many (claims vary between 13 and 19) different countries marched into the stadium. Spectators effused about how liberated they felt being in the Gay Games I Opening Ceremonies crowd (April, 1982; Salter, 1982; Treimel, 1982). Victorious Gay Games II swimmers leapt out of the pool to cheer on those who had yet to finish (Coe, 1986). A track athlete, who had already medalled, gave up his spot on a relay team that was certain to win to a friend who had not received a medal and was unlikely to get one (Snyder, 1982). In tears, Waddell presented a 44-year-old lesbian grandmother with a gold medal after she won her first-ever athletic competition in front of her children (Chui, 1982; Waddell and Schaap, 1996).

Another complexity of sameness and difference is seen with regard to the bodies of those who participate. While normalized, muscular, healthy, athletic bodies are legion, there are others with less well-toned bodies who compete, sometimes for the first time in their lives, having shunned athletics in adolescence and early adulthood due to its extremely homophobic culture. For better or for worse, the Gay Games have willingly become part of the health discourse surrounding AIDS. Preparing, training and finally participating at the Gay Games is being heralded as a panacea for people living with HIV/AIDS, providing them with purpose, hope and health, where they are imagined to have had none before. It was estimated that more than 24 per cent of Team San Francisco was HIV positive and a competitor in the Physique body building competition posed with an open chest catheter – declaring he had never felt more alive (New York in '94, 1993). The stories of this unique event continued to grow and were used often and repeatedly to claim a distinction from, yet implicitly signaled a similarity to, the International Olympics.

The incorporated 'hate' of queer shame

While these Olympic-type touches exist, the most important and most complicated reading of incorporation, for me, is how queer shame, sustained by the unresolved loss of the homophobic Olympics, motivates this entire event. As I will explain, shame cannot be expressed, only its corollary, gay pride is allowed to surface. The greater the expressions of pride, the more unacknowledged the loss is. The lost, shameful Olympics thus motivate and sustain this very successful gay pride event. In melancholic incorporation, the lost object or ideal cannot be admitted in the symbolic world. It is disavowed or tabooed. Along with losing the word Olympic, the Gay Games also had to disavow shame in the homophobic prohibition. For the Gay Games, shame cannot be admitted. Intrapsychically however, the Gay Games ego has magically taken in the shaming Olympics – unable to let them go. The Gay Games ego identifies with shame. The anger that would have been expressed towards the lost object/ideal in the world (in this case, the Gay Games' and the gay community's rage at the homophobic actions of the United States Olympic Committee) is instead taken up by the superego of the Gay Games, which berates the ego. The creation of a critical agency, otherwise known as the superego, becomes the site of aggression and rivalry. The superego expresses its rage against the ego as gay pride. As I have mentioned, incorporation is characterized by love/hate relationships with the lost or prohibited object. Counter-intuitively, gay pride then is also the expression of homophobic hate for the Gay Games (Butler, 1990, 1997).

Pride is manifested most directly in the following FGG mission statement:

> The primary purpose of the Federation of Gay Games shall be to **foster and augment the self-respect of gay women and men throughout the world** and to **engender respect and understanding from the non-gay world through the medium of organized, noncompetitive cultural/artistic** and athletics activities.
>
> (FGG Bylaws, 1989; emphasis in the original)

This statement continues that no one will be excluded from participating because of sexual orientation, gender, race, religion, nationality, ethnic origin, political beliefs, athletic/artistic ability, being physically challenged, or HIV status.

The very limited academic literature on the Gay Games reiterates this gay pride discourse, claiming the event to be resistive to heteronormative athletic events and a wonderful expression of gay and lesbian vitality and open-mindedness (Donnelly, 1996; Griffin, 1998; Krane and Waldron, 2000). Examples of this kind of gay pride include the campy tradition at gay swim meets of the Pink Flamingo Race. As Brian Pronger (1990) describes it, 'The point is for two swimmers from each team to don plastic pink flamingo hats; while one swims the arm pull of the breast stroke, the other does the kick while grasping the legs of the first; at the other end of the pool, they exchange hats and another two complete the race. Over the years this relay has grown into a camp extravaganza, with teams in radical drag making grand entrances' (1990: 275). The reclamation of once-denigrated gay traditions (in this case camp and drag) is a huge project within gay and lesbian cultures. It is a very common expression of gay pride, and has become an expected part of the aquatics competition at each Gay Games.

The Gay Games function as an important pride event for many gay and lesbian athletes who would otherwise compromise themselves in straight settings. The conventional athletic world is still extremely homophobic. Among many others, examples of this include negative recruiting for college athletics where lesbian or gay-positive coaches are maligned to parents and potential athletes, where gay male athletes fear for their physical safety and/or their lives if they come out in certain team contexts, or the ever-present paradox for female athletes where as soon as a female gendered body performs an aggressive, physical sport they are labeled a mannish lesbian (Cahn, 1994; Griffin, 1998; Pronger, 1990). Against such demonization and marginalization, the insistent reiterations of athletic homo pride have come to almost define the Gay Games. And, these overt expressions of gay pride at the Gay Games are a welcome relief for many, not just a psychically motivated necessity.

But, if left unchecked, my argument is that these expressions of pride may function as the reason for the demise of the Gay Games. The primary identification for the Gay Games, that thing which even makes them possible, is a shaming Olympics. When the superego, through expressions of gay pride, berates this ego, it is a blow to the subject. If left unchecked, the critical agency can come to embody a death drive, almost a suicide wish. The ego can withstand only so much punishment from the superego (Butler, 1990; 1997). In her 1997 book, *The Psychic Life of Power*, Judith Butler suggests that to resolve this melancholic death trajectory, the loss must be experienced again. However, the loss must be experienced differently the second time around. In the first instance, the loss of the object in the external world meant that its ideal-ness was retained as it was brought into the ego. What must happen in the second instance is that the ideal-ness of the object must be let go – the ego must confront the superego, decentering itself in the process. It is here that the melancholic Gay Games must rage against homophobic, shaming Olympics. Except this time, instead of raging against homophobia, I would like to suggest that the demands of conventional high performance sport must be subverted. Shame was not the only lost ideal in the original prohibition. The idealized Olympics were also lost, and the Gay Games must give up its identification with elite Olympic sport.

For the Gay Games this might mean breaking the attachment to one half of its double-barreled lost objects. Shame and the Olympics were lost in the original prohibition. To prescribe re-experiencing homophobic shame in order to mourn it seems like dicey territory at best. As Sally Munt (1998) reminds us, 'I don't want to reinscript a "cultural probity" of homosexual shame here, reinventing the iconography of victimization, and playing into the hands of homophobia' (1998: 4). I am not sure that this particular task is necesssary however to embrace life and escape death for the melancholic Gay Games. Perhaps it is the loss of Olympic that needs to be reworked, the other half of the shame dyad. Perhaps the Gay Games needs to lose its reliance and, arguably, fawning adherence to, the demands of conventional, high performance sport. By breaking the attachment to Olympic, and its attendant disciplinary discourses, the Gay Games might grieve its losses.

> Survival, not precisely the opposite of melancholia, but what melancholia puts in suspension - requires redirecting rage against the lost other, defiling the sanctity of the dead for the purposes of life, raging against the dead in order not to join them.
>
> (Butler, 1997: 193)

Rage against the Gay Games' homophobic loss occurred within the gay community in the late 1980s, particularly in the San Francisco area. The Visa protest and Olympic bid resistances were some examples of this.[5] Perhaps this time round, rage against the Olympics and the demands of conventional high performance sport is required. And implicit in that rage, must be a rage against the conventional heteronormative notions of masculinity and femininity, which keep homophobic shame intact. It is in this performative moment (or these kinds of performative moments) that I think a queer disruption of the Gay Games might be possible.

A queer theoretical analysis requires us to call into question certain discourses and constructions beyond those of gender and sexuality. Even though athletic participation for its own sake is lauded at the Gay Games and every event has a recreational category, sporting events are still carried out within a highly codified and organized competitive framework. When sports that have national and/or international regulatory bodies are included in the Games, every attempt is made to have the event officially sanctioned. This sanctioning indicates to the world that 'homosexuals' are 'successful' athletes. The Gay Games leaves intact the whole notion of sport, in fact, contributes to maintaining its conventional disciplinary boundaries. Only 30 sporting events are on the bill for each Games. The FGG requires 22 core sports, and the host city has some flexibility in what other options it could include. Invariably, well-established and recognizable sporting contests are chosen.

It is important to call into question how the Games use this naturalized notion of sport as a transparently good and innocent vehicle for political emancipation. Sport itself must be disrupted, called into question, its disciplinary constraints must be raged against for the Gay Games' psychic survival. Disrupting notions of 'real' sport can open up important psychic functions and discursive spaces. Because in taking apart the constitutive demands of sport, an ambivalence is produced for the Gay Games' ego, provoking an urgency for the letting go of Olympic, which will also be a disruption to a conventionally gendered form of gay:

> There can be no severing of this attachment to the object without a direct 'declaration' of loss and the desanctification of the object by externalising aggression against it... each single struggle of ambivalence loosen[s] the fixation of the libido to the object by disparaging it, denigrating it, and even as it were killing it off.
>
> (Butler, 1997: 192)

Seriously disrupting the constitutive demands of sport would mean taking apart the shaming Olympics at their core and it would radically transfigure the Gay Games. There would be huge ramifications – the event would cease to exist as it currently does. I do think, however, that if one is to queer the Gay Games, such a radical approach might be necessary. That said, I recognize that, while mourning the shaming Olympics would be a choice of life over death for the Gay Games, it cannot be read as a triumph of life over death. For there can be no final breaking of the attachment of the Gay Games from their shaming inauguration (Butler, 1997). The process of melancholia inaugurates the ego, which produces psychic and social domains. The legacies of the loss of the word 'Olympic' and the death of Tom Waddell will indelibly imprint the historicity and trajectory of the Gay Games and Cultural Events. What I am suggesting is that such imprinting might be, perhaps must be, otherwise configured for the Gay Games' future survival.

Notes

1   This chapter is based on my unpublished doctoral dissertation, '*The wannabe Olympics: the gay games, olympism, and processes of incorporation*', University of Alberta, 2003. Thanks to Sharon Rosenberg for crucial editing and loving support

2   Or more cynically, one might quote Vyv Simson and Andrew Jennings (1992) from *The Lords of the Rings*. 'So what does Samaranch's Olympic movement stand for as it approaches the twenty-first century?... [His] oratory follows a depressingly familiar pattern. First comes the evocation of the name de Coubertin, the founder of the modern Olympics. Then follows a list of nebulous Olympic slogans; "Olympism is essentially an educational movement"; "sport combined with culture"; "acting to promote peace"; "unity is our only strength"; "bringing people together in peace for the benefit of mankind". The speaker and his speeches run on auto pilot.' (p. 234).

3   San Francisco Arts and Athletics, Inc. (SFAA) was the formal non-profit society that organized Gay Games I and II.

4   The Gay Games is also a Cultural Event, an emphasis that the modern Olympics has let slide in recent decades. The cultural program draws in as many participants and perhaps more spectators than the actual athletic events. Music, film, literature, drama, art, etc., all celebrating queer culture abound throughout the event.

5   In 1987, Visa developed a default sponsorship program that supported the fundraising efforts of the USOC. Every time a cardholder put a transaction through their Visa credit card, a percentage was automatically donated to the USOC. A national gay grassroots resistance ensued with outraged letters to the editors being published in local gay newspapers and a campaign to snip Visa cards in half – sending one half to Visa, and the other to a Boston man who was going to contract a gay artist to create a sculpture of the other halves of the snipped cards. Again, in 1987, San Francisco and the Bay Area were invited to bid for the 1996 Summer Olympic Games. Gay community activists and municipal politicians formed strategic alliances to put anti-homophobic conditions on the USOC before any San Francisco bid would be supported by City Hall (Davidson, 2003).

References

April, W. (1982) 'Gay Olympics slapped with permanent injunction: Gay Games files emergency motion to nullify', *BAR*, 26 August, p. 1.

The American Run for the End of AIDS (1998) International Rainbow Memorial Run. [Information sheet]. SFPL, GLC 27, Box – FGG Business 95–6.

Athlete's package – Gay Games I. (1982) SFPL, GLC 27, Box – GG I and II in acid-free folders, File: GG I General Information.

Butler, J. (1990) *Gender trouble: Feminism and the subversion of identity*. New York: Routledge.

Butler, J. (1997) *The Psychic Life Of Power: Theories in Subjection*. Stanford, CA: Stanford University Press.

Cahn, S. K. (1994) *Coming on Strong: Gender and Sexuality in Twentieth-Century Women's Sport*. Cambridge, MA: Harvard University.

Chui, G. (1982) 'The first Gay Games ends with triumphant parade'. San Francisco Chronicle, 6 September, p.2.

Coe, R. M. (1986) *A Sense of Pride: The Story of Gay Games II*. San Francisco: Pride Publications.

Davidson, J. (2003) 'The wannabe Olympics: the Gay Games, Olympism and processes of incorporation'. Unpublished doctoral dissertation. University of Alberta, Edmonton, Alberta.

Dermody, G. (1998) 'Europe's Gay Capital Hosts Gay Games'. [Email to FGG Executive Committee]. SFPL, GLC 27, Box – Amsterdam V 1998, File: Blue Binder. August 6.

Donnelly, P. (1996) 'Prolympism: sport monoculture as crisis and opportunity'. *Quest*, 48 (1) 25–42.

Farrell, D. (1990) FGG seeks nominees for the Waddell Cup. [Press release, June]. SFPL, GLC 27, Box – FGG Business 82–94, File: Dereks' Red Binder – FGG 1989 thru 1994.

FGG Bylaws. (1989) [Bylaw document, July 3]. SFPL, GLC 27, Box – FGG Business 82–94, File – Dereks' Red Binder – FGG 1989 thru 1994.

Forzley, R. and Hughes, E. D. (eds). (1990) *The Spirit Captured: The Official Photojournal of Celebration '90 - Gay Games III and Cultural Festival.* Vancouver, BC: For Eyes Press.

Gay Athletic Games I (1982) [Official Program] San Francisco: SFAA. SFPL, GLC 27, Box 1 – GG II Hal's Notebooks.

Gildersleeve, J. and Wardlaw, L. (1982) 'Gay Olympiad I' *Coming Up!*, August: 2–3. SFPL, GLC 27, Box – Gay Games I and II In Acid Free Folders, File – GG I Press Kit.

Griffin, P. (1998) *Strong Women, Deep Closets: Lesbians and Homophobia in Sport.* Champaign, IL: Human Kinetics.

Herkenhoff, H. and Lewinstein, S. (1986) 'Guidelines for uniforms for athletics'.[Information sheet, June]. SFPL, GLC 27, Box #1, Series II, GG II – File #3, Welcoming Letters.

Krane, V. and Waldron, J. (2000) 'The Gay Games: creating our own sports culture', in K. Schaffer and S. Smith (eds), *The Olympics at the Millenium: Power, Politics, and the Games.* Brunswick, NJ: Rutgers University Press, 147–64.

Labrecque, L. (ed) (1994) *Unity: A Celebration of Gay Games IV and Stonewall.* San Francisco, CA: Labrecque.

Lorch, P. (1982) Word monopoly: Gay Olympics fights back – Court battle looms over use of word. *BAR,* 28 January, 1, 9.

Munt, S. R. (1998) 'Introduction', in S. R. Munt (ed) *Butch/femme: Inside Lesbian Gender.* London: Cassell, 1–11.

New York in '94. (1993) 'Games can change the world: Unity 94' [Corporate fundraising information package]. SFPL, GLC 27, Box – Derek GGIV NYC 1994, File – Big Blue Binder.

Peterson, R. and Kennedy, S. (1994) 'Keeping the flame lit: The Federation of Gay Games', in L. Labrecque (ed), *Unity: A Celebration of Gay Games IV and Stonewall,* San Francisco, CA: Labrecque, 12–13.

Probyn, E. (2000) 'Sporting bodies: Dynamics of shame and pride', *Body and Society.* 6 (1): 13–28.

Pronger B. (1990) *The Arena of Masculinity: Sports, Homosexuality, and the Meaning of Sex.* Toronto: University of Toronto.

Repa, B. K. (1987) 'No Gay Olympics, high court says', *San Francisco Chronicle,* 26 June, p.A1, A20.

Salter, S. (1982) 'Triumph in long race for rights: "Olympics" or not, many see event as symbolic of gays' gains'. *San Francisco Chronicle,* 29 August, p. B1.

Schaffer, K. and Smith, S. (2000) 'Introduction: The games at the millenium' in K. Schaffer and S. Smith (eds), *The Olympics at the Millenium: Power, Politics, and the Games*. New Brunswick, NJ: Rutgers University, 1–16.

Segrave, J. (1988) 'Toward a definition of olympism' in J. Segrave and D. Chu (eds), *The Olympic Games in Transition*. Champaign, IL: Human Kinetics, 149–61.

Simson, V. and Jennings, A. (1992) *The Lords of the Rings: Power, Money and Drugs in the Modern Olympics*. Toronto: Stoddart.

Snyder, W. (1982) '1986 Gaymes confirmed', *The San Francisco Sentinel*, 16 September, p. 1.

Streicher, R. (1988) 'Should the Olympics come to San Francisco? Why not?' *BAR*, 3 March, p. 6.

Treimel, S. (1982) 'Gay Athletic Games open to cheers: 15,000 watch show in Kezar Stadium', *BAR*, 2 September, p. 2, 4.

Waddell, T., and Schaap, D. (1996) *Gay Olympian: The Life and Death of Dr Tom Waddell*. New York: Alfred A. Knopf.

White, A. (1982) 'Gay Games torch arrives Sunday', *BAR*, 19 August, p. 2.

Part III

Possibilities for queer bodies and identities in sport

7 Transgendering sex and sport in the Gay Games

Caroline Symons and Dennis Hemphill

Introduction

The international Gay Games developed as an inclusive sport and cultural event engaging the communities of sexual minorities. This chapter examines the 'queering', especially the transgendering, of sex and sport, and its implications for Gay Games, especially the later games (New York, 1994; Amsterdam, 1998; Sydney, 2002). The challenge faced by organisers is development of policy that upholds the Games' philosophy of diversity, participation and inclusiveness, while responding to need/interest in conducting events in line with the ethos of mainstream sport and the expectations of regulatory bodies and corporate sponsors. Such is the conundrum and promise of the Gay Games.

'Transgendering' can be understood in the context of a larger discourse known as 'queering'. This can be understood in the following way. Against the backdrop of dominant heterosexuality, which entails an essentialistic or 'natural', as well as oppositional two-sex, two-gender human and social structure, there are sexualities (e.g. lesbian, gay, bisexual, transgender and intersex) that shape the lived experience and performance of sex (i.e. chromosomal and anatomical makeup), gender identity (i.e. self-perception as male, female, in-between, fluid), sexual orientation (sexual and romantic attraction towards others based on gender style and sexed embodiment), and gender style (the main ways that a person performs and engages with gender such as butch, butch-femme, dyke, lipstick lesbian, androgynous style, camp, Queenie, and macho). The 'heterosexing' of sport, entrenched for so long and so rigidly in sport, can make life difficult for lesbian, gay, bisexual, transgender and intersex athletes, not to mention non-athletic straight males and straight female athletes.[1]

The naturalisation of sex and sport

Most modern sports have separate categories for men and women. In fact, many sports, especially at non-elite level, have several additional categories, based on features such as age, weight and ability. These categories are usually defended on the grounds that closer competition amongst relatively evenly matched individuals or teams (the 'level playing field') will be more challenging and fair, will produce better performances and satisfaction, and validate 'personal bests' and winning.

Division based on sex may also reflect a more deep-seated notion that men are naturally better than women in sport. Physiologists have estimated that elite sportsmen on average can perform from 10–18 per cent better than elite sports-women in events emphasising strength, speed and stamina (Lamb, 1978: 300). Physiologically this difference is attributed primarily to the enhancing effects that significantly greater levels of testosterone during adolescence and early manhood have on muscle mass and strength, the production of red blood cells (carrying greater quantities of oxygen), bone thickness, muscle glycogen storage and muscle protein synthesis (Lamb, 1978: 300).

However, physiology is only a small part of the picture. Modern sport was developed and institutionalised to promote manly aggression, heroism and military readiness. It was also an important institution for men to prove their heterosexual and hegemonic masculinity and to reinforce, on quite a powerful level, the supposed superiority of men over women in Western societies. Women, at the turn of the twentieth century, were constrained by a medical discourse that discouraged vigorous physical activity and sport, and throughout the century by a media discourse that often represented women as passive sexual objects or as 'monsters', especially those who transgressed conservative gender boundaries by being lesbian, too muscular, or too good at sport (Lenskyj, 1986; Hargreaves, 1994). English (1995) argues that today's most high-profile and lucrative sports are those constructed historically around height, weight, speed, strength and power, thus giving men, statistically speaking, certain key advantages for succeeding in sport. When combined with the fact that men's sports have traditionally received a greater share of resources and rewards, what results is a social inequality disguised as a natural one.

The test of 'true' womanhood

During the time of cold war rivalry in the 1960s eastern European female athletes were so outstanding in international competition that other nations began to question their status as women (Hood-Williams, 1995: 300). Sex determination of female athletes was introduced at the Olympics and other international and national sports events with what was referred to as a 'femininity control' test. Female competitors were required to parade nude in front of a panel of medical doctors (Skirstad, 1999: 117). This gynaecological examination was replaced at the 1967 European Athletics championships by chromosomal testing – a 'real' woman being determined by the possession of an 'XX' on a microscope slide.

The International Olympic Committee (IOC) introduced a number of chromosomal 'femininity tests' from 1968 onwards, and female athletes were required to hold gender verification certificates, which included their chromosomal results (Skirstad, 1999: 117). Each had limitations, and the main test employed, the 'buccal smear,' had a 20 per cent error rate (Skirstad, 1999: 117). Out of the 3,387 female athletes that underwent gender verification at the Atlanta

Olympics, eight failed the test and had to complete further examination (Elsas *et al.*, 1997: 52).[2] Important to the notion of 'queering' sex and sport is the fact that seven of these athletes who had lived their whole lives, physically, socially and psychologically as girls and women, were classified as genetically male (XY). They had the condition Androgen Insensitivity Syndrome, which involves unresponsiveness to testosterone produced by intra-abdominal atrophic testes. In most of these cases there is no competitive advantage attributable to these genetic variations (Skirstad, 1999: 117).

There is evidence indicating that sportswomen themselves want eligibility criteria to ensure that only 'biological' women can compete in women's sporting events. This was demonstrated in the controversy over the eligibility of Renee Richards (a transgender woman with credentials as a past elite-level male player) to compete on the United States women's tennis circuit in 1976 (Birrell and Cole, 1990: 207–35). As a result of strong opposition from women's tennis associations, the United States Tennis Association, the Women's Tennis Association, and the United States Open Committee introduced a mandatory buccal smear test to determine eligibility in women's tennis. Suspicions about residual physiological advantages among male-to-female (M–F) transgenders may be understandable given the significant obstacles female athletes have had to overcome to gain parity in certain sports.

Variability of sex and gender

There are a number of sex-based chromosomal variations that do not fit humans neatly into two 'naturally' based sexes. For instance, there are people with the physical characteristics of both sexes – hermaphrodites – and people who have no gonads at all. Scouring the medical literature on intersexuality, biologist and historian of science, Anne Fausto-Sterling, conservatively estimates the incidence of intersexuality as 1.7 per cent of births (Fausto-Sterling, 2000: 51–54). Also, there are people, known in medical parlance as transsexuals, who change their sex of birth, male-to-female or female-to-male (F–M), through surgery, hormone treatment and psychosocial gender retraining to become embodied as the other sex; and those referred to as transgenders who live roles and identities across or 'in-between' genders, and who may or may not undergo sexual reassignment.

In traditional Western societies gender is often conflated with sex, and both are considered immutable. In other words, the view of gender is one where the masculine and feminine role is aligned with the 'natural' sex division of male and female. However, there is plenty of sociological and anthropological research indicating the cultural variability of gender. There exists a third gender and complex variations across gender and sex lines in some traditional societies: the berdache of the North American Indian, the Indonesian waria, the Filipino bayot, the Luban kitesha in parts of the Congo, and the mati of Suriname, for instance (Herdt, 1994: 63–72; Besnier, 1994: 285–329; Roscoe, 1994; 329–373; Shapiro, 1991: 248–79, Altman, 2001: 90–1).

The 1990s saw a growing scepticism about the immutability of the male–female sex/gender system of the West, leading some to theorise it differently. Contrary to the view that gender and sex are fixed, natural categories, Butler redescribes them as cultural performances. In her account, the body performs gender repetitively and non-voluntaristically from infancy onwards. Gender is not something we 'are', but rather something we 'do'. The largely unreflective repetition of 'bodily gestures, movements and styles of various kinds constitute the illusion of an abiding, gendered self' (Butler, 1990: 140), one which reinforces and perpetuates itself.

This is not a performance put on or off at will like a theatre act or costume, as some critics suggest. Rather, performativity must be understood 'not as a singular or deliberate "act", but, rather, as reiterative and citational practice by which discourse produces the effects that it names' (Butler, 1993: 1). Butler uses drag performances to illustrate how big hair, protruding breasts, fake eyelashes, overdone eye make up and exaggerated hip movements have no origin in the female body, as such. Rather, they stand in contrast to the 'normal' or mainstream bodily performance of masculinity and femininity, a performance equally shaped by certain gendered ideals and fantasies.

The sexed anatomy of the body is not the origin of gendered performance. Rather this material body is brought to life by the over-determined and polarised gender performance demanded by normative heterosexuality. In Butler's words:

> Because there is neither an essence that gender expresses or externalises nor an objective ideal to which gender aspires, and because gender is not a fact, the various acts of gender create the idea of gender, and without those acts, there would be no gender at all. Gender is, thus, a construction that regularly conceals its genesis; the tacit, collective agreement to perform, produce, and sustain discrete and polar genders as cultural fictions is obscured by the credibility of those productions – and the punishments that attend to not agreeing to believe in them.
>
> (Butler, 1990: 140)

Feminist academic Barbara Brook sums up the centrality of this understanding of the body to Butler's work: 'This interpretation is crucial to her disruption of that continuity between sexed anatomy, gender, and sexuality, which privileges the sexed anatomy as the origin of a singular, sexual identity' (Brook, 1999: 116). Butler insists that there is no body that pre-exists discourse and that we are never out of a gendering framework. Furthermore, performances that transgress gender norms, such as drag acts, queerness, lesbianism, butch and camp homosexuality and the like have the 'deviant' status they do only in the context of the entrenched performances of males and females along traditional heterosexual lines.

While it is understandable why mainstream sport might be threatened by participation of lesbian, gay, bisexual, transgender and intersex athletes, the Gay Games could be seen as a haven for diverse sexualities. However, the queering of the Gay Games is not without its own problems, some to do with tensions between diversity and mainstreaming, and others to do with acceptability of transgender, transsexual and intersex individuals within the Gay Games. Transgenders, transsexuals and intersex individuals find themselves in the middle of controversy, yet again, and it is to the transgender queering of the Games that this chapter now turns.

Political tensions within the Gay Games

Transgender involvement and inclusion in the Gay Games did not become significant until Gay Games IV, in 1994, the first Games to have a specific transgender policy. This was due to a number of complex historical and political factors. The Gay Games was envisaged as an exemplary sporting event for gay and lesbian communities worldwide. Gay and lesbian peoples from diverse sporting abilities and age groups, as well as from diverse racial, ethnic, religious and political backgrounds, were to be brought together in a spirit of mutual understanding and celebration. It was believed that this would be achieved through 'wholesome' involvement in sporting competition, with events that emphasised inclusion, participation and doing one's best.

For early Gay Games organisers (San Francisco, 1982; San Francisco, 1986; Vancouver, 1990) sport was seen as an excellent vehicle to mainstream gay men and lesbians, that is, to 'normalise' them in the eyes of straight society. Showing that gays and lesbian athletes were involved in vigorous sports, especially those involving the demonstration of strength, power, speed and combat, could subvert many of the negative stereotypes haunting this community, including the supposed effeminacy of gay men, the supposed obsession of all gay people with sex, and their supposed irresponsible, hedonistic and 'deviant' lifestyles. There was also growing interest in, and pressure on organisers to ensure that events were run along conventional sporting lines, with standardised conditions for competition, officiating and recording of results, to gain sanctioning from mainstream sport bodies and attract corporate sponsorship. This conservative gendering of early Gay Games resulted in downplaying of more leather, camp or sexually flamboyant elements of participation, producing its own in-house tensions.

Notwithstanding these challenges, organisers were concerned with making the Games as accessible as possible. Gay Games organisers have had to overcome significant obstacles to staging the Games, including the devastating AIDS crisis (and resultant restrictive United States immigration policy), public attacks by conservative religious groups, obstruction by public officials, and legal battles with the United States Olympic Committee (USOC) over the use of the word 'Olympics'.[3] In spite of this, Games' organisers formed policies and implemented practices to live up to the Games' philosophy of diversity, participation and inclusiveness. These included promotion of more sexual diversity on organising committees, developing 'outreach' programmes to increase women's participation in general, and that of gays and lesbians with HIV/AIDS or from non-Western countries in particular, all the while trying to balance the competitive sport ethos with that of participation. For instance, there were no qualifying standards to enter the Gay Games. Most sports had novice to advanced levels of competition. Official medal tallies and Games records were as a matter of policy not recorded and all registrants received a participation medal.

Most importantly, transgender and intersex communities were only beginning to form at this time and were not aligned with broader gay and lesbian communities within the United States and other Western nations. Understanding this community formation is essential to the context of transgender and intersex participation policy within Gay Games IV, V and VI. It is a subject addressed in the remainder of this chapter.

Transgender and intersex community formation

Transsexual and transgender peoples are some of the most discriminated and stigmatised in many societies (Smit, 1998: 22–6; Perkins *et al.*, 1995: 62). Discrimination comes in a variety of forms and from a variety of sources. Califia (1997: 256) sees strong parallels with the hostility directed against gay men and lesbians and transgender people: 'Straight culture reads much of the public expression of gay identity as gender transgression. To them, we're all part of the same garbage heap of sex-and-gender trash'. A popular view portrays transgender people as homosexuals or extreme transvestites (Califia, 1997: 256–57). In sport, the Renee Richards case pointed out the deep suspicion that women's tennis associations had toward M–F transsexuality.

Yet, discrimination does not always come from straight society and organisations. Hostility towards transgender people also emanated from separatist lesbian feminist collectives during the 1980s. Janice Raymond established the theoretical basis for this hostility in her influential book *The Transsexual Empire* (1979). According to Ekins and King (1997: 12–13) and Califia (1997: 86–120), Raymond's work was used to silence dissenting views amongst academics concerning transgender issues, and in some circumstances to justify significant intolerance. Califia documents a number of incidents where transsexual women who identify as lesbians were excluded from lesbian-only events and organisations within the United States (1997: 106–7). Similar exclusionist practices appear to have occurred in other Western countries. There was also significant prejudice experienced by transgender people within the gay male scene (Califia, 1997: 156–7 and Perkins *et al.*, 1995: 58).

There was another social factor that militated against the formation of transgender and intersex community identity: the discourse of pathology by the medical establishment. Underpinned by heterosexual normativity, doctors used hormones, surgery and gender re-training to 'cure' the 'condition' of gender dysphoria and produce 'healthy' feminine heterosexual women and masculine heterosexual men. In the case of intersex individuals, surgery was used to rectify ambiguous genitalia. With intersex infants, doctors were put in the position of deciding sex: clitorises too large were excised, and penises too small, transformed into female genitalia (Money and Ehrhardt, 1972: 52, 167 and 171; Fausto-Sterling 2000, 45–77).

Pat Califia comments in her groundbreaking coverage of the history and politics of transgenderism that gate-keeping power by the medical establishment 'had a huge impact on the way transsexuals viewed themselves and the way they presented themselves to each other and to the public' (1997: 48). Once cured of their dysphoria, transsexuals were expected to assimilate quietly into their new 'normal' lives. Many transsexuals wished to do this anyway, and did not want to be associated with another 'deviant' (i.e. gay and lesbian) community. In fact, homophobia is not uncommon amongst transgenders and transsexuals, and sex/gender normalisation, shaped as it is by the discourse of heteronormativity, is what many desire.

Transgender activism started in the 1970s and principally consisted of challenging laws against female impersonation and policies that made it difficult for transsexuals to change identification and other public records. It also involved lobbying for greater access to sex reassignment, raising public awareness concerning transexuality and transvestism, and forming support and social groups for transgender people (Califia, 1997: 221–2). Only in the early to mid 1990s did transgender activism became more radical. One of the main organisations representing this politics was Transgender Nation, developed from the gay and lesbian action coalition to transcend identity politics – Queer Nation (QN). Activism by people with intersexed conditions began within the United States during the early 1990s (Chase, 1998: 196–7).

By the mid 1990s community formation became more visible and fulsome, and affiliations were established with the broader lesbian and gay community. By the new millennium it became common practice to speak of the lesbian, gay, bisexual, transgender, and intersex community – with intersex being the most recent addition. Queer theorising of gender during this time emphasised transience, fluidity and performativity. In Kate Borestein's *Gender Outlaw*, this translates to: 'the ability to freely and knowingly become one or many of a limitless number of genders for any length of time, at any rate of change. Gender fluidity recognizes no borders or rules of gender' (1994: 52).

Deconstruction, Foucault and Judith Butler's theory of 'gender performativity' provided the basis of much of this queering. Furthermore, coalition politics in the United States, which developed with ACT UP[4] and the fight against government indifference and community prejudice over AIDS, inspired queer and difference activism. Gay men, lesbians, transgender, drug users, prostitutes, straight people, of all races were activists together in this life-threatening struggle.

Legal issues

In the context of pathologising transgender and intersex individuals, and their growing activism, came legislative definitions and determination of rights. Anti-discrimination legislation covering areas of education, housing, accommodation and workplace was introduced in San Francisco in 1994 (Califia, 1997: 238–39). By 1996 it became firmly established in European law that it was unlawful to discriminate against a transsexual person in employment (1997: 238–39). The

Netherlands at this time had comprehensive anti-discrimination legislation in place protecting the rights of transgender people, and included provisions to enable post-operative transsexuals and people who were in serious 'gender transition' to participate in sport in the sex that they lived. By the mid 1990s most states in Australia had legislation protecting the human rights of transgender and inter-sexed peoples, including those who were transitioning (Comben, 1996: 15–18).

However, there are exceptions within the law that apply to sport. According to legislation in New South Wales (NSW), the host Australian state for the Sydney 2002 Gay Games, a transgender person 'can be excluded from participation in any sport activity for members of the sex with which the transgender person identifies' (Opie, 2001: 375–404). During debates over this exemption, which occurred in the Legislative Council of NSW in 1996, The Women in Sport Foundation supported the exclusion clause with the following statement:

> We believe that postoperative male transsexuals have an unfair physical advantage over females in sport because of their pre-existing superior anatomical and physiological characteristics, which develop as a result of puberty.
>
> (Quoted in Sharpe, 1997: 40)

A similar debate was being conducted within the Australian Federal legislative sphere during the formulation of the 1995 Commonwealth Sexuality Discrimination Bill (ASC, 1995). Transgender lobbyists, human rights advocates, medical experts and the Australian Sports Commission (ASC) took the position that postoperative M–F transgenders did not necessarily possess physiological advantages. This was due to the fact that they had to continually undergo hormone therapy, which significantly increased their oestrogen levels, and their bodies no longer produced testosterone. The ASC quoted Doctor Elizabeth Ferris in their official submission:

> Transgenders who have had an operation and take oestrogens are being as typically womanly as possible and will not do anything to tip their physical appearance over to the masculine side. The assumption that anyone exposed to testosterone at puberty will be a star athlete is untrue 'it's like saying anyone over 5'10 will be a good volleyball player.'
>
> (ASC, Additional Comments on the Sexuality Discrimination Bill 1995)

The ASC also cited the only exercise physiology research that they were aware of on an M–F transsexual athlete that had been competing within NSW. This research had been conducted at the University of NSW and indicated that this athlete fell within the 'normal' range for female athletes (ASC, *Additional Comments*, 1995). The ASC recommended further research, although they were content to see the Sexuality Discrimination Bill proceed (ASC, *Additional Comments*, 1995).[5] Generally, sporting authorities within Australia and internationally have been very slow in responding to the rights and challenges presented by the existence of transgender and intersexed persons.

Transgendering Gay Games' policy and practice

Gay Games IV: New York

The Gay Games movement faced significant challenges in relation to developing a transgender and sport participation policy in the lead-up to the New York Games in 1994. Deb-Ann Thompson, Vice-President of the Federation of Gay Games (FGG), consulted one of the main authorities representing transgender people within the Unites States – the International Foundation of Gender Education – in her policy deliberations (Thompson, interview, 2001). What resulted was policy based largely on criteria established by the medical and psychological professions in determining the gender transitioning process. Participation criteria for the Games were similar to those that needed to be met by a transgender person before they could undergo sex realignment surgery (SRS). The criteria are as follows.

1   Proof of a completed legal name change to match the desired gender role.
2   Letter from a medical physician stating that the participant has been actively involved in hormone treatment for a minimum of two full years without any time lapse. Letter also needs to explain current health condition.
3   Letter from a mental health professional therapist stating that the participant has been actively involved in psychotherapy for a minimum of eighteen months. Letter also needs to state that this participant had emotionally and psychologically transitioned into the desired gender role and why it would be impossible or severely detrimental for this individual to participate in their biologically born gender.
4   Proof of participant's cross-living in the desired gender role for a minimum of two years.[6]

According to Thompson, the intent of the FGG's policy was to include people who lived their lives fully as members of the sex they had transitioned to, but didn't necessarily involve SRS. This was thought appropriate due to the fact that a number of medical conditions prohibited SRS surgery, such as being HIV+, having herpes or hepatitis C, and SRS itself was expensive and out of reach for the most seriously transitioned.[7] The requirement for continuous hormone treatment over an ongoing two-year period was considered adequate to place the transitioning person in the acceptable sports performance ranges for the gender they lived, and to ensure fair competition, especially in the events emphasising strength, stamina and physique.

Within the New York transgender community, this policy was controversial, and views were divided. The most radical transgender organisation, Transsexual Menace (TM) held a press conference and threatened to boycott the Games on the ground that this policy was discriminatory, as it relied too much on the authority of 'experts'.[8] For TM, gender identity was a deeply personal matter for the individual concerned, not a pathology to be cured by doctors and psychologists.

There were also practical difficulties with the policy, including the fact that changing one's name was not a straightforward process in some countries, and that on-going consultation with a medical or mental health professional was an unlikely occurrence for people who had already transitioned and lived their 'true' identity for a number of years (interview with Riley, 2001).[9] Furthermore, it appears that transgender people undergoing surgical procedures requiring general anaesthetic are required to cease their hormone treatment for up to four weeks beforehand to reduce the risk of Deep Vein Thrombosis, a lapse that would, thereby, constitute an infringement of Games' policy (interview with Riley, 2001).

Gay Games' operations manager, Roz Quarto, also faced challenges with this policy. The Sports Co-Chairs, who were responsible for organising sports competitions for these Games, raised serious concerns about how inclusion of transgenders in the Games, and the 'bad' publicity it was generating, could jeopardise much-needed sanctioning by mainstream sport bodies and funding by corporate sponsors. Quarto and the Sports Co-Chairs also voiced concerns about insurance coverage and litigation in the event that a female athlete in contact sports such as flag football or soccer was injured by a presumably stronger M–F transitioning athlete (interview with Quarto, 2001).

The Gay Games of 1994 appears to have been the first international sports event to include transgender participants within its policy and procedures, including those who were in transition or who could not complete their sex change for financial and/or medical reasons. Whilst the policy did not go far enough for the more radical TM, it reflects difficulties facing organisers of these Games. That is, organisers were attempting to balance the competition and participation ethos, and be responsive to the needs and interests of a growing number of sexualities in the Games, all in a world that was still deeply prejudiced towards gays and lesbians, let alone transgenders.

Gay Games V: Amsterdam

In drafting transgender participation policy at these Gay Games, legal advice had to be sought to ensure that policy was in line with equal opportunity legislation of the Netherlands. A ruling was sought from the Netherlands Equal Opportunity Board (EOB) and the following policy was established:

> **Special Needs – Transgender Issues**
> Gay Games welcomes everyone, regardless of his or her sexual orientation or gender. For participants whose passport meets their gender the following is not applicable. In order to be treated equally as their gender identification implies, participants must provide, upon request, proof of the following conditions to the Board Gender Identification Committee of Gay Games Amsterdam 1998:
>
> Proof of completed gender transition in active daily life for at least two years (photographs, personal correspondence, etc)

Letter from a medical physician stating that the participant has been actively involved in hormone treatment for a minimum of two full years without any time lapse. Please pay attention to the regulations on drug testing. [10]

This policy is considerably less involved than that used in Gay Games IV. It overcomes the difficulty of proving a name change, is more flexible in its demands on proving gender transitioning, and does not use language or stipulate requirements that pathologise transgender persons. It also makes reference to the issue of drug testing in the bodybuilding and power lifting events, a situation where F–M transgenders could produce a positive drug test if done immediately after taking one of their required and regular doses of testosterone. However, as with Gay Games IV, people with intersex conditions were not catered for in this policy.

There were a number of transgender participants at the Amsterdam Gay Games who were unhappy with this policy. It appears from evidence given during development of the transgender participation policy for Gay Games VI that reasons for this included: difficulties with the no-time lapse requirement due to medical complications, difficulties with proof of name and identity change, and what was perceived as still an over reliance on medical experts in proof of transitioning.[11]

Gay Games VI: Sydney

Transgender and intersex peoples were enabled to participate in Gay Games VI through development of a most inclusive 'Gender Policy' that defined gender in terms of social identity.[12] This development was a drawn-out process taking over eighteen months and involving community consultation with main stakeholders. These included the FGG, the Board of Management of Sydney 2002, Sydney 2002 National Indigenous Advisory Committee, Moana Pacifika (Sydney 2002 Pacific Island Working Group), Sydney 2002 Women's Advisory Group, Sydney 2002 Asia Committee, the Gender Centre (Sydney) and Australian Intersex Support (Australia).[13] The process began with a community forum held at Gay Games headquarters on April 10, 2001.[14] At this meeting it was accepted in principle that an inclusive policy enabling transgender and intersex persons to participate in the Gay Games should be developed.

By the end of 2001 the Amsterdam policy was presented as the best inclusive option. However, there was still much opposition to it. In the context of NSW anti-discrimination legislation, the Amsterdam policy was seen as discriminatory, as it requires transgender persons to prove their sex/gender identity when the same is not required of other participants.[15] Transgender groups deemed the policy 'inadequate in relation to the medical and social reality of many transgender persons,' arguing that indigenous, Asia Pacific, African and other 'ethno-local' transgenders do not have access to Western medical practices, and their identities are often based on indigenous customs and belief systems rather than Western discourses of transgenderism. Some called for separate transgender sports events, while others pointed out that the policy did not provide for intersex conditions (Buckle, 2002). Some members of the Sydney 2002 Board of

Management, echoing previous Games' concerns about fairness and risk management, took exception to the policy's implication that purely identity-based transgenders (not undergoing any hormonal transitioning) could compete in women's events (Buckle, 2002).

Elizabeth Riley proposed a compromise policy, one sensitive to the fairness issue as well as to objections to policies that pathologise transgenders and, in her words:

> Place the onus of proof on all members of the transgender community to safeguard the Games against the unlikely situation of a non genuine participant seeking to gain some gender based advantage from the verification regimes they are subjected to. This is a tiresome burden that transgenders are often subjected to in all walks of life and one that is insulting to, and undermining of, our identities. If you have been a woman for twenty years it is really annoying to have to keep proving it.[16]

Her recommended and eventually accepted policy did not require proof of identity or transitioning at the point of accreditation. Accordingly, all participants should be presumed to be the sex they assert they are without further question unless a complaint is made amongst competitors in contention for medals. This complaint has to be based on valid grounds and should be dealt with by an Appeals Board which uses the Amsterdam policy to determine the sex and gender identity of the competitor in question.

FGG sports representatives in wrestling voiced concern over the possible safety issues and insurance risks entailed by the participation of transgender athletes, the assumption being that F–M transgenders may be at a serious disadvantage in the men's competition (Borrie, 2003: 113). This issue was resolved within the final policy in the following way:

> **Safety**
> In events which involve body contact, the technical officials implementing the rules of the event have discretion in determining the circumstances which place participants at risk of injury and to take action to avoid such injury. Where the technical official at the event level is of the opinion there may be a risk of injury, subject to the rules of the particular sport, they may rule that an individual may not participate in that event/class/division. Where a technical official makes a decision on these grounds the affected person will be provided written notice of the decision and the reason.
>
> (Sydney 2002, Gender Policy: 10)

Essentially, the policy devolved responsibility for safety into the hands of technical officials, who, being close to the action, could make decisions on a case-by-case basis.

All Gay Games VI participants were required to complete an accreditation process before they could participate in official Games' programmes. At accreditation all people registered in a sport organised under male and female divisions were asked which gender division they wished to compete in. They were required to produce legal documentation such as passports, birth certificates, and other identification to verify gender identity. Where a person's 'official' gender identity differed from the one they wished to participate in the Games, a number of alternative verification steps were available. These included:

1   A letter from a medical practitioner is provided stating that the participant has been actively involved in hormone treatment for a minimum of two full years; and/or
2   Proof of the participant living as the chosen or self-identified gender for a minimum of two years.

(Sydney 2002, Gender Policy: 9)

Proof of condition 2 could be verified by legal documents, drivers licence, evidence of employment, testimonials and statutory declarations, bank accounts and the like. Sydney 2002 accreditation officials had discretionary powers to determine gender identity exclusively on condition 2 (Sydney 2002, Gender Policy: 9). For indigenous transgenders, testimony from a bona fide indigenous community organisation or Australian indigenous community worker was also acceptable for Transgender/Sistergirl status (Sydney 2002, Gender Policy: 9).

There were a couple of thorny issues relating to the sports programme and transgender participation. One of these was the breaking of (state, national or international) records by transgender and intersex peoples. Sydney 2002 Gay Games officials stated that they would make every effort to encourage sporting bodies and technical officials governing sanctioned and non-sanctioned sports events to recognise the gender identity verified during accreditation. However, officials also acknowledged that they could not 'enforce such policy on autonomous sporting or cultural bodies or associations' (Sydney 2002, Gender Policy: 8). As a result, Games officials left it to the sanctioning body to determine the recording of records and performances where legal identity documents did not agree with social gender identity on accreditation.

Drug testing during the Gay Games presented further difficulties. For instance, there was the risk of M–F transgender participants, who had not undergone hormonal or surgical 'treatment' and so had testosterone levels of average males, competing in female sports divisions. This may have had an impact at the top performance level in the power and strength events and would be detected through drug testing. Furthermore, F–M transgenders on hormone therapy would likely test positive for anabolic steroids. These unresolved situations highlighted tensions between the competition ethos, supported implicitly by the FGG push for drug testing (Borrie, 2003: 108–10)[17] and the participation ethos, which would not require such surveillance.

Netball and transgender participation

The sport of netball at Gay Games VI is an interesting case, not just because of the large participation rate of transgenders, but also for the challenges that diversity presented for the organisers (interview with Mueller, 2003).[18] Netball, along with volleyball, experienced the largest numbers of transgender participants during Gay Games VI. There were eight indigenous netball teams (representing 56 per cent of all netball participants), of which seven identified as transgender (representing 44per cent of all netball participants). These players originated from Palm Island, Northern Queensland (Sistergirls), Samoa (fa'afafine), Tonga (fa'afafine) and Papua New Guinea.

Netball was a non-sanctioned event, and minimal assistance was given in organising and officiating the competition by Netball NSW or Australia.[19] The competition attracted a total of 157 registrations and 15 teams (interview with Mueller, 2003). There were divisions for teams of men, women, mixed and transgenders. Individual transgenders could compete in any division; however, transgender teams could not play against biological women's teams. This was due to physical disparity between biological women and some transgender participants. As a result, transgenders played in a separate women's division. Five transgender teams entered this women's division, one entered the men's competition and all transgenders played in the mixed competition. Individual transgenders played in the biological women's team, however, competition rules allowed one transgender player per team. In the mixed team division, with a ruling of six men and four women, transgenders were counted as men to minimise injury and promote fair competition.

The competition draw evolved and changed in the weeks preceding, and also during, the Games, requiring flexibility in management of the event. This was due to a number of factors; including unavailability of email in aboriginal and islander communities, confusing registration details (e.g., transgender players were allowed to use up to three names and identities based on passport name, birth name, or stage/persona), and uncertainty of players about participation divisions and categories. There were, at times, disputes between transgender teams over the credentials of some sistergirls, and cultural differences in the interpretation of competition rules and ethos, both requiring negotiation amongst officials and players. Notwithstanding the major complexities in organisation of the netball competition, it was described as very enjoyable, playful and rewarding. The event culminated with a medal ceremony and party, colourful costuming and music marking the indigenous and transgender heritage of participating teams. Due to the variety of competition categories and a number of themed awards, practically all participants received a medal.

The Gender Policy of Sydney 2002 was the most comprehensive and inclusive of Gay Games to date, and went some way to reducing what many transgenders considered demeaning gender verification regimes. The need for these regimes in the first place points to the influence that the traditional (competitive) sport ethos has within the Games. The policy took the sports programme beyond Western conceptions of sex/gender/sexuality, as traditional indigenous transgender identities were included explicitly within the sports and cultural programmes. Indigenous Australian Sistergirls, Indonesian Waria, Thai Kathoey, South Asian Hijra and Samoan Faafafine were able to play the sport of their choice in the gender in which they lived. While the Sydney Gay Games can claim success, it also revealed the difficulties formulating and implementing policy for an ever-expanding number of sexualities that have a stake in the Gay Games.

Future considerations

Full inclusion of transgender and intersex people within the Gay Games certainly tests the principles of the Games and highlights tensions between mainstreaming and transformative sports agendas. While it goes beyond the scope of this chapter, there are several procedures future Gay Games organisers may want to consider to improve inclusive participation while preserving fair competition.

The first is to organise sports not along traditional gender or transgender lines, but to organise them in such a way that ability and handicapping are the primary measures used to create a fair, inclusive and competitive environment. Masters swimming, for example, organises heats according to common times rather than by sex, while golf has a long tradition of handicapping. The other is to introduce team sports that are designed to encourage interaction between all participants. Korfball comes to mind here, and other team sports could be adapted or developed along similar lines. A cue can be taken from English (1995), who suggests the invention or revision of sports, so that they feature a variety of combinations of fitness and motor skills in order to neutralise or compensate for any possible competitive (strength, speed, power and socialisation) advantage related to 'biological' males or non-medicalised transgenders.

On the other hand, the gender-based categories of sport competitions provide enjoyment and a sense of common identity for many participants. On a social level, women and men often enjoy sporting involvement in segregated teams – as has been demonstrated by the community, identity, friendship, loving and sexual relationships enjoyed by many lesbians who have played team sports such as softball, hockey, soccer and cricket (Faderman, 1992; Caudwell, 2004; Cahn, 1994, Lenskyj, 1995; Krane and Romont, 1997, Rowe and Symons, 2001). Most Games' participants are relatively well-off white gay men and lesbians who believe in the 'naturalness' of the two-sex system. Furthermore, most were socialised into traditional ways of doing sport – and this is what they enjoy and want to do well in. A plethora of gender styles still have the supposed bedrock of two sexes. The plethora of sexualities – orientations, pleasures, and practices – are still bound up in certain anatomically sexed configurations. The majority – gay men desire men's bodies and lesbians desire women's bodies. Or is it this straightforward? Queering sex, understanding the ambiguity of sex and gender – emphasising differences as well as celebrating a vast variety of sexed and gendered identities may be the way to go.

The communities of the Gay Games – gay, lesbian, bisexual, transgender, intersex and queer people of the world – have little in common except their sex and gender transgression. They challenge heteronormativity and the dominant gender order. Both the sports and especially the cultural events of the Gay Games, at least since Gay Games IV, have provided opportunities to include and affirm a diversity of gender styles and sexualities. The Gay Games are leaders in these inclusive policies and practices, but they may need to stage a more imaginative and transformative sports program if the Gay Games are to realise their promise.

Notes

1 For further discussion of issues raised in this chapter, please see 'Transexed conundrums' and other related chapters from the unpublished PhD thesis, "The Gay Games: The play of sexuality, sport and community', by Caroline Symons, Victoria University, 2004.
2 According to Ferguson-Smith this proportion is broadly consistent with what had occurred in previous Olympic Games (1998: 360–64).
3 The Gay Games were originally named the Gay Olympic Games, however, the USOC prevented the founding organisers from using this title with a costly legal battle. The USOC under US federal law had monopoly use of this word. The USOC had not objected to the Armchair Olympics, Armenian Olympics, Special Olympics, Handicapped Olympics, Police Olympics, Dog Olympics, Xerox Olympics, Diaper Olympics, Rat Olympics and Crab Cooking Olympics, all events held within the USA during the 1970s and early 1980s (Waddell and Schaap 1996: 150–51). Gays were deemed an unsuitable group and the USOC feared that their Olympic association could jeopardise the budget of the official Olympics to be held in Los Angeles in 1984.
4 ACT UP – Coalition To Unleash Power. Founded in the US in the early 1990s with offshoots in Europe and Australia. A radical coalition of peoples dedicated to protest, civil disruption and political action that highlights the plight of HIV/AIDS sufferers and the perceived lack of action by government and health authorities on this issue.
5 The ASC stipulated a sunset clause on this bill to allow for medical research into the sports performance of M–F post-operative transgenders to assess this fairness issue. Whilst research was conducted transgender athletes should be able to compete in sport.
6 Federation of Gay Games minutes, March 1992 – and outlined in Policy and Procedures of Gay Games IV and Cultural Festival. Athletics Registration Book, 1994. Archived in San Francisco Public Library: Federation of Gay Games Archive, Box 2, Series V, folder 10.
7 According to Thompson, less than 10 per cent of M–F's live as desired sex through SRS within the United States. Due to the more expensive and invasive procedure, and even less satisfactory SRS of F–M (hysterectomy, inability to construct a viable penis, etc.), even fewer F–M undergo full SRS, with most stopping at a radical mastectomy.
8 Transsexual Menace are silent in print on these practical issues – although their activism against being pathologised is well documented.
9 Elizabeth Riley is the Director of the Gender Centre in Sydney, the peak advocacy and welfare organisation for transsexual and transgender persons in NSW. Riley was the main advisor on the transgender policy for Gay Games VI in Sydney 2002.
10 Policy on Transgender Issues, contained in Special Needs section of Gay Games V website at address: http://www.gaygames.nl/Amsterdam/specialneeds/index.html, accessed 23 July 1998.

11 From ongoing correspondence with Gay Games VI organisers. The exact nature of these complaints was queried, but no response was received from the organisers in Amsterdam who were involved with the implementation of this policy.

12 One hundred and twenty transgender people indicated an interest in participating in Sydney 2002. Forty-one actually registered as transgendered (cf. Symons, 2004).

13 See Memorandum on this Transgender Policy, written by Quentin Buckle, Director of Equity and Diversity Portfolio, Sydney 2002 Gay Games Board. This memorandum was emailed to interested parties by Suganthi Chandramohan, Outreach and Community Development Manager, Sydney 2002 Gay Games Ltd, dated, Thurs December 6, 2001, 11.05 a.m. Also see Sydney 2002, *Sydney 2002 Gay Games VI Gender Policy*, Adopted 10 July 2002 (final policy), p. 7.

14 This meeting was made known through two interviews: one with the Chair of the Women's Advisory Committee of Sydney 2002, Kate Rowe; and the other with Elizabeth Riley. These interviews were conducted by phone in May and July of 2001 respectively and notes were taken during the course of the interviews.

15 It must be presumed that a person is of the sex they assert they are. From legal notes attached to Women's Golf Australia's Transgender Participation policy. These notes and the policy were written by Moira Rayner – past Equal Opportunity Commissioner of Victoria.

16 Memorandum from Elizabeth Riley, dated 16 July, 2001, p. 2.

17 Borrie cites the FGG as strong proponents of drug testing during the Gay Games in his final report as the Director of Sport for Sydney 2002.

18 Phone conversation with Chris Mueller, manager of the netball competition, Sydney 2002 Gay Games. Conducted on 12 October 2003.

19 Netball Australia promoted participation in the Games through membership mailouts and emails, but with little response. Mueller used his networks with more success, eventually recruiting a retired senior office bearer from Netball NSW to act as the competition manager and advisor.

Archival material

'Special Needs' Policy Document, Gay Games V website, <http://www.gaygames.nl/amsterdam/specialneeds/index.html.> (accessed 20 June and 23 July 1998).

SFAA, *Gay Games IV Policies' Gay Games IV and Cultural Festival. Athletes Registration Book*, 1994, Archived in San Francisco Public Library: Federation of Gay Games Archive, Box 2, Series V, folder 10.

Unity '94, *Gay Games IV Policies' Gay Games IV and Cultural Festival. Athletes Registration Book (1994) p.7*, 1994, Archived in San Francisco Public Library: Federation of Gay Games Archives, Box 2, Series V, folder 10.

Quentin Buckle, Director of Equity and Diversity Portfolio, Sydney 2002 Gay Games Board, *Memorandum on Transgender Policy, Gay Games VI, Thursday 6 December, 11:05 am*, 2001, Archived in Victoria University Library: Caroline Symons Gay Games Personal Archive.

Elizabeth Riley, Director of the Gender Centre, *Observations Concerning the Gay Games IV and V Policies. Facsimile Addressed to Caroline Symons, Dated 16 July, 2001*, Archived in Victoria University Library: Caroline Symons Gay Games Personal Archive.

Sydney 2002 Gay Games Ltd, *Sydney 2002 Gay Games VI Gender Policy (final), Adopted 10 July, 2002*, Archived in Victoria University Library: Caroline Symons Gay Games Personal Archive.

Interviews

Chris Mueller, October 12, 2003 (by phone).
Roz Quarto, December 2001, New York.
Kate Rowe, May 2001 (by phone).
Elizabeth Riley, July 2001 (by phone).
Deb-Ann Thompson, October 2001 (by phone).

References

Altman, D. (2001) *Global sex*. Crows Nest, NSW: Allen & Unwin.

ASC (1995) Additional Comments Submitted to the Australian Federal Government During Formulation of the Sexual Discrimination Bill 1995: Australian Sports Commission.

Besnier, N. (1994) 'Polynesian gender liminality through time and space', in *Third Sex, Third Gender: Beyond Sexual Dimorphism in Culture and History*. New York: Zone Books, 285–329.

Birrell, S. and Cole, C. (1990) 'Double Default: Renee Richards and the Construction and Naturalisation of Difference', *Sociology of Sport Journal*, 7 (1): 1–21.

Borestein, K. (1994) *Gender Outlaw: On Men, Women and the Rest of Us*. New York: Routledge.

Borrie, S. (2003) *Sydney 2002 Gay Games and Cultural Festival Sports Department Final Report – March '03*. Archived in Victoria University, Sunbury Campus: Caroline Symons Gay Games Personal Archive.

Brook, B. (1999) *Feminist Perspectives on the Body*, Longman, Harlow.

Butler, J. P. (1990) *Gender Trouble: Feminism and the Subversion of Identity*. New York: Routledge.

Butler, J. P. (1993) *Bodies that Matter: On the Discursive Limits of 'Sex'*. New York: Routledge.

Cahn, S. K. (1994) *Coming on Strong: Gender and Sexuality in Twentieth-century Women's Sport*. Maxwell Macmillan, Canada: Free Press.

Califia, P. (1997) *Sex Changes: The Politics of Transgenderism*. San Francisco, CA: Cleis Press.

Caudwell, J. (2004) 'Out on the field of play: women's experiences of gender and sexuality in football contexts', in S. Wagg (ed) *British Football and Social Exclusion*. London: Routledge, 127–46.

Chase, C. (1998) 'Hermaphrodites with attitude: mapping the emergence of intersex political activism', *Journal of Gay and Lesbian Studies, The Transgender Issue* (edited by Susan Stryker), 4 (2): 189–213.

Comben, L. (1996) 'Transgender issues in sport: problems, solutions and the future', research paper submitted for Master of Laws, Faculty of Law, University of Melbourne.

Ekins, R. and King, D. (1997) 'Blending genders: contributions to the emerging field of transgender studies', *The International Journal of Transgenderism*, 1 (1): 1–17.

Elsas, L., Hayes, R. and Muralidharan, K. (1997) 'Gender verification at the Centennial Olympic Games', *Journal of Medical Association of Georgia*, 86: 50–8.

English, J. (1995) 'Sex equality in sport', in J. Morgan and K. Meier (eds) *Philosophic Inquiry in Sport*. 2nd edn. Champaign, Illinois: Human Kinetics

Faderman, L. (1992) *Odd Girls and Twilight Lovers: A History of Lesbian Life in Twentieth-century America*. London: Penguin.

Fausto-Sterling, A. (2000) *Sexing the body: gender politics and the construction of sexuality*, New York: Basic Books.

Ferguson-Smith, M. (1998) 'Gender verification and the place of XY females in Sport', in M. Harries *et al.* (eds) *Oxford Textbook of Sports Medicine*, 2nd edn. Oxford: Oxford University Press, 360–64.

Hargreaves, J. (1994) *Sporting Female: Critical Issues in the History and Sociology of Women's Sports*. London: Routledge.

Herdt, G. (1994) 'Introduction' in G. Herdt (ed) *Third Sex, Third Gender: Beyond Sexual Dimorphism in Culture and History*. New York: Zone Books, 63–72.

Hood-Williams, J. (1995) 'Sexing the athlete', *Sociology of Sport Journal*, 12: 290–305.

Krane, V. and Romont, L. (1997) 'Female athletes' motives and experiences at the Gay Games', *Journal of Gay, Lesbian and Bisexual Identities*, 2: 123–38.

Lamb, D. (1978) *Physiology of Exercise Responses and Adaptations*. New York: Macmillan.

Lenskyj, H. (1986) *Out of Bounds: Women, Sport and Sexuality*. Ontario: The Women's Press.

Lenskyj, H. (1995) 'Sexuality and femininity in sport contexts: issues and alternatives', *Journal of Sport and Social Issues*,18 (4): 19–33.

Money, J. and Ehrhardt, A. A. (1972) *Man and Woman, Boy and Girl: The Differentiation and Dimorphism of Gender Identity from Conception to Maturity*. Baltimore, MD: Johns Hopkins University Press.

Opie, H. (2001) 'Medico-legal issues in sport: The view from the grandstand', *Sydney Law Review*, 23 (3): 375–404.

Perkins, R., Griffin, A. and Jakobsen, J. (1995) *Transgender Lifestyles and HIV/AIDS Risk*, Kensington, NSW: School of Sociology University of New South Wales.

Raymond, J. (1979) *The Transexual Empire, The Making of the She-Male*. Boston, MA: Beacon Press.

Roscoe, W. (1994) 'How to become a berdache: towards a unified analysis of gender diversity', in R. Herdt (ed) *Third Sex, Third Gender: Beyond Sexual Dimorphism in Culture and History* New York: Zone Books, 329–73.

Rowe, K. and Symons, C. (2001) 'Girls Just Wanna Have Fun'. Unpublished Report on lesbian participation at EuroGames 2000, and implications for the Sydney 2002 Gay Games: NSW Dept. of Sport and Recreation.

Shapiro, J. (1991) 'Transsexualism: reflections on the persistence of gender and the mutability of sex', in J. Epstein and K. Straub, *Body guards: The Cultural Politics of Gender Ambiguity*. New York: Routledge, 248–79.

Sharpe, A. (1997) 'Naturalising sex differences through sport. An examination of the New South Wales transgender legislation', *Alternative Law Review*, 22 (1): 39–42.

Skirstad, B. (1999) 'Gender verification in competitive sport: turning from research to action', in T. Tannsjo and C. Tamurrini, *Values in Sport: Elitism, Nationalism, Gender Equality and the Scientific Manufacture of Winners*. London: E & FN Spon, 117–21.

Smit, I. (1998) 'Transexuals marginalised', *Wordt Vervolgd, Gay Rights, Special Edition*, July/August, 22–26.

Symons, C. *The Gay Games: The Play of Sexuality, Sport and Community*. PhD Victoria University, 2004

Waddell, T. and Schaap, D. (1996) *Gay Olympian: The Life and Death of Dr. Tom Waddell*. New York: Alfred A. Knopf Inc; Distributed by Random House.

8   Catching crabs

Bodies, emotions and gay identities in mainstream competitive rowing

Gareth Owen

Introduction

> We should not ignore that the Twickenham regatta had a moment of its own, when the umpire starting the heats of the Delta RC [gay rowing club] v Thames Tradesmen in the men's veteran coxless four, announced:
>   'I will not start this race till you are both straight.'
>   After a quick conference amongst the Delta crew, they decided to ignore the umpire and row anyway.
>   Various spectators were wondering why the rest of the Delta boys collapsed in laughter.
>
> (Tideway Slug: Jan–June 2001)

This extract from the Tideway Slug,[1] derives its humour from the sometimes ironic position of gay men within the compulsory heterosexual world of mainstream competitive sport. The scene also suggests that visible gay bodies have the potential to undermine heteronormativity; but the image of a 'quick conference' before deciding to row, also hints at the tensions and contradictions of performing 'out' gay masculinities in mainstream competitive sport.

So what are the decisions that need to be made before deciding to 'row anyway'? What motivates gay men to row in the rough waters of mainstream competitive sport, and how are gay masculine identities performed in competition? Is there anything at stake when a gay crew goes head to head with an assumed heterosexual crew, and why row as a gay crew anyway?

In this chapter I explore these issues using my experience as a participant observant novice rower in an English gay rowing club. Using a reflexive ethnographic approach I focus on my body as an instrument of data collection and explore how sporting narratives can be used to investigate the complex relationships between the body, emotion and the construction of gender and sexual identities. I examine how writing the self into ethnographic narratives helps the researcher to engage with the sensuous and emotional aspects of embodiment, and how self-narrative can be used as a sensitising tool to 'open up' the data collected from fieldwork and interviews. In this study, I view competitive sport as an *emotionally charged arena* in which gender and sexual identities are performed relationally within the prevailing discourses of heteronormativity.

Background

Emotions in sport

The significance of sport as an embodied experience is only brought to life by the amplificating effect of emotions. Elias and Dunning (1986) demonstrated that a principal function of sport is the 'arousal of pleasurable forms of excitement' in an arena structured by competition, rules and regulations which create tension and facilitate a 'controlled decontrolling of emotions'.

Reviews of emotion in sport sociology have been undertaken by Ferguson (1981) and Duquin (2000), but emotions tend to remain an incidental rather than a central category of analysis in the sociology of sport. Maguire (1992) in particular, has attempted to draw our attention to the importance of emotions in sport, and building on the work of Elias, has suggested a dialogue with other perspectives.

Recent scholarship from the sociology of emotions proposes that emotions are the essential link between agency and structure (Bendelow and Williams, 1998; Layder, 1997). Barbalet (2002: 1) argues that 'without the emotions category, accounts of situated actions would be fragmentary and incomplete' because 'all actions and indeed reason itself, require appropriate facilitating emotions if successful actions or reason are to be achieved'. Emotions power our desires, cognition, decisions and actions by amplifying the significance of our social interactions.

Kemper (1978) developed a socio-relational perspective of emotions from a general analysis of empirical studies which consistently shows that power and status are fundamental dynamics in all social relations. Kemper uses this to develop a predictive model of emotion, which demonstrates that much of human emotion arises from the 'real, anticipated, recollected, or imagined outcomes of power and status' in social relations (1984: 371). According to Kemper, emotions therefore arise out of the dynamics of *power* and *status* between 'self' and 'other' in social interaction – different emotions arising depending on whether the dimensions of power and status are in excess, adequate or insufficient. The advantage of Kemper's theory of emotion is that relations of power and status, as well as being the fundamental dynamics of competitive sport, are also at the heart of Connell's (1987) theory of the gender order. Kemper (1990: 221) highlights the centrality of emotion in social practice by pointing out that 'if power and status are useful dimensions for descriptive and analytic purposes they should also be useful in accounting for social processes in which relationships are the focus'. Emotions are therefore the 'energising factor' in the 'dynamic interplay between power and status' in competitive sport and the gender order.

Having established the ubiquitous nature of power, status and emotion in social relations, I now focus on shame and pride, which I suggest are important emotions in the gay 'coming out' process as well as being of particular significance in the practice of sport.

The shame/pride nexus

Probyn (2000: 13) has argued that dynamics of competition in sport focus attention on the body as 'a frequently shamed entity', which reminds us 'of the visceral
dynamics of pride, shame and bodily affect in ways that have been notably missing from much feminist and cultural analysis'. Turning her attention to the Gay
Games, Probyn points to linguistic manoeuvres which recast 'competitors' as
'participants' in order to redefine gay sport as an all-inclusive co-operative activity. It is claimed that participants win not by beating other participants but by
achieving their personal best, and in this way pride becomes the only officially
recognised emotion at the Gay Games. With no competition and no losers, the
emotion of shame has been erased. Though it is debatable if such a manoeuvre
changes the dynamics of competition, it is an attempt to make sport more accessible to those who have felt excluded by ability, age, gender or sexuality.
However, such manoeuvres to deny or erase the emotion of shame from gay sport,
inevitably suggest shame's fundamental power in human interaction. Probyn
argues:

> One of the most striking features of the narratives of gay pride... is the way in
> which pride operates as a necessity, an ontology of gay life that cannot admit
> its other. Of course, gay and lesbian accounts of pride are not alone in the
> erasure of shame. It is perhaps more intriguing that sociological accounts of
> sport in the main refuse to enter into the dynamics of competition and the
> bodily experience of shame that so often accompanies sport.
>
> (Probyn, 2000: 26)

Therefore 'if we are to continue to mobilize the figure of Pride', we must also pay
attention to its mirror image and 'far from jettisoning shame, competition and
the other deeply corporeal affects found in a queer/sport nexus', they should be
taken into our theories (Probyn, 2000: 26).

To incorporate shame into our theories we need an operational definition,
and for this we can call upon Scheff's (1990, 2003) careful analysis of shame
from the works of Cooley, Freud, Elias, Lynd, Goffman, Lewis and Tomkins.
Scheff's conceptual definition views shame as 'the large family of emotions that
include many cognates and variants, most notably embarrassment, guilt,
humiliation, and related feelings such as shyness that originate in *threats to the
social bond*' (2003: 255: emphasis in original). For Scheff, the maintenance of
social bonds is fundamental to human motivation, and threats to these bonds,
however slight (for example arising out of failure, criticism, sarcasm, inadequacy, misunderstanding or rejection), give rise to feelings of shame. This gives
shame a central position in social interaction and Scheff (2003: 239) names it
'the master emotion of everyday life'.

Gay masculinities in competitive sport

Having established that emotions link social actor with social structure and that they arise out of the dynamics of power and status in social relations, we can now link this to Connell's (1987: 98) framework of the gender order as 'a historically constructed pattern of power relations between men and women'. If emotions arise out of power relations they are potentially implicated as the 'energising factor' in the production of masculinities and femininities. The highly emotional tenor of sport is therefore a productive arena in which emotions might be used as an analytical lens on gender performance.

According to Connell (1995: 54) sport has become the 'leading definer of masculinity in mass culture'. Pronger (1990, 2000) and Griffin (1998) have highlighted that mainstream sport in North America and Europe is a heteronormative arena which remains generally hostile to the visible presence of lesbians and gay men, although discrimination is often experienced in subtle rather than explicit forms (Hekma, 1998; Elling *et al.*, 2003). The exclusion of gay men from sport is in part driven by the need to expel sexuality from a homosocial space which allows men opportunities for physical contact and emotional bonding. It is also perhaps to ensure that Messner's (1996: 225) 'normalizing equation' of 'athleticism = masculinity = heterosexuality', still adds up.

Kimmel (1994: 129) argues that 'masculinity is a homosocial enactment' demonstrated through 'an exaggerated set of activities' to other men who define and confirm the attainment of manhood. This creates a competitive dynamic where men are continually ranking themselves against each other. Sport is perhaps the most obvious arena where 'an exaggerated set of activities' is performed to demonstrate masculinity. However, as a place of performance there is an ever-present fear of failure and in this failure lurks a man's shame.

Sport is the arena where men *feel* close to that most exalted ideal of authentic heterosexual masculinity – the powerful, dominating figure of athletic manhood. Men use this competitive arena to measure up against this figure, and through their imitative performances get a sense and feeling for their own masculine identities. This is the process of masculine identification. The question here is, how do gay men identify with this hegemonic figure of *heterosexual* athletic masculinity in competitive sport? A number of authors have pointed to the contradictory position of gay men in the gender order (Connell, 1995; Edwards, 2005). If the acquisition of masculinity depends upon the repudiation of homosexuality as well as femininity, then gay men are left in an awkward position. The problem is well stated by Edwards.

> All of this leaves us with something of a conundrum, for if gay men are not real men at all, or if they are gender deviants whose relationship to masculinity is essentially one of lack, then how does this square with their attempts to reclaim the masculine, if only by desire?
>
> (Edwards, 2005: 51)

So, the visibility of gay men in sport has the potential to challenge the hetero-normative exclusive ownership of masculinity by straight men. However, the potential to challenge hegemonic masculinity is significantly compromised, because for some gay men at least, it would mean that they are challenging the very masculinity that they desire.[2] As Bersani (1988: 208) put it, 'the logic of homosexual desire includes the potential for a loving identification with gay man's enemies'. This may be implicated in Pronger's (2000) observation that gay community sport tends to reinforce rather than challenge the structures of mas-culine dominance and exclusivity in sport.

The study

Context and social setting

Rowing in the United Kingdom has a conservative image popularly defined by the University Boat Race and Henley Royal Regatta. The elitism of rowing stems from the idea of the 'gentleman amateur' which excluded anyone who

> competed for money, or have received payment for any kind of athletic exer-cise, or belong to a club containing 'mechanics or professionals' or be a 'mechanic or artisan' himself. The amateur also had to be an officer in the fighting or civil service, educated at a University or public school, or be a member of the liberal professions.
>
> (cited in ARA, 2004)

This discrimination persisted until 1956 when the sport was brought together under the governance of the Amateur Rowing Association (ARA). Nowadays the ARA promotes 'sport for all' and has an 'equity action plan' which aims to raise awareness and promote participation of minority groups. At grassroots level there is now much greater inclusively, but the hegemonic position of rowing as 'sport for men', is still maintained by the greater prestige men enjoy over women's rowing, particularly through elite events like Henley and the University Boat Race.

The Gay Rowing Club was founded in 1997 by a group of experienced rowers who came together to compete in the Amsterdam Gay Games. They were origi-nally attached to one of the existing mainstream rowing clubs, but decided to become a separate gay-identified club and were affiliated to the ARA in 1999. In 2001 the club successfully applied for an 'Awards for All' lottery grant, to buy equipment and to develop coaching. The significance of a gay-identified group of rowers did not go unnoticed within the mainstream rowing community. For instance, it originally rowed out of a mainstream club which had the commonly abbreviated name of 'A.K.', which in some quarters, was ironically converted to 'Gay. K.'. However, the club has been generally well accepted in the mainstream rowing community and it is affiliated to a mainstream club who provide a base in their boathouse for the club's equipment and social needs. The club usually has an active base of between 40 and 60 members and has introduced more than 100 people to rowing through its annual beginners courses. Membership tends to be predominantly white professional gay men spread across a wide age range and includes an active veteran squad. Women have rowed with the club but participation declined and during the period of this research there were no active women members. The club's main focus was to 'build a seriously competitive club with a recognised record of success,' as well as offering a 'busy social calendar'. The club regularly competes in mainstream rowing events around the country including the historic annual Head of the River Race[3] and at international gay sporting events.

Data collection

This is an ethnographic study of a gay rowing club and the main method of data collection was participant observation supported by in-depth interviews and documentary analysis. The participant observation part of the study was carried out between September 2001 and March 2003. Permission was obtained to conduct the research from the club's committee. I entered the club as a full participant novice[4] rower with no previous experience. The intensive training, which is a common feature in rowing clubs, began with an induction course followed by training sessions on the water and in the gym, usually three and sometimes four times a week. The study included participation in winter head races, summer regattas, training camps, ergometer tests[5] and full immersion in the social life of the club. In-depth interviews were conducted and fully transcribed with twelve key participants including six novices, two seniors, two coaches/committee members, and two gay men who rowed for mainstream clubs. Documentary analysis included information from the club's website, emails and general rowing sources.

Reflexive ethnography

Reflexive ethnography is a form of inquiry where the researcher uses his or her experience of participation in a culture 'to reflexively bend back on self and look more deeply at self–other interactions' (Ellis and Bochner, 2000: 740). Through reflexivity and narrative, the experience of the researcher is integrated and studied alongside the experience of other cultural members.

Entering the field of gay rowing, what struck me most was how my body became an instrument of data collection. The experience of learning to row focused attention on my body, through an intense coaching experience which aims to discipline power, movement and emotion. As well as focusing attention on embodied physical sensations such as exhaustion or blistered hands, I also noted that my body was central to an emotional experience induced in the dynamics of competitive sport. These experiences included comradeship, the elation of physical exertion, the shame of letting my crew down, pride in winning, desire for success and the disappointment of failure. As Ellis and Bochner

(2000: 741) point out, 'reflexive ethnographers ideally use all their senses, their bodies, movement, feeling and their whole being – they use the "self" to learn about the other'.

De Garis (1999) developed a form of reflexive ethnography from his experience as an active participant in the pro wrestling ring. Here he found there was a level of understanding which could only be achieved by attending to physical feelings, smells, taste and sounds. This he defines as 'sensuous ethnography' which as an epistemological framework 'requires ethnographers to reflect on, evaluate, and integrate their own sensuous experiences into the ethnographic text' (1999: 73). Sands (2002) has worked from a similar perspective in his research as a competitive sprinter and football player. Performance-based ethnography, or what Sands calls 'experiential ethnography', potentially brings the ethnographer closer to the cultural reality of team mates, through the rites of passage of shared somatic and kinaesthetic experience. For Sands (2002: 137), 'the nature of sport ethnography presents an exciting opportunity to use the tools of contemporary ethnography, especially reflexive narrative, to study athletes, sport and sport cultures. In this perspective, sport ethnography sits on the cusp of ethnographic innovation in methods and strategy'.

By emphasising emotions as a way of knowing in this study, I propose a form of reflexive investigation which may be termed *emotional ethnography*.

Sporting narratives

Rail (1998: xv) calls for postmodern accounts of sport to create 'critical space for diverse narratives and as many stories of the everyday relations of power, domination, resistance and struggle in sport, as they are articulated through issues of race, ethnicity, gender and sexuality'. I take this up in this chapter, working on a sporting narrative which explores the performance of gay identities, by drawing on the emotional and embodied experience of sport. Writing the self into narrative is a central feature of reflexive ethnography and has 'the potential to challenge disembodied ways of knowing' (Sparkes, 2002: 100). Rowing narratives in sociology have been used previously by Porterfield (1999) who examined her experience of becoming an athlete in her forties, and by Tsang (2000) who explored aspects of identity in top-level international women's rowing.

Here I attempt what Richardson (2000: 11) describes as 'an evocative representation' by telling the tale of rowing up to the start of a race, in a layered narrative woven with personal reflection, quotations from interviews, field notes and emails. In this way I tell a story which combines my voice with the voices of other gay rowers, to create a poly-vocal text. The narrative is layered with interpretation, where I start making connections to theory. I draw attention to the 'fictional' aspects of my writing, in that the text is constructed as a device to present my experience and interpretation. The reflections, events and voices quoted, have all taken place, but not necessarily within the linear sequence of the narrative.

Catching crabs

Motivations

> A perfect mid summer's day in England. We are about to launch our boat for
> the last time, a culmination of ten months intensive training. At stake is our
> final opportunity to end the season by moving up the hierarchy of amateur
> rowing from novice to senior 4.
>
> Lowering the boat to the water we take our seats and make ready. I focus
> on the task ahead, determined to prove myself a competent oarsman and
> motivated towards that special experience of pride and fellow feeling by win-
> ning with my crew.
>
> But my stomach is already churning, anticipating rowing my body over
> the pain threshold, and even then, the possibility of failure. For a moment I
> find myself thinking:
>
> 'Why are we doing this?'

Motivations for joining the gay rowing club were generally framed by the desire
to participate in a sporting club where gay identities could be assumed rather
than explained or hidden. In addition, many rowers emphasised the social opportunities and camaraderie which the club provided, outside of the bars and clubs
of the gay scene. Some club members related previous experience of homophobia
in sport, although this was more commonly expressed as an alienation or discom-
fort with the prevailing atmosphere of heterosexism in mainstream sport clubs.
For instance:

Jeff: A lot of clubs are quite homophobic, I tried a couple and just thought if I
am going to invest a lot of time in this, I want to be comfortable to be out,
because I am too old to mess about in the closet really.

Another common motivating factor was to reclaim a feeling of pride which had
been stolen during shaming experiences of sport at school David remembers:

> I still carried with me this idea of the skinny, slightly awkward, not particu-
> larly athletic [boy]... so I suppose in quite a good way, I was able to challenge
> all those assumptions I had been handed at school... which is all about
> reclaiming the space for me really.

Perhaps the most complex motivator was a desire to engage with the dynamics of
competition. For most of the senior members of the squad, the desire to compete
and win was a significant feature of their motivation. However, the competitive
nature of amateur rowing came as a surprise to some of the new novice rowers.
For instance, Tom explains:

> It was strange because when I started I was going along socially but when I
> got there I found that rowing was very competitive and I realised that they

wanted to form teams, and teams to win. And that was an aspect I never thought would be in existence. But you know I can go with that – at times it was sort of tiresome but ultimately because we won that season it was worth it, yeah.

There is a tension between the club's aim of 'making rowing a fun activity for rowers at all levels' and trying to 'build a seriously competitive' squad in mainstream competition.[6] A tendency towards exclusion by ability would be a common structural feature of small clubs with limited resources but this also becomes a consequence of a commonly held vision in the club, as expressed here by Steve:

> I felt I had something to prove to the rest of the world, the rowing world – that gay rowers can be as good as straight rowers - this was always one of my core motivations. Which is why I am not really interested in having a separate gay rowing club which is not competitive.

Shame and performance

Now the boat is launched and we proceed slowly up the river towards the start. Rowing is not just about muscular power and physical fitness. A rowing boat is a fragile unstable shell which must be balanced by delicate adjustments of body in relation to crew, boat and water. It is about disciplining the body to move in perfect synchrony. Sometimes it happens – instinctive harmony, kinetic ecstasy, rowing in the zone – this is the indescribable jouissance of sport.

Sadly the jouissance of our novice rowing has been somewhat dampened by crabs this season. Catching a crab is a catastrophically bad stroke caused by failure to extract the oar from the water cleanly. I remember catching a crab – the oar ripped violently from my hands, knocking me backwards as the boat lurched alarmingly from side to side. Forward momentum suddenly lost, I fought to recapture my oar as my startled crew worked to reset and balance the boat. Catching that crab induced performance anxiety and an experience of shame, worrying that I was the weakest link and letting my crew down.

How does shame affect our experience in sport?

Catching crabs can be difficult to shake from the mind for they cling to memory, and become a heavy burden to carry in your next race. The shaming potential of catching a crab was explained by David:

David: Because rowing is such a choreographed thing, because there are eight people doing supposedly exactly the same thing – if one of you gets it wrong – firstly it is very visible, and secondly, it buggers it for everybody because it knocks the rhythm of the boat. It is the fear of being the one

who is screwing up and being seen to screw up. So, 'Let it not be me!' is
the big prayer you utter at the start.

GO: Is it attached to shame in any way?

David: Oh yes. Shame is about – 'Let it not be seen to be me' – you know, I don't
want to be *seen* to fail in front of all these people.

So catching crabs are moments of exposure where sporting performance has been
interrupted by failure, and to use Probyn's (2000: 23) words the body is 'covered
in shame'. Catching a crab becomes a painful negative 'experience of the self by
the self' (Tomkins, 1995: 136) where the inadequacy of your performance is
exposed to crew, competitors and further magnified by the presence of spectators.
It also hints at shame being an experience of non-conformity where one is out of
step and less competent in the choreography of life. Thinking back to Scheff's
(2003) model of shame – catching a crab signals a threat to the social bond
within the crew, and therefore serves as a powerful motivator to reconnect by
restoring pride through better performance.

One crew member had been unfortunate enough to catch crabs in several of
our races and as a result seemed to carry a heavy burden of shame. During the
post-race debrief – or 'debitch' as the cox liked to call it – the crab catcher stood
slightly outside the circle, silent with head down, bringing to mind Sedgwick's
evocative description:

Shame floods into being as a moment, a disruptive moment... Indeed, like a
stigma, shame is itself a form of communication. Blazons of shame, the
'fallen face' with eyes down and head averted – and to a lesser extent, the
blush – are semaphores of trouble, and at the same time of a desire to recon-
stitute the interpersonal bridge.

(Sedgwick, 1993: 5)

Camp and butch rowing

We stop rowing for a while and wait in the sunshine as a queue of boats
edge closer to the start. We are wearing our one piece lycra rowing kit,
fetishised by some because of the way it displays muscle and – if it is big
enough – that powerful symbol of masculinity, the phallus. In a rather camp
tension breaker, crew members 7 and 8 pull the straps off their shoulders to
ensure an even tan. Our kit has been a focus for gender subversion before,
with remarks like 'does my bum look big in this'. I also remember proudly
wearing my new kit in front of a friend, rather hoping that my display would
create the desired association with athletic masculinity. Unfortunately he
read it rather differently, and castrated my strutting ego by suggesting it
looked like I was wearing a woman's bathing costume. So much for the
phallus.

How do we perform gay masculinities in sport?

Butching it up and camping it up were both stylistic features of rowing in a gay crew and the shared ironic understandings were important in maintaining bonds and camaraderie. As Tom explains:

> I felt comfortable in Delta because people could laugh at the same jokes... I can be camp and because they know what I was talking about I didn't fear having to hide that.

A speculative subversion of the masculine image of rowing became a recurring conversation in the pub after training. We imagined ourselves rowing in hooped skirts, another time in tartish drag and then in long white Audrey Hepburn gloves. However, these were private imagined moments of subversion, while in public we tended to conform to 'appropriate' masculine behaviour, ironically policed by reminders to 'butch it up'.

At one regatta, high after winning a race, we discussed how our opposing crew might feel in defeat against gay men. Speculative drag appeared again – this time imagining the enhancing effect of victory in pretty bonnets or 'big hair' wigs. We enjoyed the idea until reminded how silly we would look in defeat, and saw the shameful spectacle of our wigged and vanquished crew attempting to vacate the scene unnoticed.

These discussions showed an awareness of the contradictory position of gay masculinities in mainstream rowing and the potential to subvert performances of hegemonic masculinity. But this was never the primary objective, which was emphasised by one of our coaches in the dictum 'you are rowers first and gay men second', and most of the oarsmen seemed to agree with this. However, despite the rule of conformity the visible presence of a gay-identified crew still provided some opportunities to challenge the heteronormativity of the sport, for instance in public shows of affection between gay partners at regattas. Indeed, it is important not to underestimate how difficult it still is for some men to be publicly identified as gay. For instance, returning to our rowing kit once more, Rob explains how:

> I found it difficult when we went to competitions because for the very first time I was wearing that little black number which singled me out as gay, which is what I had been avoiding my whole life. It was a very big test with conflicting emotions of trying to compete as well as being '*out*'.

The persistent shame of being identified as gay is hinted at here and serves to remind us that the edifice of gay pride may still be a shaky one, for as Munt (1998: 4) points out, we have 'imposed a heterodoxical sense of pride' and 'its counterpoint of shame is no more (or less) real'.

Desire and identification in sport

We now turn the boats and prepare to line up with our opponents. It's that same crew who we have raced twice before already this season. On both occasions we led until our chances were scuppered by catching a crab. I try hard not to look at my opposite number in seat 6, remembering him very well from our first meeting. In a show of cocksure bravado he had shouted over to us before the race, asking if we were their opponents. He had taken his shirt off to reveal an impressive physique of muscle and hairy chest, topped off by a crew cut. Snatching a quick look I experienced conflicting emotions. Part of me did feel intimidated by his confident display but this also made me more determined to win the race. But perhaps the most disconcerting feeling was that I desired his dominant beef-cake masculinity. This feeling had to be sublimated because we were about to go head to head, and this was the arena of competitive sport not the arena of homosexual desire.

How do we negotiate masculine desire in competitive sport?

Masculine identification and the erotic side of participating in sports were both acknowledged as motivating factors for involvement in rowing. For instance:

Steve: I could see the erotic side when we went to regattas. It used to be very exciting.

Dominic: It was a really hot day and most of the guys took their shirts off and although I didn't fancy any of the guys *per se*, just the whole thing, the naked flesh and the sweat and the sunshine, was really homoerotic.

The work of Bech (1997) might be used to interrogate my conflicting emotions in the above episode. For Bech, masculinity is in part constituted by men through a process of gazing at each other. This gazing puts men in relation to one another, and each man assesses his masculinity both in relation to other men, and in relation to the cultural fantasy of the *ideal* man. Muscle is an obvious signifier of masculinity, and Bech uses the practice of building muscle to illustrate how the gym is a social space which allows men to discreetly gaze at each other in the process of 'modelling oneself as a man' (1997: 50). A man must constantly make the decision to be a man, and he must gaze at other men to compare and rate himself between the poles of ideal and failed masculinity. It is a process of comparison which provokes 'a wish, a longing, a desire' to be more like one man and less like another.

Reflecting on this I could detect 'a wish, a longing, a desire' to be like my opposite number in seat 6, for he embodied a form of masculinity with which I would most like to be identified as a man. However, to lose the race implied – in a symbolic sense at least – a lack of masculinity in relation to my chosen model, and within this failure I experienced a feeling of shame. However, my desire to identify with this man and my desire to prove my masculinity in relation to him, was further complicated by a layer of sexual desire. These observations illustrate the complexities, difficulties and possibilities of sport as a place of masculine identification and desire. This theme is further highlighted by Bech below:

But the connections between wish, longing, body images, togetherness, sharing, security, excitement, equality and difference in relation to other men which are intrinsic to identification make it impossible to keep it apart from eroticism...Identity wish and identity experience are not the same as erotic wish and erotic experience, but they turn into one another, unless one prevents them from doing so.

(Bech, 1997: 55)

The possibility that identification might turn to erotic desire, explains why boundaries are drawn around explicit homosexuality in sport. Paradoxically, the same connection hints at why gay sports groups might reinforce rather than challenge the oppressive features of mainstream competitive sport, for as suggested here and by Bersani (1988: 208), the ability to challenge hegemonic masculinity may be compromised by its erotic attractions. This might be further compromised where gay men experience the linking of homosexuality with femininity as gender shaming, increasing the desire to identify and conform to hegemonic masculine ideals. For instance:

Dominic: If I am gay then what does it mean? Does it mean I am not a man? Does it mean I am some kind of hermaphrodite? And so I think, well for me it is important to be able to identify role models who could show that you could be stereotypical male and gay.

GO: Stereotypical male and gay?

Dominic: I am thinking somebody who is a leader, strong, made a mark on history, a good fighter, a good soldier, sporting. Those are all traits that you associate with a man.

Dominic illustrates how gay masculine identification can be a contradictory position in the gender order, becoming both subordinate and complicit with hegemonic masculinity.

Queer sport – concluding comments

Finally we are called to the line. It is now our turn to race – our turn to prove ourselves in the arena of masculinity – a test of strength, skill, power and determination to win. The tension builds as the tetchy umpire waits for the coxes to bring the boats into line. My heart is pounding my chest. Adrenalin floods my body. Feeling sick – is this fight or flight? Our cox calls, 'Come forward to row', and we move up the slide with our oars squared in the water, our bodies compressed like coiled springs. This is it. Last chance. 'Let it not be me'. And the umpire calls:
   'ATTENTION'!
   'ROW'.

So what is at stake when these two crews line up to race? On one level there is the dynamic of competition structured by winning and losing – pride and shame. On another level the visibility of a gay crew can queer the heteronormativity of sport. The dynamics are described here by Steve:

> Intrinsically sport is competitive. It is about beating someone else or another team or another crew. It is about being faster, fitter, being stronger, better skilled, whatever the activity is. In some way you are proving you are better than them. In some way that competitiveness is often mixed with this macho thing – you know – traditionally a macho thing is about being stronger, about being bigger, about being more courageous, whatever, than the other person, or team. So for somebody to sort of challenge that by – 'Well I am gay actually' – you know it doesn't sit comfortably. It contradicts.

However, it would seem that the challenge of a gay crew in mainstream sport is primarily framed by proving that gay men are as masculine as straight men, and this can only really be confirmed by winning the race. The political limits of the challenge are summed up by Jeff:

> I can stand until I am blue in the face and argue for gay pride, gay rights and stuff. But for a lot of people it will just go over their heads. I mean I could say that we are as strong as you are, we are as fit as you are, but until they have been beaten by us and we are standing there holding the pot, it doesn't quite hit home. It is a tightrope because equally – if we do badly – we reinforce the negative image of gay men [as] a bunch of 'Marys'[7] who couldn't quite cut it.

It seems that by trying to disavow the association of femininity and homosexuality by proving our masculine status in competition, we are rowing a 'tightrope' between gay pride and gay shame. The visibility of gay men in sport might indeed trouble the normative equation of 'athleticism=masculinity=heterosexuality', but hegemonic masculinity is still reproduced by the mandatory performance of *competitive* masculinities in conventional sport.

Notes

1   The Tideway Slug is a popular satirical rowing website, commenting on recent happenings in the many rowing clubs based on the river Thames in the United Kingdom. (http://www.twrc.rowing.org.uk/slug/slug.htm)
2   Desire here can be both on the level of identification and libidinal.
3   The Head of the River Race was founded in 1926. It is a processional race for men's eights rowed on the River Thames over the 4¼ mile University Boat Race course in reverse. With 420 novice, senior and elite crews and 3,750 competitors, it is believed to be the largest single rowing race in the world.
4   Rowers are classified by the Amateur Rowing Association (ARA) as novice, senior (4/3/2/1) and elite. Rowers move up through the divisions by winning races. Divisions are also made by age, gender and weight.

5 Indoor rowing machines which test muscle strength and endurance. The tests are used to rank levels of fitness and can be used in crew selection.
6 Taken from the club's website on 3 September 2001. The issue of providing opportunities for recreational rowing in a largely competitive club structure has also been noted by the ARA (see endnote 5).
7 Slang implying feminine men.

References

Amateur Rowing Association (2004) <http://www.oara-rowing.org/about/whatara.php> (accessed 5 October, 2004).

Barbalet, J. (ed) (2002) *Emotions and Sociology*. Oxford: Blackwell.

Bech, H. (1997) *When Men Meet: Homosexuality and Modernity*. Cambridge: Polity.

Bendelow, G. and Williams, S. J. (eds) (1998) *Emotions in Social Life: Critical Themes and Contemporary Issues*. London: Routledge.

Bersani, L. (1988) 'Is the rectum a grave?' in D. Crimp (ed), *AIDS: Cultural Analysis, Cultural Activism*. London: MIT Press.

Connell, R. (1987) *Gender and Power*. Cambridge: Polity.

Connell, R. (1995) *Masculinities*. Cambridge: Polity.

de Garis, L. (1999) 'Experiments in pro wrestling: toward a performative and sensuous sport ethnography', *Sociology of Sport Journal*, 16 (1): 65–74.

Duquin, M. (2000) 'Sport and emotions' in J. Coakley and E. Dunning (eds), *Handbook of Sports Studies*. London: Sage.

Edwards, T. (2005) 'Queering the pitch? gay masculinities', in M. S. Kimmel, J. Hearn and R. W. Connell (eds), *Handbook of Studies on Men and Masculinities*. London: Sage, 51–68.

Elias, N. and Dunning, E. (1986) *Quest for Excitement: Sport and Leisure in the Civilising Process*. Oxford: Blackwell.

Elling, A. de Knop, P. and Knoppers, A. (2003) 'Gay/lesbian sport clubs and events: places of homo-social bonding and cultural resistance?' *International Review for the Sociology of Sport*, 38 (4): 441–56.

Ellis, C. and Bochner, A. (2000) 'Autoethnography, personal narrative, reflexivity: researcher as subject', in K. Denzin and Y. S. Lincoln (eds) *Handbook of Qualitative Research*. Thousand Oaks, CA: Sage, 733–768.

Ferguson, J. (1981) 'Emotions in sport sociology', *International Review of Sport Sociology*, 16 (1): 15–23.

Griffin, P. (1998) *Strong Women, Deep Closets: Lesbians and Homophobia in Sport*. Champaign, IL: Human Kinetics.

Hekma, G. (1998) '"As long as they don't make an issue of it...":Gay men and lesbians in organized sports in the Netherlands'. *Journal of Homosexuality*, 35 (1):1–23.

Kemper, T. D. (1978) *A Social Interactional Theory of Emotions*. New York: Wiley.

Kemper, T.D. (1984) 'Power, status, and emotions: a sociological contribution to a psychophysiological domain', in K. R. Scherer and P Ekman (eds) *Approaches to Emotion*. Hillsdale, NJ: Erlbaum, 369–383.

Kemper, T. D. (1990) 'Social relations and emotions: a structural approach', in T.D. Kemper (ed.), *Research Agendas in the Sociology of Emotions*. Albany, NY: State University of New York Press, 207–37.

Kimmel, M. S. (1994) 'Masculinity as homophobia: Fear, shame, and silence in the construction of gender identity', in H. Brod & M. Kaufman (eds) *Theorizing Masculinities*. London: Sage.

Layder, D. (1997) *Modern Social Theory: Key Debates and New Directions*. London: UCL Press.

Lewis, H. (1971) *Shame and Guilt in Neurosis*. New York: Science Editions.

Maguire, J. (1992) 'Towards a sociological theory of sport and the emotions: a process-sociological perspective', in E. Dunning and C. Rojek (eds) *Sport and Leisure in the Civilizing Process: Critique and Counter-Critique*. Basingstoke: Macmillan, 96–120.

Messner, M. (1996) 'Studying up on sex', *Sociology of Sport*, 13 (3): 221–37.

Munt, S. (1998) 'Introduction', in S. Munt (ed) *Butch/Femme: Inside Lesbian Gender*. London: Cassell.

Porterfield, K. (1999) 'Late to the line: starting sport competition as an adult', in J. Coakley and P. Donnelly (eds), *Inside Sports*. London: Routledge, 37–45.

Probyn, E. (2000) 'Sporting Bodies: Dynamics of Shame and Pride', *Body and Society* 6 (1): 13–28.

Pronger, B. (1990) *The Arena of Masculinity*. London: GMP Publishers.

Pronger, B. (2000) 'Homosexuality and sport: who's winning?' in J. McKay, M. Messner and D. Sabo (eds) *Masculinities, Gender Relations, and Sport*. Thousand Oaks: Sage.

Rail, G. (ed.) (1998) *Sport and Postmodern Times*. New York: SUNY.

Richardson, L. (2000) 'New writing practices in qualitative research', *Sociology of Sport Journal*, 17 (1): 5–20.

Sands, R. (2002) *Sport Ethnography*. Champaign, IL: Human Kinetics.

Scheff, T. J. (1990) *Microsociology: Discourse, Emotion and Social Structure*. Chicago: University of Chicago Press.

Scheff, T. J. (2003) 'Shame in self and society', *Symbolic Interaction* 26 (2): 239–62.

Sedgwick, E. K. (1993) 'Queer performativity: Henry James's *The Art of the Novel*', *GLQ: A Journal of Lesbian and Gay Studies*, 1 (1): 1–16.

Sparkes (2002) *Telling Tales in Sport and Physical Activity: A Qualitative Journey*. Champaign, IL: Human Kinetics.

Tideway Slug (2001) <http://www.twrc.rowing.org.uk/slug/slug.htm> (accessed 8 September, 2004)

Tomkins, S. (1995) *Shame and its Sisters: A Slivan Tomkins Reader*. Ed. by E. K. Sedgwick and A. Frank. Durham, NC: Duke University Press.

Tsang, T. (2000) 'Let me tell you a story: a narrative exploration of identity in high-performance sport', *Sociology of Sport Journal*, 17 (1): 44–59.

9 Femme-fatale

Re-thinking the femme-inine

Jayne Caudwell

Introduction

This chapter, using a particular sport subculture, intends to inform understanding of normative gender and sexuality. Discussion relies on research from a larger ethnographic study of an 'out' lesbian football/soccer team. The research includes analysis of archival materials and club documents, semi-structured interviews with six players and participant observation.[1] The specific focus is how femme-ininities are [re]articulated in football spaces, such as on the pitch, in changing rooms, at training, during warming up and cool downs. The use of the term, prefixed with 'femme', is to denote femininity/ies as detached from immediate heterosexual relations. The inclusion of femme identifies and asserts femininity that is chosen, possibly for the female gaze. The intention is to generate further exploration and analysis of the spatiality of sporting femininity/ies from a feminist–queer perspective.

In many ways an out lesbian football team can be understood as offering resistance and challenge to compulsory heterosexuality. It is this disruption of normative sexuality and the dislocation of the regime of heterosexuality that can be understood as queer. Given evidence of obdurate heteronormativity in most sporting arenas (Griffin, 1998; Veri, 1999) the team can be described as a queer community. However, critical engagement with what constitutes normative and anti/non-normative, and how sex–gender–sexuality configurations are regulated within the subculture, is required before making claims that predominantly lesbian football teams are queer and/or that only lesbians queer sport spaces. Grosz (1995) stresses that lesbian and gay are not always synonymous with queer and she points out that queer relies on individuals setting 'themselves outside both the heterosexual as well as the gay communities, which, many claim, function as coercively, and as judgementally as each other' (1995: 216).

Relatively little is known about social relations that exist within lesbian sporting communities or how [hetero]normative lesbian communities can be. In other words, the possibility that lesbian players might reinforce the values, beliefs and status of normative culture. Through engagement with femme-inine players the chapter highlights how processes of marginalisation are complicated, multilayered and shifting. Such a project must remain mindful of Jagose's (1996) contention that:

> The inflection of queer that has proven most disruptive to received under-
> standings of identity, community and politics is the one that problematises
> normative consolidations of sex, gender and sexuality... and is critical of all
> those versions of identity, community and politics that are believed to
> evolve 'naturally' from such consolidations.
>
> (Jagose, 1996: 99)

In this vein, focus on femme-ininity/ies problematises the frequently imagined
normative consolidation of women–masculine–lesbian within footballing communities (Caudwell, 1999; 2003; Cox and Thompson, 2000; 2001; Mennesson
and Clement, 2003; Scraton *et al.* 1999; Williams, 2003).

In many ways analysis relies on the idea of identity, and it is worth making the
point at the outset, that advocacy of a fixed gendered/sexual identity is problematic. Some feminists, including queer theorists, have contested identity as stable
and authentic. Scott (1991, cited in Turner, 2000) goes so far as to argue that
claims of fixed identity are otiose to political projects. That said, identity has fea-
tured in critical accounts of gendered and sexual hierarchies and some feminists
deploy identity strategically to make visible women's lived experiences of power
relations. Given these tensions, this chapter refers to gendered and sexual 'identities' as a way to explore the complex [re]production of femme-ininity/ies.

[Sport]feminism and femme-ininity/ies

The relationship between feminist thought and an understanding of femininity is
not straightforward. Probably one of the most challenging moments, for me, was
when Germaine Greer publicly reprimanded Suzanne Moore's choice of hairstyle
and shoes ('fuck-me shoes'). Moore (1996) responded with an analysis of feminism, femininity and class. In short she argued: 'As someone who grew up with
punk and Madonna, I take it for granted that women dress to please themselves
and not men...' (1996: 294). Presentation of a feminine body, by women, in public spaces is an important issue for discussion. Moreover, embodiment of
femininity by women in the public domain of sport arenas continues to engage
sports feminists.

Theberge (1991) suggests that, for women in sport, femininity becomes spectacle. The body is central to this process and as a dressed and decorated object is used
to visually signify gender (Paechter, 2003). In addition to adorning signs of gender,
such as clothing, make-up and hairstyle, the body articulates gender via size, shape
and bulk, and gesture. Sports feminists have paid attention to femininity as artifice
and critical analysis of the operation of femininity for women actively involved in
sports discursively marked as 'male' provides testimony to the social construction of
gender. For example, Wesely (2001) argues that women body builders 'discipline
their bodies' (2001: 165) in order to adhere to the rules of [normative]femininity.
Through swimwear, breast implants, make-up, hairstyle and walk, bodies are made
to comply with normative gender ideals. Mennesson (2000) found that women
boxers also ensured they acted in conventional feminine ways, which included

walking and talking appropriately: 'All the respondents were keen to confirm their feminine identities both in and out of the ring. This affirmation involved choosing appropriate attire for the ring ("something sexy"), wearing mini skirts after competition, and having long hair' (2000: 28).

Brace-Govan (2002) argues that women's sporting bodies are judged within the confines of heterosexual desirability and Christopherson *et al.* (2002) clearly highlight the ways this happens for US soccer players in the 1999 Women's World Cup. It seems that women in sport must negotiate practices and discourses that operate to mark them as unquestionably feminine and heterosexual (Theberge, 1991). Critical accounts that expose these processes successfully illuminate sport as a hetero-patriarchal institution. However, returning to the dispute between Greer and Moore, I argue it is important to explore the complexities, intricacies and nuances of femininity and the possibilities femme-ininity presents for potent disturbance to heteronormativity. Therefore I advocate further interrogation of the political potential of femme-ininity/ies within feminist and queer thinking.

The research questions

Critical reflection on my previous research highlights the centring of female masculinity in analysis of gender and sexuality, and sports' power relations; hetero-patriarchy, heteronormativity and homophobia. Importantly, this research sought to illuminate the 'figure'[2] of the lesbian butch in football in England, and make legitimate the lesbian butch gender identity in sport. However, in the wake of this research it is apparent that focusing on butch has occluded in-depth understanding of the complexities and range of sporting femme-ininity/ies. Interestingly, Creed (1995) argues that lesbian bodies are imagined in particular ways. She identifies three stereotypes, within popular culture, as follows: 'the lesbian body as active and masculinized; the animalistic lesbian body; the narcissistic lesbian body' (1995: 88). It seems that the lesbian body has not been imagined as femme-inine and active.

Exclusive attention on the butch figure has been heavily criticised by an emerging queering of femininity (Brushwood Rose and Camilleri, 2002; Gomez, 1998; Harris and Crocker, 1997; Hurst, 2004). For example, Brushwood Rose and Camilleri seek to celebrate and complicate 'femme as a gender experience on its own terms, as an experience that expands, exceeds, and troubles the familiar framework or 'norms' of lesbian (butch) femme' (2002: 13). In short, the femme's contribution as a site/sight for recoding and re-articulation of gender and sexuality has been marginalised by the centrality of the butch. Femme-ininity/ies is/are often understood myopically, as belonging to butch or the butch–femme equation. In this way the femme is misunderstood and often dismissed as incomplete, fragile and duped. Harris and Crocker (1997) argue that within feminism specifically, femme-ininity/ies is/are understood pejoratively, as patriarchally imposed. They advocate a rereading of femme and femininity as radical, critical, subversive, empowering, transgressive, disruptive and chosen. This chapter's intent is not to position female masculinity and female femininity as binary opposites but to begin to think about how sporting practices and discourses, on a local level, impact on femme-ininity/ies.

The research question that informs the chapter reflects a concern with articulation and materialisation of femme-ininity/ies, and the possibility that femme-ininity/ies disrupt normative sex–gender–sexuality. Therefore, the research question is – how does femme-ininity/ies appear in a footballing subculture and what are the responses to its presence?

The research and the team

The team is part of a larger club, established in 1986 as a result of a group getting together after meeting on a 'Football for Women' class organised by a London Borough. As advertised on the club's website, the club 'was the first totally women-run team and the first predominantly lesbian team in London, possibly the UK'. At inception the club and team was set up 'in line with feminist principles of collective responsibility in decision making and also for a non-competitive squad selection policy to operate' (Huggett, 1997: 3). The main aims of the club, on foundation, were to promote football to women regardless of skill and ability. The club stood for a sense of lesbian community within the traditionally lesbian-phobic world of sport. Scorelines were deemed irrelevant. Lesbian visibility, lesbian solidarity and the pleasure of playing, for its own sake, and socialising were the main drivers. Committee meetings ran on a consensus system, which meant they could go on for hours since outcome was based on all players agreeing any decision.

Research for this chapter, drawn from a larger research project, includes participant observation during two playing seasons. The participant observation can be described as covert, although team and club are now aware of the research and the documentation of players' experiences. The disclosure was a result of feeling uncomfortable with the traditions of covert participant observation and believing that it is important to request permission to [re]tell women's stories. Previous research into women's football cultures relied on semi-structured interviews because covert participant observation seemed to undermine principles of feminist methodology (cf Stanley and Wise, 1993). However, after over ten years as an 'insider', playing for teams in London, the West Midlands and Yorkshire, it was felt that this status afforded valuable insights that would otherwise go untold. As Wheaton (2002) argues, 'there are some private worlds, including certain sport cultures, where only insiders have access to respondents' (2002: 240). An out lesbian team is such a sport culture. Participant observation seemed the best way to discover the everyday experiences of players. In addition, it allowed access to sport spaces, such as changing rooms and the field of play, which is central to any analyses of the spatiality of sexuality (Eng, 2003; Fusco, 1998; Pronger, 1994 and 1999).

The club is unusual in that it is one of few all-women run football clubs with a socio-political association. At the time the club was founded, members drew up a constitution which continues to underpin practice and policy. For example, members continue to acknowledge the original equal opportunities policy:

3.2 In the spirit of the club, all members will uphold the rights of all women to be free from oppressive, prejudicial and discriminatory treatment on the grounds of their gender and we challenge all sexism.

3.3 [...]We reject all forms of anti-lesbian and anti-gay behaviour. We challenge all forms of heterosexism and homophobia.

3.4 We uphold the rights of Black women, women of colour and women of all nationalities and cultures to be free from abuse and discrimination on the grounds of their colour, race, culture and/or nationality. We challenge all racism.

Similar statements exist for disabled women, older women and working-class women. In the early years members were encouraged to look at 'who is empowered and who is silenced in the group' (Huggett, 1997: 25). The alignment with lesbian feminism is also apparent in lyrics to songs players compiled for events such as the Gay Games and Gay Pride Marches.

I am LESBIAN, a big butch LESBIAN,
That's why I'm marching here today.
Nobody tells me who can love me,
So you can take all your CLAUSES away

I am a DYKE, Mum, a (hairy/happy) Dyke, Mum,
I want the world to know I'm GAY.
So please don't blank me, you should thank me.
Cos' I'm marching for all Women today.

(extract from *Songbook, Pride 1993*)

Reference to 'clauses' signals UK legislation (Section 28, 1986, introduced by a Conservative government) and right wing attempts to regulate (lesbian) sexuality.

The club has challenged numerous forms of homophobia including direct assault, charges of bringing the game into disrepute, disparaging comments from spectators and players, and more recently homophobic violation of the website. Copies of letters to the Greater London Women's Regional League (GLWRL), correspondence with the Women's Football Association (WFA, pre 1991) and the Football Association (FA, post 1991) detail incidents that occur on the field of play. One example follows:

... being a lesbian wasn't easy. You know, in the early 90s, the attitude you got from other teams, you know, we got kicked to pieces on a five a-side game, by a team that was good at football but were just kicking us. We reported the things they did to us and things they said to us but the league was powerless to deal with it effectively (extract from interview with former club secretary).

Direct assault is the most brutal form of homophobia experienced by players and an incident took place at a training venue booked by the club. A men's side refused to finish their session at the allocated change-over time and records detail how the coach (Gill) was treated after she asked the men to leave the pitch. One of the men pushed then punched her, then when she fell to the ground he started kicking her. The club minutes also record:

> Ali tried to intervene, Gill tried to defend herself, [the man] threw punches at Ali... [he] eventually backed off. 'Come on Mick its only a bunch of women' 'It's not a woman it's a lesbian'. [He] backed off shouting abuse, threatened to come back and get us 'fucking bunch of lesbians'.
>
> (Minutes from club meeting 28.01.95)

This is a chilling reminder of how violently men can mark football space and public space as male and heterosexual. The club wrote several letters demanding that fences surrounding the pitch be repaired, that the area be patrolled and that a member of security be present at change-over, surveillance cameras and improved lighting in the area be installed:

> What price do we have to put upon women's safety? Surely any commitment to equal opportunities must mean commitment to providing women with a safe opportunity to play football. Men do not face verbal or physical assault just for 'daring' to ask for a pitch they have pre-booked. We are in no position to intimidate men off of the pitch...
>
> (extract from letter sent to: leisure facility; local authority; local police and Sports Council, 1995)

The team now trains and plays at a different venue. League and cup games under observation constitute GLWRL fixtures and took place on Hackney Marshes. Hackney Marshes is a huge expanse of grassland in the heart of North East London. Within footballing folklore the mass of football pitches covering this open space are understood as an integral part of white working-class urban football culture. However, more recently the whiteness of Hackney Marshes and the many men's teams that occupy its countless pitches, marked out side-by-side and back-to-back, have been contested. In a national newspaper article entitled 'The United Nations of Hackney Marshes' (*The Guardian*, 21 May 2004) we are introduced to various teams: The Caribbeans, The Albanians, The Arabs, The Asians. Despite essentialist references to ethnicity, the account highlights emerging erosion of whiteness in grass roots football and within traditional working-class urban football space. Unfortunately, the account falls short of a complete overview of Sunday fixtures. Unsurprisingly, it fails to acknowledge The Women and The Lesbians; teams that play on the same pitches on a Sunday afternoon after the men have had the privilege of using the playing space first. The reason I specifically mention The Lesbians is because during research, three 'out' lesbian teams played their home fixtures on Hackney Marshes.

It is evident that football spaces are where power is materialised and where women's bodies are controlled and regulated. Football fields are places where processes of 'othering' occur. However, as van Ingen (2003) argues, 'lived space also produces critically important counterspaces that are the spaces for diverse, resistant and oppositional practices' (2003: 204). Focus on a lesbian-identified team helps illuminate some of the ways players create and produce footballing space, counter to popular cultural representations. Although such contestation is important, the aim of this research is to look beyond lesbian resistance, as founded on collective political identity, in order to explore complexities of sex–gender–sexuality.

The femme-inine player/defender

Since football is understood as male, and concomitantly assumed masculine, most work that explores players' experiences of embodiment and gender tends to capture accounts that reveal negotiation of [tom]boyish and butch (Caudwell, 1999; 2003; Cox and Thompson, 2000; 2001; Mennesson and Clement, 2003; Scraton, *et al.* 1999; Williams, 2003). Focus on female masculinity and football works either to celebrate the butch (Caudwell, 1999; 2003) or view her as a troublesome presence on the field of play; she is often seen as having potential to devalue 'women's' footballing status. Within lesbian feminist politics, butch similarly occupies a contentious position. Very simplistically, she is both abhorred (Jeffreys, 1993) and valorised (Case, 1998; Munt, 1998; Nestle, 1989; Roof, 1998). According to Morgan (1993) some aspects of feminism not only maligned butch but also the femme. Instead of viewing femme as having political power to redefine femininity (Nestle, 2002), it can be argued that some aspects of feminism have affected women's relationships to femininity, therefore squandering the potential of femininity as an effective challenge to heteronormativity.

Focus here on femme and butch reflects some discourses evident in the team. During participant observation it was noted that reference to butch and femme was frequent, and appeared to be understood as reclaimed lesbian-gender identification. For example, pre-match team talks, which usually take place in changing rooms or on the side of the pitch, provide a discursive space for marking players and the team according to notions of femme and butch and the butch–femme equation. More specifically, sitting in a grotty changing room (Hackney Marshes have a single storey quadrant of about 15 changing rooms and 'men's toilet' facilities) one Sunday afternoon with debris of the morning's and previous day's men's matches on the floor, benches and hangers, the person in charge of organising the side seemed stuck over where to position players on the pitch. During the brief moment of silence, a player suggested we line up butch–femme-butch–femme and so on. The line up reflects the spatiality of the team within the boundaries of the pitch and the assumed coupling of butch–femme. This coupling is contested when another player suggests that this might upset the cohesion of the butch back line; a suggestion that demonstrates the existence of an established line up. The 'butch back line' refers to the four defenders that form the last line of defence in front of the goalkeeper.[3] Interestingly, the reference to a butch back line [re]produces normative butch lesbian-gender on the football field. In this particular sport space the butch is produced as a viable player/defender, which is unusual given the social construction of sporting butch as an abject and abhorrent athlete (Caudwell, 1999). In changing rooms and during a pre-match team talk she is re-produced as a valuable member of the team; she is capable of protecting the goal and preventing the opposition from scoring and possibly winning. However, at the same time the butch is celebrated, the femme and femme-ininity are dismissed. The femme player is not recognised as a defender within the spatial arrangement of team line up. In this way, team tactics privilege the butch and marginalise the femme, and this practice alludes to assumptions of femme-ininity generally and more specifically within a lesbian-identified football team; too fragile.

Clearly this was a playful moment within football tactical team talk where, in this case, what is understood as lesbian-gender is used to articulate sexuality on the field of play. Those involved in marking players and the team in this way tend to be lesbian players who have been with the club for some time, or lesbian players who self-identify as femme or butch. In fact, these players often publicly squabble before or after games over who is more or less femme or more or less butch. Conversations take place as the team warms up or cools down together, either jogging in a group or forming a circle to stretch. Again this discursive ritual is playful, however, it indicates the ease with which lesbian players [re]claim and celebrate aspects of lesbian gender. However, in moments when the femme and butch figures suffuse football's landscape – in changing rooms, warming up/cooling down, on the field of play – it is the butch who becomes signified by football iconography as authentic. In other words, footballing attire is more likely to reify female masculinity than female femme-ininity. Not only is the butch visually signified, she is discursively marked given football's masculine tradition. Butch display is easier and therefore does not always represent subversion. The articulation of femme-inity is not so easy and the femme is often invisibilised or forced to work hard to establish her subjectivity.

Analyses of women's active involvement in sports defined as male, such as boxing (Halbert, 1997; Hargreaves, 1997; Mennesson, 2000), rugby (Carle and Nauright, 1999; Howe, 2001; Wright and Clarke, 1999), ice hockey (Theberge, 2000) and body building (Brace-Govan, 2002; Holmlund, 1997; Johnston, 1996; Wesely, 2001), indicate many ways participants embody femininity in order to present a body that is read as woman. It is usual to assume that such feminine display either functions to appease male gaze or is the corollary of hetero-patriarchal control and regulation. Such a reading forgets lesbian femme-ininity/ies and the lesbian gaze. Interestingly, given these arguments, and a return to the football team, it is evident that femme-ininity is marginalised on the field of play. In addition, playing attire is distinctly non-feminine. However, some players manage to femme-inize the process of wearing boots, shorts and shirts. Again, in changing rooms before a league game, Kate, a white player who has played field hockey for many years, a sport where skirts have been traditionally worn, begins to advocate the wearing of skirts for football as well (in the UK, field hockey has traditionally been a predominantly white and middle-class sport). She argues that she feels more comfortable in a skirt and that she enjoys wearing a hockey skirt because it feels right around her hips and thighs. Known for her lesbian femme-ininity she resists the usual wearing of shorts low on the hips and pulls the waistband to waist level. She displays the curves of her body which, incidentally, does not conform to 'ideal' size. There is a mixed response, some smile, some are indignant. A few gazes linger on her visible curves, enjoying her display. The mixed response can be understood if we consider the symbolic transgression her body, in the football changing room, offers. Kate's lesbian femme-ininity challenges the butch stereotype and assumptions that surround women footballers (Caudwell, 1999; Cox and Thompson, 2000; Williams, 2003), which also have currency within the team. Many players have successfully re-claimed woman–masculine–lesbian to an extent that can be understood as normative. In this specific context lesbian femme-ininity dislocates the public imagination (woman–masculine–lesbian *and* woman–feminine–heterosexual) and the 'locker room' practices (butch display) of a particular sport subculture.

Kate's embodied femininity reminds me of how another player, Kirsha, often turned up to summer games and training, ready to play, in tight, very short, bright coloured shorts and matching tight, small strapped top. As she arrived, players often greeted her with comments about her choice of clothing – too small, too tight, too much skin, too much leg, and too much body, instead of the usual 'hello'. I was privy to a conversation between three white players, who identify as lesbian, when they questioned why a heterosexual woman (Kirsha) would appear in a predominantly lesbian club dressed as she does. The comments alluded to a [mis]understanding of her femme-ininity as sexual display. It was not clear if the players further interpreted her sexual display as pointless because there were no men present in the team/at training, or that the presumed sexual display teased the lesbian gaze. Either way, the comments reflect the functioning of heteronormativity. Focus on her attire and her body sexualised, and pathologised, her femininity. Kirsha identifies with the term Black British. For me, comments about her corporeal femme-ininity conflate her 'femininity', ethnicity and sexuality. It is because of her ethnicity that her femme-ininity and sexuality are understood, within the 'rules' of heteronormativity, as excessive.

As Skeggs (2004) has documented, Black femininity and white working-class femininity are often understood as tasteless and sexually deviant. Within the subculture of the team, femme-ininity is unintelligible when it is evidenced as Black heterosexual 'femininity', but not when white middle-class lesbian-femme-ininity is present. Kirsha's team mates call into question her gender and sexuality and in this way she is not recognised as socially viable (Butler, 2004). According to Butler (2004), the process of recognition relies on 'undoing gender' (and the sexed body and sexuality) and this process is a site of power. In this case, power constitutes more than Foucault's (1976) privileging of sexuality. Power is also racialised as well as sexualised. Through her 'conforming' to popular modes of gender, it can be argued that Kirsha disorientates the very 'femininity' she exudes. Therefore, and given the context, we can understand her femme-ininity as paradoxical and this opens a way for new possibilities of gendered identifications and sexual dissidents.[4]

For the team, playing attire can provide an opportunity for expression of lesbianism and for summer tournaments the club usually disregards formal long sleeved shirts and wears more casual T-shirts. T-shirts have been deployed to articulate club identity, for example, a range from C & A (UK department store) with the C and A rainbow striped across the chest were worn as a way to display the freedom flag and symbolically represent gay pride. For one weekend tournament, three seven-a-side teams represented the club. As was usual practice, each team decides its playing strip. A conversation occurred between two players, both of whom are white and identify as lesbian. Both seem keen to select and acquire T-shirts for their side that go against football's masculine tradition. In the changing rooms after a game they talked about the style of kit they would prefer. One suggested 'polka dot tops' and they both agreed it would be something they'd like to wear.

It is difficult to establish the extent to which their suggestion illustrates femme-inine display. The comment appeared to be understood by other players who were listening as a reference to femme-ininity and a move to feminising the playing kit. Players standing nearby expressed, through non-verbal communication, their uncertainty/disbelief towards the suggestion. Given the team's privileging of the butch these responses are not surprising. The suggested playing attire clearly disrupts the gendering of football *and* the normative gendering of lesbianism as wholly masculine.

Clearly femme subjectivity is complex, as Suzanne Moore highlighted during the incident with Germaine Greer (see p.146). More can be done to explain how femme-ininity, as subversive, is articulated in sport spaces. If we are to understand women's experiences of sport and 'femininity' it is important to consider femme-ininity/ies as it/they function both inside and outside lesbian gender-desire. Such critical discussions are important to understanding the spatiality of sexuality in sport. As Harris and Crocker (1997) argue, lived experiences of femme-ininity are often missing from discussion: '[F]emme voices that could teach us much about the intersections of feminist, lesbian and queer identities are often overlooked... [A] mainstream feminism has not analysed femme as a model of critical reshaped femininity and assertive sexuality' (1997: 1).

Femme-ininity can disrupt normative sex–gender–sexuality and provide transgressions that dislocate heteronormativity. Analysis of processes that surround articulation of femme-ininty in footballing spaces may well reveal the complicated and multilayered ways that heteronormative sexing and gendering of these spaces are contested.

Conclusions

Little is known about femme-inine bodies beyond critical discussion of compulsory heterosexual femininity and the operation of heterosexual hegemony in the production of femininity. Critical discussions are important to understanding women's experiences of sport, however, everyday experiences of femme-ininity/ies as subversive and having political potential are often missing from accounts. In some ways the traditional focus of feminist sport sociology neglects femme-ininity and [re]produces femininity as duped. Exploring women's experiences has, to date, paid little attention to how femme-ininity/ies can disturb sex–gender–desire imperatives.

In this chapter I argue that [hetero]normative is multi layered and we need to seek out disruptions that contest the familiar. Queer has many meanings and here it has been used to identify an 'out' lesbian football team *and* criticise practices within this sport subculture that maintain [hetero]normative alignments of sex–gender–sexuality. It is evident that the cultural backdrop of sport, especially football, functions to re-produce femininity in familiar ways and we need new approaches to re-imagining femme-ininity in sport to illuminate hegemonic power relations in the formation of heteronormativity.

Notes

1 This research also supports discussion that has been presented to two journals: *Soccer and Society*; *Gender, Place and Culture. A Journal of Feminist Geography*.
2 Research in the mid–late 1990s (Caudwell, 2001) evidenced the assumption that women footballers must be butch. Players were often understood as male/boy because of wanting to play, and the over-simplistic conflation of gender and sexuality equated to the presence of a ubiquitous butch(-lesbian) figure. She functioned as an abject presence and seemed to haunt the playing fields.
3 United tend to play the 4–4–2 formation, this involves four defenders, four mid-fielders and two strikers.
4 Important critical discussion on femininity as complex appears in the cultural studies literature. For example, Pini (2001) and Bakare-Yusuf (1997), both cited in Carrington and Wilson (2004), explore club and music subcultures to highlight challenge to the confines of normative heterosexual white femininity. And Holland (2004) provides an important account of *Alternative Femininities* from her research with adult women negotiating 'alternative' and/or 'freaky' feminine identities.

References

Brace-Govan, J. (2002) 'Looking at bodywork, women and three physical activities': *Journal of Sport and Social Issues*, 26 (4): 403–20.

Brushwood Rose, C. and Camilleri, A. (eds) (2002) *Brazen Femme: Queering Femininity*. Vancouver: Arsenal Pulp Press.

Butler, J. (2004) 'Undoing Gender', paper presented at *The(o)ries; Advanced Seminars for Queer Research*, Women's Education, Research and Resource Centre, University College Dublin, 28 September, 2004.

Carle, A. and Nauright, J. (1999) 'A man's game? Women playing rugby union in Australia', *Football Studies*, 2 (1): 55–73.

Carrington, B. and Wilson, B. (2004) 'Dance nations: rethinking youth subcultural theory', in A. Bennett and K. Kahn-Harris (eds) *After Subculture: Critical Studies in Contemporary Youth Culture*. London: Palgrave, 65–78.

Case, S.-E. (1998) 'Making butch: An historical memoir of the 1970s', in S. Munt (ed) *Butch/Femme: Inside Lesbian Gender*. London: Cassell, 37–46.

Caudwell, J. (1999) 'Women's football in the United Kingdom: theorising gender and unpacking the butch lesbian image', *Journal of Sport and Social Issues*, 23 (4): 390–402.

Caudwell, J. (2001) 'Women's experiences of gender and sexuality in football contexts in England and Wales'. Unpublished PhD Thesis, University of North London.

Caudwell, J. (2003) 'Sporting gender: women's footballing bodies as sites/sights for the [re]articulation of sex, gender and desire', *Sociology of Sport Journal*, 20 940; 371–86.

Christopherson, N., Janning, M. and McConnell, E. (2002) 'Two kicks forward, one kick back: a content analysis of media discourses on the 1999 Women's Championship', *Sociology of Sport*, 19 (2): 170–85.

Cox, B. and Thompson, S. (2000) 'Multiple bodies – sportswomen, soccer and sexuality', *International Review for the Sociology of Sport*, 35 (1): 5–20.

Cox, B. and Thompson, S. (2001) 'Facing the bogey: women, football and sexuality', *Football Studies*, 4 (2): 7–24.

Creed, B. (1995) 'Lesbian bodies: tribades, tomboys and tarts', in E. Grosz and E. Probyn (eds) *Sexy Bodies: The Strange Carnalities of Feminism*. London: Routledge, 86–103.

Eng, H. (2003) 'Sporting sex/uality: doing sex and sexuality in a Norwegian sport context'. Unpublised PhD thesis, The Norwegian University for Sport and Physical Education.

Foucault, M. [1976](1990) *History of Sexuality*. London: Penguin.

Fusco, C. (1998) 'Lesbians and locker rooms: The subjective experiences of lesbians in sport', in G. Rail (ed) *Sport and Postmodern times*. New York: SUNY.

Gomez, J. (1998) 'Femme erotic independence', in S. Munt (ed) *Butch/Femme: Inside Lesbian Gender*. London: Cassell, 101–109.

Griffin, P. (1998) *Strong Women, Deep Closets*. Leeds: Human Kinetics.

Grosz, E. (1995) *Space, Time and Perversion*. London: Routledge.

Halbert, C. (1997) 'Tough enough and woman enough: stereotypes, discrimination, and impression management among women professional boxers', *Journal of Sport and Social Issues*, 21 (1): 7–36.

Hargreaves, J. (1997) 'Introducing images and meanings', *Body and Society*, 3 (1): 33–49.

Harris, L. and Crocker, E. (eds) (1997) *Femm: Feminists, Lesbians, and Bad Girls*. London: Routledge.

Holland, S. (2004) *Alternative Femininities: Body, Age and Identity*. London: Berg.

Holmlund, C. (1997) 'When autobiography meets ethnography and girl meets girl: The 'dyke docs' of Sadie Benning and Su Friedrich', in C. Holmund and C. Fuchs (eds) *Between the Sheets, in the Streets. Queer, Lesbian, Gay Documentary*. London: University of Minneapolis Press, 127–43.

Howe, P. D. (2001) 'Women's rugby and the nexus between embodiment, professionalism and sexuality: An ethnographic account'. *Football Studies*, 4 (2): 77–92.

Huggett, J. (1997) 'We can't even shoot straight – issues of power and safety in a feminist lesbian football team'. Unpublished MA dissertation, Institute of Education, London.

Hurst, R (2004) 'Theorizing femme identities', paper presented at *Queer Matters Conference*, Kings College London, 28–30 May.

Jagose, A. (1996) *Queer Theory: An Introduction*. New York: NYU Press.

Jeffreys, S. (1993) *The Lesbian Heresy: A Feminist Perspective on the Lesbian Sexual Revolution*. London: The Women's Press.

Johnston, L. (1996) 'Flexing femininity, female body-builders refiguring "the body"', *Gender, Place and Culture. A Journal of Feminist Geography*, 3 (3): 327–40.

Mennesson, C. (2000) '"Hard" women and "soft" women. The social construction of identities among female boxers', *International Review for the Sociology of Sport*, 35 (1): 21–33.

Mennesson, C. and Clement, J.-P. (2003) 'Homosociability and homosexuality: the case of soccer played by women', *International Review for the Sociology of Sport*, 38 (3): 311–30.

Moore, S. (1996) *Head Over Heels*. London: Viking.

Morgan, T. (1993) 'Butch–femme and the politics of identity', in A. Stein (ed) *Sisters, Sexperts, Queers: Beyond the Lesbian Nation*. New York: Plume 35–46.

Munt, S. (1998) *Heroic Desire: Lesbian Identity and Cultural Space*. London: Cassell.

Nestle, J. (1989) *A Restricted Country: Documents of Desire and Resistance*. London: Pandora.

Nestle, J. (2002) 'Genders on my mind', in J. Nestle, C. Howell and R. Wilchins (eds) *GENDERqUEER. Voices from Beyond the Sexual Binary*. Los Angeles: Alison Books.

Paechter, C. (2003) 'Reconceptualising the gendered body: learning and constructing masculinities and femininities in school', paper presented at *British Educational Research Association Annual Conference*, Heriot-Watt University, 11–13 September, 2003.

Pronger, B. (1994) *The Arena of Masculinity: Sports, Homosexuality and the Meaning of Sex*. New York: St Martin's Press.

Pronger, B. (1999) 'Outta my end zone: sport and the territorial anus', *Journal of Sport and Social Issues*, 23 378–89.

Roof, J. (1998) '1970s lesbian feminism meets 1990s butch-femme', in S. Munt (ed) *Butch/Femme: Inside Lesbian Gender*. London: Cassell, 27–36.

Scraton, S., Fastings, K., Pfister, G. and Bunuel, A. (1999) 'It's still a man's game? the experience of top-level European women footballers', *International Review for the Sociology of Sport*, 34 (2): 99–111.

Skeggs, B. (2004) *Class, Self and Culture*. London: Routledge.

Stanley, L. and Wise, S. (1993) *Breaking Out Again*. London: Routledge.

Theberge, N. (1991) 'Reflections on the body in the sociology of sport'. *Quest*, 43 (2): 123–34.

Theberge, N. (2000) *Higher Goals: Women's Ice Hockey and the Politics of Gender*. New York: SUNY.

Turner, W. B. (2000) *A Genealogy of Queer Theory*. Philadelphia: Temple University Press.

van Ingen, C. (2003) 'Geographies of gender, sexuality and race. Reframing the focus on space in sport sociology'. *International Review for the Sociology of Sport*, 38 (2): 201–16.

Veri, M. (1999) 'Homophobic discourse surrounding the female athlete', *Quest*, 52 (4): 355–68.

Wesely. J. K. (2001) 'Negotiating gender: bodybuilding and the natural/unnatural continuum', *Sociology of Sport*, 18 (2); 162–80.

Wheaton, B. (2002) 'Babes on the beach, women in the surf: researching gender, power and difference in the windsurfing culture', in J. Sugden and J. Tomlinson (eds) *Power Games: A Critical Sociology of Sport*. London, Routledge, 240–266.

Williams, J. (2003) *A Game for Rough Girls? A History of Women's Football in Britain*. London: Routledge.

Wright, J. and Clarke, G. (1999) 'Sport, the media and the construction of compulsory heterosexuality: a case study of women's rugby union', *International Review for the Sociology of Sport*, 34 (1): 5–16.

10 Heterosexual femininity

The painful processes of subjectification

Rebecca Lock

Introduction

This chapter considers the relationship between pain and heterosexual femininity in the context of women's ice hockey. Heterosexuality and pain are
commonly understood as natural phenomena rather than as discursively shaped
and constituted. Here, I explore the latter perspective. In exploring the discur-
siveness of pain, I suggest that essentializing and universalizing ways of
understanding pain are politically problematic and reductive.

According to, Kleinman, Brodwin, Good, and Delvechio-Good (1992), 'It is
[...] reasonable to assume that pain is a universal feature of the human condition'
(1992: 1). Prefacing this is the explanation that people of all ethnicities, social
classes, genders, and ages report pain, and that neuroscientists consider pain to
be a principal aspect of the nervous system. What is at stake in claims of universalism? What does this claim do? To refer to pain as a universal, speaks to the
importance of pain on account of 'its' ubiquity and establishes commonality
across different experiences of pain. However, it also erases the multiplicity of
discursive strategies that construct experiences of pain; and implicitly designates
'physical pain' as actual pain while silently pushing psychic pain and psychic
dimensions of pain somewhere else.

To address the social construction of pain, I draw upon queer theory. While
queer theory is a diverse and contested term, a major interest for some queer theorists has been the examination of various social processes that enable
contemporary normative heterosexuality to appear natural. Two such theorists are
Michel Foucault and Judith Butler, whose insights broadly guide the way I deploy
queer theory. Foucault's (1980) analysis of sexuality questions the modernist idea
of sexuality as an identity. He discusses sexuality in terms of the processes through
which different discourses come to constitute sexuality as an identity. He argues
that sexuality is manifest through disciplinary and regulatory practices, which
simultaneously shape social relations and the production of subjects. I take from
Butler (1999), the insight that sex, gender, and sexuality are co-constitutive of
one another.[1] That is, to be understood as a real female you must also be feminine,
and identify as heterosexual. By the same token, to be read as authentically feminine you must be female and heterosexual; and finally, if you are to be recognized

by others as heterosexual as a woman, you should appear as a woman and that entails behaving in a way that is recognized as feminine.

Taking these two aspects of queer theory, I consider how pain is utilized in women's ice hockey to construct female athletes. The question tackled is: how are women who engage in a sport that is commonly understood as a male-appropriate activity, reined in as heterosexually feminine subjects? Some authors (Nixon, 1996; Young and White, 1995) suggest that when women engage in masculine sporting practices, such as ice hockey, they are emulating the values and practices of conventional masculinity. One aspect of this masculinity concerns pain. Playing a collision sport like hockey involves pain, and tolerating pain is normatively understood as a display of masculine toughness. Contrary to this, I argue that how hockey is regulated specifically for women, formally and informally, constitutes the kind of pain that women experience, in ways that contribute to the construction of female hockey players as heterosexually feminine subjects.

To understand how pain is gendered in sport, it is necessary to understand some of the discourses on pain that heterosexual femininity is in part constructed through. Therefore, I begin by outlining three different discourses of intelligible female pain: rape, birthing, and pain in medical contexts. Western discourses on pain consolidate women's experiences of pain with norms of female heterosexuality. In order to grasp the complicated way in which female pain is regulated in ice hockey, I discuss the grammar and social script of these three kinds of pain. In short, I argue that many of the norms from these three discourses are manifest in how pain is regulated in women's ice hockey. Furthermore, it is my contention that discussion about sport should consider other aspects of the social world because sport is always woven into a broader social fabric. Sport is permeated by values and discourses that at a cursory glance appear to have very little to do with sport, but are the means by which normative practices in sport are intelligible to us.

Constructing heterosexual femininity through pain

Rape

The discourse of rape produces women as victims, and males as more powerful than women. It is sensible then that women fear rape because within this discourse women are rapable by virtue of being women. In considering the effects of rape, Cahill (2001) explains, 'The typical reactions of a rape victim, marked by overwhelming guilt and self-loathing, are the reactions of a person who should have known but temporarily forgot that she was constantly at risk' (2001: 164). When women forget their rapableness they are thought of as being at their most vulnerable. Presumably, the alternative is to have a constant consciousness of oneself as being in danger from men, being weaker than men, and being responsible for not staying within realms of safety.[2] Furthermore, this construction of women as inherently rapable affirms the need for women's protection by benevolent men, and the law.

Instead of understanding rape as derived from facts about women's powerlessness, Marcus (1992) puts forward the idea of rape as a 'linguistic fact', enabled by narratives that structure women's lives (1992: 389). He refers to rape as an interaction that is socially scripted (1992: 390). The rape script solicits women to behave in conventionally feminine ways and invites men to behave in conventionally masculine ways. Women are characterized as violable, passive, weak, paralyzed by fear, and unable to fight back; men in contrast are perceived to be subjects of violence, more powerful than women, and entitled to women's sexual services (1992: 390). This script produces women as rapable and produces men as powerful enough to rape. Marcus explains that the *gendered grammar of violence* provides the organizing pattern of the rape script (1992: 392). This grammar constitutes the rules and structures that assign roles within the script: men as the subjects of violence and women as the objects of violence. Furthermore, Marcus argues that the gendered grammar of violence is not isolated in rape, but is continuous with everyday norms of heterosexual femininity and masculinity.

Women on the whole are encouraged to perform heterosexually feminine norms. However, given that this performance makes women rapable, the current effort to prevent rape is punishment by judicial systems. As Marcus (1992) points out, the logic of law is to dissuade men from raping. The possibility of preventing rape lies with men. This protects femininity from criticism of being implicated in disempowering women in rape attacks. The defence of the accused rapist positions the woman as bringing the alleged rape upon herself, and so she stands as responsible for the rape, in effect undermining its classification as rape. Rape is a form of pain that benign men and a masculinized legal system desire to protect women from, but the gendered grammar of violence produces rape as a female-appropriate pain because rape is coherent with heterosexual femininity.

Birthing

A second female-appropriate pain is birthing. Birthing is not only an exclusively female pain, but it marks a woman's entry into the heterosexually feminine role of mothering.[3] A crucial feature of heterosexually feminine pain is its construction as a sacrificial pain. Like rape, birthing also has a social script and grammar. Women suffer pain in birthing, and this pain is made sense of with language that reiterates conventions of heterosexual femininity.

Women are expected to fear the pain of birthing. Counters to birthing anxiety include breathing exercises and analgesics, to help women relax while in pain (Bergum, 2004). Bergum argues that, 'the offer of medication confirms the fear that, yes indeed, we will not be able to stand it' (2004: 5). In affirming this fear, there is a suggestion that women have a lower capacity to tolerate pain than men and that women cannot stand pain.

Women are understood as vocal about their pain. For example, in Bergum's phenomenological study, crying out in pain emerges as a theme, indicating that crying out is a salient aspect of many women's experience in birthing. The pain of birthing is not a senseless pain.[4] There is an acknowledgement of birthing as exceptionally painful, as significant, precisely because it constitutes birthing as an intelligible sacrifice. The significance of the sacrifice is that it marks a woman as self-less, giving of her-self, and giving up her-self in order to nurture the child. Buytendijk (1961) sums up the relationship between birthing pain and sacrifice as, '[T]he purpose of pain... *lies exclusively in the opportunity given to the suffering women to participate directly and consciously in the objective process of a new life coming into being and freeing itself from the old one: the mother may actually sacrifice herself for the new life*' (191: 156, emphasis in original). Although dated, Buytendijk's (1961) thoughts about birthing pain and sacrifice are echoed in common sense understandings of being a 'good mother'. The 'good mother' puts the needs and interests of her children before her own. Or more absolutely, the first interest and desire of the mother becomes caring for her children.

There is a sense, then, that if birthing women are unable to cope with pain, their response is recognizable as leaning toward hysteria rather than stoicism; the expressiveness of their pain signals emotional and physical weakness in tolerating pain. Reading birthing women in this way heterosexually feminizes them, because it implies their inferiority to men. There is also the implication that the pain of birthing is symbolic of the female role of sacrifice for others. Nurturing and caring for others is the occupational role of women as wives and mothers. The grammar of birthing, the rules and structures that assign women to their position in this script, includes a conflation of screaming with intolerance and inability to cope. Medication is not the innocent relieving of legitimate pain, but an indication that a woman is too weak to bear the pain. Women's sacrifice in birthing is not hailed as heroic, but as nurturing. The grammar of birthing predicates dissolving women as subjects with their own needs and desires, and produces a subjectivity based on servicing others.

Medical (treatment of) pain

In this section, I discuss how medical personnel make sense of their patients' pain. Unlike rape and birthing, pain in this context pertains to men as well as women. In this, we might hope that scientific notions of objectivity and universalism would lead to treating women's pain as adequately as it treats men's pain. Unfortunately, not only is the pain of women not adequately treated, but the factors that lead to inadequate relief are also implicated in the production of the heterosexually feminine subject.

Marcus' (1992) notion of script refers to social norms that make a predictable and familiar story. The predictable story about the difference between male and female pain in the medical context echoes some of the heterosexually feminine norms described in rape and birthing. Criste (2002) describes two consistent findings in sex differences for pain: females have lower pain thresholds than males, and females have a lower pain tolerance than males.[5] Given that there is no current biological explanation of the difference, the author notes the socialization of males to be stoic and unemotional as the distinction. It is here that a script for male and female medical pain becomes evident.

The belief that women exaggerate pain occurs because they are assumed to be more expressive than men; the consequence of this belief is that, 'female pain patients are less likely than their male counterparts to be taken seriously and are more likely to receive sedatives rather than opioids for the treatment of their pain' (Hoffmann and Tarzian, 2001: 20). Females are read as behaving in a heterosexually feminine way in response to pain, and so their pain is less adequately treated. The grammar that organizes male and female behaviour and the reading of that behaviour is tautological. The grammar presumes and produces women as heterosexually feminine and men as heterosexually masculine. The common reading of the stoic male response to pain is that men have higher pain thresholds and pain tolerance (than women). However, men perform the stoic role because of their socialization to behave in a way that indicates that they have higher pain thresholds and pain tolerance (than women). The logical implications of this tautology create a further dangerous tautology for women. If men are stoic they are in pain, if men in pain are compelled to scream and complain then they are in unbearable pain. On the other hand, if women are expressive about their pain it is because they have a lower pain threshold and tolerance, if they are inexpressive, they are not in pain. Not only is the male response to pain a socialized practice that does not indicate level of pain, but it is treated as the standard by which pain is judged. The extent to which females deviate from the male response to pain is the extent to which they exaggerate (Criste, 2002); but, because exaggeration has been seen as the female response to pain, all female expressions of pain are presumed to exaggerate the degree of pain felt. However, an interesting recent finding of sex differences in patient-controlled analgesia indicates that men consume 2.4 times more medication than women (Miaskowski and Levine, 1999). Unfortunately, the conclusions drawn reiterate the idea that the male response to pain is still the standard. Instead of questioning whether males are intolerant of their pain when they do not have to express it to anyone, it is suggested that opioid analgesics are more effective in relieving the pain of females. The conclusion once again implies women to be the ones who are different and men as 'normal'.

The positioning of men as 'normal' constitutes the legitimacy of men's response to pain, whatever that response. If women's response to pain was seen as legitimate, that is, if women were taken to authentically express their level of pain, heterosexual masculinity would be damaged, as heterosexual masculinity is predicated on men having a response to pain that is more stoic than women's response. To maintain continuity of heterosexual masculinity, to help make it appear ontological, women must be interpreted differently when in pain; otherwise, they cease to have continuity as heterosexually feminine subjects. Contrary to Melzack's (1990) claim that people tragically suffer from needless inadequately treated pain, I suggest that pain is strategically used to produce and maintain an intelligible heterosexual society.[6]

Women's ice hockey in Canada

There is no simple script and grammar of women's pain in sport for the following related reasons. First, because athletic pain is recognized as playing a role in defining men as masculine (Howe, 2001; Nixon, 1992, 1993, 1996; Pringle, 1999; Roderick *et al.*, 2000; Young *et al.*, 1994), there is resistance to women experiencing it at all. Second, because of discourses of equality women are no longer excluded from sports therefore some pain is inevitable. Third, given that the implicit objective is to ensure women are heterosexually feminine, but that some kinds of pain that undermine heterosexual femininity will occur, the strategy is to counter this in three ways:

• Allow women to experience pain that least contravenes their heterosexual femininity;
• Prevent females from experiencing pain most strongly associated with heterosexual masculinity;
• Use other strategies that heterosexually feminize female athletes.

In short, there is fundamental conflict between the gesture toward gender equality in organized sports and athletic pain defined as heterosexually masculine pain. Therefore, a constant process of compromise and negotiation occurs between multiple strategies that are used to heterosexually feminize female athletes.

To articulate the attempts to construct women as heterosexually feminine subjects in sport, I discuss women's ice hockey in Canada, as it provides particularly good examples. I demonstrate how productions of heterosexual femininity are materialized through permitted and expected female pains (rape, birthing, medical treatment). In discussing women's ice hockey, I draw upon these discourses to show how regulation of the pain women experience in this sport functions to materialize them as heterosexually feminine. I also take up the stigmatizing use of the term 'lesbian' as threateningly deployed to police female hockey players into appearing heterosexually feminine. To do so, I draw upon theories that consider the process of subjectification in terms of experience and materialization.

In some sense, women's very presence in sport, particularly in contact sports, undermines their heterosexual femininity, because women are willingly engaging in activities that are painful. In the scripts of rape, birthing, and medical pain, women are normatively understood as unable to cope with pain. In relation to rape, women need to have a constant sense of safety, the protection of the law and benevolent men. In birthing, women fear pain and cry out because they are unable to cope with it. In the medical context, women are also vocal about their pain, and are presumed to call for relief from even the smallest pain. Playing sports that are painful undermines women's categorization as people who avoid pain and need protection from pain wherever possible. However, given that women do play sports, an important way of reining them in as heterosexually feminine is to prevent them from particular kinds of pain associated with masculinity.

Rules of hockey pain

Women's hockey is distinct from men's because women are penalized for checking one another whereas men are not (Hockey Canada, 2003).[7] The utility of checking is to stop a player from having possession of the puck, but it is likely to cause pain and/or injury. A hard check potentially reduces a player's ability to play effectively, either because they are intimidated or because they are hurt. Sometimes, in men's hockey, if a 'big' player from one team checks a smaller player from the opposition it causes a fight.[8] In elite women's hockey, there are very different ways of penalizing players who fight than in elite men's hockey.[9] Men are penalized with a five minute penalty, whereas women are penalized with a five minute penalty, a game misconduct, and will be evaluated for, and likely to receive, a suspension (Hockey Canada, 2003). Penalizing women for checking and fighting prevents women from suffering pain and from inflicting pain on one another in particular ways. There is continuity here with the grammar of rape, which refuses women as subjects of violence. And like benevolent men and laws around rape, Hockey Canada is arguably assuming this same role as the male protector that prevents women's pain. Furthermore, as medical discourse on female pain demonstrates, authoritative interpretations of the pain that females can tolerate are necessary because women's interpretations of their own pain are inaccurate. A further important reason for preventing women from being subjects of violence is that it protects their subject position as mothers who are caring and nurturing.

Penalizing women for checking and penalizing them more harshly than men for fighting, ensures that women's painful experiences of hockey are different from those of men. Scott (1992) usefully problematizes experience in the following way: 'It is not individuals that have experience, but subjects that are constituted through experience' (1992: 5–26). Preventing women from experiencing certain kinds of pain is therefore not the innocent act of preventing individuals from suffering. Instead, preventing pain alters the experiences of women hockey players so as to encourage them to understand themselves as needing protection from pain and to think of it as inappropriate for them to inflict pain on others. Importantly, by having different rules that lead to different experiences, women hockey players think of themselves not as hockey players *per se*, but as 'female hockey players'.[10] Scott's (1992) distinction between an individual having experiences and a subject constituted through experiences is not to say that the 'having' does not occur. The sense of having experiences problematically presumes the identity of the person that has the experience. Scott's (1992) point is that there is no ontological identity before experience, that experience creates and reiterates identity, and provides the continuous fabric to identity that makes it feel like an ontological unity that is prior to particular experiences. The constituting of experience is one and the same with the feeling of having experience.

A third rule applied to women and not men is that they must wear full face protection (Hockey Canada, 2003). Epidemiological studies of hockey injuries have shown that whether or not players wear full face shields affects the kinds of injuries that occur. In a Minnesota high-school league with full face protection, 34 per cent of players were reported to have suffered concussion or concussion symptoms, whereas facial injuries were so minimal as to not warrant categorization (Gerberich et al., 1987). However, in Jørgensen and Schmidt-Olsen's (1986) study of elite Danish hockey players, for whom full face shields are not mandatory, the incidence of concussion and concussion symptoms is only 14.3 per cent, but the incidence of facial and dental injuries is 13.8 per cent. The claim that face shields make the difference between the kinds of injuries that hockey players received in these two studies is supported by Bishop et al.'s (1983) biomechanical analysis of how the face shield changes the centre of mass and moment of intertia of the head. The full face shield causes the centre of mass of the head to move forward[11], and because the centre of mass has moved forward the forcearm increases.[12] The increase in the forcearm puts increased rotational force on the neck,[13] which amounts to greater movement of the head in whiplash, and a greater strain on neck muscles that try and prevent whiplash. The increased movement of the head (whiplash) can cause the brain to contact the inside of the skull causing concussion and/or symptoms of concussion.

Given that there is research that indicates that full face shields are likely to cause more serious injuries to hockey players than not wearing face shields, it seems that attempts to protect women in hockey have limits. As we have seen in other discourses of gendered pain, the priority is not to protect women at all costs, but to protect women from pain that contravenes their heterosexual femininity and to allow them pain when it reaffirms it. Facial injuries, lacerations, facial bruising, eye and dental damage that occur without a full face shield are arguably aesthetically unpleasing on a woman's face; they undermine her desirability as an object for the visual consumption of men. For women to suffer mild to severe brain injury on the other hand does not make them any less attractive visually. As with the medical discourse on pain, women suffer more severely than men when preventing their pain would require treating men and women similarly with regard to pain, and thus not rendering them heterosexually masculine and feminine respectively.

There are two ways in which wearing a full face shield materializes the female hockey player as the heterosexually feminine subject: when on the ice women appear to have more protection because they have covered faces and; when off the ice women show an absence of facial injuries. Butler's (1997) comments on how materialization and investiture are coextensive in the prison can provide insight into the materialization of the female hockey player as heterosexually feminine. Butler claims:

> [T]here is no prison prior to its materialization; its materialization is coextensive with its investiture with power relations; and materiality is the effect and gauge of this investment. The prison comes to be only within the field of power relations, more specifically only to the extent that it is saturated with such relations and that such a saturation is formative of its very being.
>
> (Butler, 1997: 91)

The heterosexually feminine hockey player does not exist prior to a woman's participation in hockey. For example, it is only by wearing a full face mask and having no facial injuries that a woman materializes as this subject. Her materialization as this subject requires the power relations that demand her to wear a full face shield. Heterosexual femininity is not already there and then responded to with facial protection, instead, it is the effect of power relations that insist on the shield being worn. The untainted face of the heterosexually feminine hockey player is *formed* by facial protection, not protected by it. The rules in hockey actually materialize the female hockey player as different from the male, by reiterating social norms of heterosexual femininity in specific and novel, but nevertheless recognizable ways. It is the continuity with and similarity to other iterations that give the impression of a prior heterosexually feminine subject.

The lesbian threat

Women are discouraged from assuming the masculine subject position associated with playing hockey. Although hockey is adapted to make it a sport suitable for women, the idea that women want to play hockey, traditionally a game for men, brings into question their sexuality (Cahn, 1994; Griffin, 1998; Lenskyj, 1986). This illustrates the fragility of attempts to make a heterosexually feminine version of hockey. Following Derrida (cited in Namaste, 1996), one way of articulating this fragility is through the notion of the supplement. The attempt of securing the meaning of women's hockey, so that it is not masculine, is by contrasting women's hockey to men's hockey. Therefore, for the women's game to be intelligible as a game for women, it is necessary to invoke the men's game. Women's hockey is contaminated by men's hockey because of the necessary play of presence (women's hockey) and absence (men's hockey). The masculinity that women's hockey has tried to posit as an outside is always already fully inside it. The material symptom of masculinity that manifests in women's hockey is 'the lesbian'.

The first women's ice hockey world championship in 1990 provides a good example of how influential the fear of lesbianism is in hockey. Etue and Williams' (1996) report that many parents of the female players in Canada objected to the roughness and masculinity of the game, and there were rumors of lesbianism. To counter these 'unfavorable' insinuations about women's hockey, the representative colors for Canada were pink and white! Furthermore, Etue and Williams' (1996) reported that players did not openly object to the uniforms, even though they felt the marketing strategy to be sexist, for fear of expulsion from the national team. Moreover, these women were sanitized from the stigma of being lesbians by being posited as daughters, a safe familial role for females, and by being dressed in pink – a tried and trusted strategy from birth. Their resistance to heterosexual feminizing was quashed with the threat of losing their places on the national team. Women's participation in hockey is arguably impacted by reiteration of the stereotype that women hockey players are lesbians. Women who fear the accusation of lesbianism (both because they feel it is right and because they feel it is wrong) may be discouraged from playing hockey. Women who are homophobic, a popular attitude in Canada, may also feel repelled from playing hockey. If a woman is not put off from playing ice hockey by this lesbian threat, given that its purpose is to insult and shame women, and if women are concerned to stave off the stigma of lesbianism, they will feel compelled to perform heterosexual femininity in other respects.

In a number of different ways, actual and potential women hockey players who fear being labeled as lesbian struggle with what Davies (2000) refers to as being spoken into existence as lesbians. Another way in which Davies puts this is hailing – being called upon as a certain kind of subject. Davies (2000) refers to hailing and the potential ways in which one may respond, as a process of subjection, which 'entails a tension between simultaneously becoming a speaking, agentic subject and the corequisite for this, being subjected to the meanings inherent in the discourse through which one becomes a subject' (Davies, 2000: 27). While there is a simultaneous 'becoming' of the agentic subject and subjection to the discourse this becoming is part of an ongoing history of and between the subject and the discourse (Butler, 1997). In being hailed as a lesbian one can respond in a number of ways. However, in assuming a subject position by speaking, one is subjected to the discursive regulations of that position. For the women on the national team, who were ostensibly hailed as lesbians, the CAHA[14] produced them as heterosexually feminine by dressing them in colors that cohered with heterosexual femininity. In other words, giving the women pink and white uniforms was to 'hail' the players as heterosexually feminine. The players knew that if they objected to the uniforms (and disputed the way they were 'hailed') they would be assuming a transgressive subject position (the lesbian) that would result in them losing their place on the team. In wearing the uniforms, they were subjected to the discourse of heterosexuality. The effect of the CAHA 'hailing' female hockey players in this way, with the threat of excluding them from the team, provides incentive for women to be complicit rather than resistant to assuming a heterosexually feminine subject position. While the incentive of being on that national team provided a practical readiness to turn to the hailing, there is also a readiness in that female hockey players have a history of negotiating the discourse of heterosexuality. Although the subject is produced in the moment of hailing, the readiness to turn to the hailing indicates that the subject is, in the moment, negotiating the familiar discourse of heterosexuality in a specific and partially new way.

Psychic pain, physical pain, universalism and masculinity

In the previous section, I outlined two different ways in which female hockey players are produced as heterosexually feminine subjects. The first entails policing the kinds of pain they experience. The second involves various threats including those of a homophobic and sexist nature and in the case of the women's first World Cup, the threat of exclusion from the national team if one does not perform as heterosexually feminine. It is my contention that both of these strategies are painful processes of subjection, and both of these subject-constituting pains are obscured by the notion that pain is universal and that tolerating pain is a masculine behavior.

Pain and gender are inextricably linked in construction of the subject; males and females differentially experience pain, because they are produced and policed to experience different kinds of pain, and because their expressions of pain are read differently. To claim that pain is universal collapses these differences into an apolitical point of commonality. The danger and irony of the apparently universal compassionate gesture of recognizing that everyone experiences pain is that it erases the politically troubling ways in which pain is harnessed to produce normal heterosexual subjects.

The suggestion that pain is universal, because it is a principal aspect of the nervous system, universalizes pain on a certain set of terms. Excluded from this notion of pain is the psychic dimension. Pain that is felt physically, perhaps as a result of injury or disease, always has a psychic dimension (Melzack and Wall, 1982; Morris, 1991). If pain did not have this dimension, it is questionable whether we could consciously experience pain at all. The erasing of the psychic dimension of pain, in the wake of a universal biology, renders pain that is principally psychic as not a painful experience at all.

Using the term lesbian as an insult may make the hailed person feel uncomfortable, unsafe, hurt, ashamed, embarrassed, or ridiculed. To give national team players the choice of following sexist, homophobic, and heteronormative rules for how they have to appear, or to be excluded from the team, can also be expected to cause feelings of distress. Any lesbian on the team who is told that their sexuality is something that should be hidden and replaced with apparent heterosexuality is likely to experience psychic pain. Regardless of sexuality, anyone on the team might feel forced to publicly tolerate prejudices contrary to their own beliefs, which is also likely to be distressing.

In identifying how women endure pain, as less about women assuming a masculine subject position and more about them assuming a heterosexually feminine position, I am displacing the simple connection between masculinity and tolerating pain. The key to undermining this connection is to not consider pain as a universal phenomenon, a trivial insight with politically dangerous repercussions. As I have argued, pain is culturally shaped and culturally shaping. Tolerating pain is no more aligned with norms of heterosexual masculinity than it is with norms of heterosexual femininity. Both are intricately bound up with pain, but necessarily different kinds of pain.

It is within a universal notion of pain that male pain is rendered legitimate and visible. The women's game has protective rules and so it seems obvious that the men's game is likely to be a more painful practice. It is because 'physical pain' is foregrounded in a universal notion of pain, that psychic pain is excluded from recognition and legitimation as pain. However, once we open up our understanding of pain to include that which the universalizing of pain obscures, it is possible to see how pain is culturally shaped to make women's pain appear lesser than men's pain. It is also then possible to recognize as pain the common practice of 'hailing' hockey players as lesbians as not an appropriate way of ensuring socially desirable appearances, but another painful way of heterosexually feminizing them.

Conclusion

Considering the meanings of particular pains and particular subjectivities as an effect of the same productive force infinitely complicates understanding of pain. As I have tried to show, pain in women's hockey, must be understood in relation to men's hockey, discourses of rape, birthing, and medical treatment of pain, as well as homophobic 'hailing'. It is important to consider pain in its social context because the meanings it has, the ways in which people respond to it, are caught up in how a given pain is interwoven with other discourses.

Limitations to studying pain, when one wants to respect and address its complexity, compel me to return to the claim of pain as universal, because it continues to trouble me. Having argued that pain plays a role in construction of the feminine subject in a multitude of ways I refute the universalism of pain. In making this case, I implicitly question the authenticity of those who believe that pain is universally bad and in need of relief, because people do not act in accordance with that belief.

I am deeply troubled to think of pain as used in the production of heterosexually feminine subjects, even though I know pain cannot stand outside of discourse. Therefore, one of the implications of this chapter is a need for proliferation of discursive articulations of how pain produces subjects. This is a means of refuting the singular value that universalism posits to all pain. A second way to interrupt the universalism of pain is to address the normative conceptualizing of experience that it implies. While pain happens in the temporal sense of being an embodied event, as being an experience, this implicitly posits the experience as the complementary particular to the universal. However, the notion of experience articulated by post-structural thinkers, such as Scott (1992) and Derrida (1973), provides the possibility of understanding experience as constituting of both subjects and universalism.

Notes

1 This idea does not originate from Butler (1999), Butler cites Wittig's notion of the heterosexual matrix.
2 Discursively, realms of safety include the home, marriage, well-lit streets, and the company of others. Of course, the home is a location that may also protect the rapist, as is the institution of marriage.
3 I consider mothering to be a heterosexually feminine role, because even though lesbians may mother, only heterosexual women are presumed to mother. The normative way of getting pregnant is through heterosexual sex. If you come out as lesbian, and your parents were hoping to be grandparents, a common assumption parents make is that you will not have children. I expect that when people see women with children in public, even if they deviate somewhat from a heterosexually feminine appearance, the likely presumption will be that they are heterosexual.

4 Birthing rhetoric sets up birthing pain as not being senseless, because it has the reward of a new life, and this new life makes the pain worthwhile, and it functions as something of a crux in the process of the materialization of the subject 'mother'. The pain that produces this new subject is celebrated, as worth it, perhaps even as a beautiful and joyful pain. Here pain is beautiful because it produces a new subject position for the woman, the good subject position of being a mother.

5 'Pain threshold is defined as the minimum amount of stimulation that reliably evokes the report of pain... Pain tolerance is the amount of time that a continuous stimulus is endured ... or the maximum amount of painful stimulus endured' (Criste, 2002: 478).

6 Melzack's (1990) essay is a widely known one in which he objects to the conservative use of opioid analgesics for pain patients. The fear of medical personnel is that liberal use of this medication for pain will lead to addiction. Contrary to this Melzack argues that the stingy use of analgesics only results in needless pain because many studies show that pain patients, with no prior drug addiction problems, do not develop addictions when drugs are given for pain relief.

7 A woman will get at least a minor penalty for checking, but depending on the severity of the check a major penalty or a game misconduct may be called.

8 If the check is a good clean check, it is unlikely to cause a fight, but if it is a 'cheap shot', it could. A cheap shot would be if the check could have been called as a penalty but is not, or trying to hit the player harder than necessary and hurting him. However, the attack by Todd Bertuzzi on Steve Moore was instigated by Steve Moore's check on Marcus Naslund, a check that is commonly understood as a clean check.

9 In my use of the terms, elite men's hockey refers to the NHL (National Hockey League), and elite women's hockey refers to national level competition.

10 Theberge's (1995) study on what women think of the differences between men's and women's hockey provides some good examples of a self understanding of women players as having a heterosexually feminine subject position

11 The centre of mass is the point where a force is seen to be acting.

12 The axis of rotation is the neck. If you draw a line from this axis to the top of the head, the forearm is the distance between this line and the centre of mass.

13 Torque, the rotational force acting on the neck, is the product of the rotational force multiplied by the forearm. This makes any increase of the forearm significantly impact the pressure placed on the neck.

14 Canadian Amateur Hockey Association (now known as Hockey Canada).

References

Bergum, V. (2004) Birthing pain. *Phenomenology Online*. Available from <http://www.phenomenologyonline.com/articles/bergum.html> (Aaccessed 22 March 2004).

Bishop, P. J., Norman, R. W., Wells, R. P., Ranney, D., and Skleryk, B. (1983) 'Changes in the centre of mass and the moment of inertia of a headform induced by a hockey helmet and face shield', *Canadian Journal of Applied Sport Science*, 8 (1): 19–25.

Butler, J. (1997) *The Psychic Life of Power*. Stanford, CA: Stanford University Press.

Butler, J. (1999) *Gender Trouble: Feminism and the Subversion of Identity*. London, UK: Routledge.

Buytendijk, F. (1961) *Pain*. Westport, CT: Greenwood Press, Publishers.

Cahill, A. J. (2001) *Rethinking Rape*. Ithica, NY: Cornell University Press.

Cahn, S. (1994) *Coming on Strong: Gender and Sexuality in Twentieth Century Women's Sport*. Free Press: Toronto, Canada.

Criste, A. (2002) 'ANNA journal course. Update for nurse anesthetists. Gender and pain', *ANNA Journal,* 70(6): 475–80.

Davies, B. (2000) *In a Body of Writing: 1990–1999*. CA: Altamira Press.

Derrida, J. (1973). *Speech and Phenomena: And Other Essays on Husserl's Theory of Signs*. Evanston, IL: Northwestern University Press.

Etue, E. and Williams, M. K. (1996) *On the Edge: Women Making Hockey History*. Toronto, Canada Second Story Press.

Foucault, M. (1980) *The History of Sexuality: An Introduction: Volume 1*. New York, NY: Vintage Books.

Gerberich, S. G., Finke, R., Madden, M., Preist, J. D., Aamouth, G. and Murray, K. (1987) 'An epidemiological study of high school ice hockey injuries', *Child's Nervous System*, 3: 59–64.

Griffin, P. (1998) *Strong Women, Deep Closets*. Champaign, IL: Human Kinetic.

Hockey Canada Official Playing Rules (2003). Ottawa, Canada: Hockey Canada, 60th edn.

Hoffmann, D. E. and Tarzian, A. J. (2001) 'The girl who cried pain: A bias against women in the treatment of pain', *Journal of Law, Medicine and Ethics*, 29 (1): 13–27.

Howe, D. (2001) 'An ethnography of pain and injury in professional rugby union', *International Review for the Sociology of Sport*, 36 (3): 289–303.

Jørgensen, U. and Schmidt-Olsen, S. (1986) 'The epidemiology of ice hockey, injuries', *British Journal of Sports Medicine*, 20 (1): 7–9.

Kleinman, A., Brodwin, P.E., Good, B. J. and Delvechio Good, M. (1992) 'Pain as human experience: an introduction', in: M. Delvechio Good, P.E. Brodwin, B. J. Good and A. Kleinman (eds) *Pain as Human Experience: An Anthropological Perspective*. Berkeley, CA: University of California Press, 1–28.

Lenskyj, H (1986) *Out of Bounds: Women, Sport and Sexuality*. Toronto, Canada: Women's Press.

Marcus, S. (1992) 'Fighting bodies, fighting words: A theory and politics of rape prevention', in: J. Butler and J. W. Scott (eds) *Feminists Theorize the Political*. New York, NY: Routledge, 385–403.

Melzack, R. (1990) 'The tragedy of needless pain', *Scientific American*. 262 (2): 27–33.

Melzack, R and Wall, P. (1982) *The Challenge of Pain*. New York, NY: Penguin Books.

Miaskowski, C. and Levine, J. (1999) 'Does opioid analgesia show a gender preference for females?' *Pain Forum*, 8 (1): 34–44.

Morris, D. B. (1991) *The Culture of Pain*. Berkeley, CA: University of California Press.

Namaste, K. (1996) 'The politics of inside/out' in: S. Seidman (ed.) *Queer Theory / Sociology*. Cambridge, MA: Blackwell, 194–212.

Nixon, H. L., II (1992) 'A social network analysis of influences on athletes to play with pain and injuries', *Journal of Sport and Social Issues*. 16 (2): 127–35.

Nixon, H. L., II (1993) 'Accepting the risks of pain and injury on sport: Mediated cultural influences on playing hurt', *Sociology of Sport Journal*. 10 (2): 183–96.

Nixon, H. L., II (1996) 'Explaining pain and injury attitudes and experiences in sport in terms of gender, race, and sports status factor', *Journal of Sport and Social Issues*. 20 (1): 33–44.

Pringle, R. (1999) 'The pain of sport: socialization, injury and prevention', *Journal of Physical Education New Zealand*, 32 (1): 14–16.

Roderick, M., Waddington, I. and Parker, G. (2000) 'Playing hurt: managing injuries in English professional football', *International Review for the Sociology of Sport*, 35 (2): 165–80.

Scott, J. W. (1992) 'Experience', in: J. Butler and J. W. Scott (eds) *Feminists Theorize the Political*. New York, NY: Routledge, 22–40.

Theberge, N. (1995) '"Same sport different gender": A consideration of binary gender logic and the sport continuum in the case of ice hockey', *Journal of Sport and Social Issues*. 22 (2): 183–98.

Young, K. and White, P. (1995) 'Sport, physical danger and injury: The experiences of elite women athletes', *Journal of Sport and Social Issues*, 19 (1): 45–61.

Young, K., White, P. and McTeer, W. (1994) 'Body talk: male athletes reflect on sport, injury, and pain', *Sociology of Sport Journal*, 11 (2): 175–94.

Index